The Art of Dying
and Living

The Art of Dying and Living

Lessons from Saints of Our Time

Kerry Walters

ORBIS BOOKS
Maryknoll, New York 10545

Founded in 1970, Orbis Books endeavors to publish works that enlighten the mind, nourish the spirit, and challenge the conscience. The publishing arm of the Maryknoll Fathers and Brothers, Orbis seeks to explore the global dimensions of the Christian faith and mission, to invite dialogue with diverse cultures and religious traditions, and to serve the cause of reconciliation and peace. The books published reflect the views of their authors and do not represent the official position of the Maryknoll Society. To learn more about Maryknoll and Orbis Books, please visit our website at www.maryknollsociety.org.

Library of Congress Cataloging-in-Publication Data

Walters, Kerry S.
  The art of dying and living / Kerry Walters.
      p. cm.
  Includes bibliographical references (p.   ).
  ISBN 978-1-57075-924-6 (pbk.)
  1. Death—Religious aspects—Christianity. 2. Death. I. Title.
  BT825.W29 2011
  248.4—dc22
                                    2010042873

For Robin Jarrell
Priest, biblical scholar, author, friend

Ex umbris via imaginatio in veritatem

CONTENTS

ACKNOWLEDGMENTS

First, thanks to Robert Ellsberg, editor-in-chief and publisher of Orbis Books, whose patient and wise steerage made this book much better than it would've otherwise been. I'm grateful also to the Reverend Robin Jarrell for reading and improving portions of the manuscript, and to Georgianna Roscoe and Basil Rastignac for helping me work through some of the book's ideas. Although she may be surprised to learn it, the Rev. Lynn Carter-Edmands helped set me on the path of thinking about the connections between living and dying many years ago. So did the many patients to whom I ministered during my stint as a hospital chaplain, fellow chaplains Ricky Phillips and Elaine Brock, and Mark McCullough, John Jobson, James Edwards, and Jim Gardner. I'm grateful to all of them. And of course I continue to be thankful to Kim and Jonah, who every day lovingly tutor me in the art of living and better prepare me for The Great Test of dying.

INTRODUCTION

An *Ars Moriendi* for Today

"This new ars moriendi is not a manual for intensive care units, hospice, or the bedroom at home. The motto of this ars is to 'live fulfilled,' to do so all of one's life and as a result 'to die in peace.'"

"I don't know how to do this"

I once knew a lovely woman who, when she found herself at the final stages of a long and dreadful disease, confessed: "I don't know how to do this. I've no experience at dying." She was a woman of deep faith, generous goodness, and many years of happy life. Her words weren't meant to express desperation or terror so much as bewilderment in the face of a situation for which she felt unprepared.

It's a bewilderment that awaits each of us. How could it be otherwise? Like my friend, we've no experience at dying. Even thinking about it comes hard. The sheer uncanniness of death—of ceasing to be an embodied person who enjoys the aroma of freshly cut grass, the laughter of children, the sound of rain, the thrill of a good book or film, the caress of a loved one—numbs the spirit. How can it possibly be that the world will continue in my absence? The mere thought of it is surreal.

Samuel Johnson once famously noted that the prospect of impending execution wonderfully concentrates the mind. But this kind of clarity in the face of death isn't a given. For many of us, awareness of imminent death scatters our thoughts in a thousand panicky directions or, if it *does* concentrate our minds, focuses them on a frenzied and futile struggle to hang onto life. Both are bad ways to die. As part of my preparation for ordination, I served a couple of years as a chaplain at a major hospital. During that time I ministered to dozens of patients dying from cancers, heart disease, diabetes, kidney failure, AIDS, respiratory failure, and injuries. Almost without exception, they and their families did everything they could to avoid acknowledging that the end was near. It was as if there was an unspoken rule of etiquette that forbade any mention of death. It was hard for me to break through this silence in order to help patients ready themselves for death. Too often, when death came for them, they were utterly unprepared. I can count on two hands the number of patients I knew who died well.

It was a sobering experience. It's unnerving to watch someone die flailing in horror and desperately begging doctors, nurses, chaplains, and anyone else who's present to save them. It's not just that there's a sad unseemliness to this kind of end. More to the point, it robs the dying person of the opportunity to be present at her own death. Too distracted by terror to focus on what's happening to her, she misses the chance to be an active participant in the final scene of her life. For non-religious people, it's a lost opportunity to conclude life with a dignified and mindful departure. For persons of faith, it's a missed opportunity to prepare spiritually for the transition from bodily existence to whatever comes afterwards.

Watching someone stubbornly fight to the last breath is equally distressing. It's not just that the struggle is hopeless or that it usually burdens the patient and family with additional physical and emotional distress. More significantly, there's something improper about refusing to bend to the law of nature which dictates that all living things must die. In saying this, I don't mean to defend fatalism. There are lots of situations in which it's entirely appropriate (and sometimes even obligatory) to resist threats to our lives and struggle mightily to survive. But the end of life isn't one of them. Refusing to go gentle into that good night when it's clear that dusk is falling isn't heroic. It's defiant to the point of arrogance. For Christians who die like this, the rebellion isn't merely against nature. It's also against God. By refusing to submit to death gracefully, we claim for ourselves ultimate authority over our lives, a prerogative relinquished even by Jesus (see Phil 2:5–11). Our last earthly act becomes one of disobedience.

It's probably inevitable that the prospect of death frightens and saddens us. Unless we're in tremendous physical or emotional pain, no one welcomes the end of life. This is as true for people of faith as for anyone else. But, at the same time, surely none of us really wants to leave the world in terror that rips us apart or in bullheaded and anguished defiance. In spite of our fear of it, we sense that dying is one experience in life too important to miss.

We should trust that intuition. Dying *is* important. It's both universal—*all* living creatures will die—and intimately mine—*I* will die, *my* life will end. When my time to die comes, I will go through something that every other member of the human family must experience. This shared fate, which connects me to all past, present, and future generations, by itself makes the end of my life a noteworthy event because it stretches beyond just *me*. But my dying, because it's also uniquely *mine*, offers me the opportunity to trace the lineaments of my life, to reconcile and take leave, and to open my mind, spirit, and body to an experience that no one else can have or even share with me. Approaching our dying with a full appreciation of its importance can make it an act of completion and fulfillment rather than an incomprehensible nightmare.

All of us yearn for this kind of completion. We want to be able to look back on life when our end comes and see that our life had a purposeful direction, that it told a story worth the telling, and that we found in the living of it not simply what we may have wanted but what we genuinely needed. (I think it was Henry David Thoreau who said that his greatest fear was realizing on his death bed that he'd never really gotten around to living.) Our dying can be the final, fulfilling chapter in our life, one that doesn't abruptly or arbitrarily break off our story so much as complete it. This is the kind of end that's traditionally been viewed as a good death. My guess is that it's the death most of us wish for ourselves and our loved ones. If we have to die, this is the way to go.

But how do we do it?

Learning to Die

Many of us die badly not because we're wicked or weak people, but because we simply haven't been taught how to die *well.* The unwillingness of patients to talk forthrightly about death that I ran across as a hospital chaplain permeates our culture. Dying is frightening enough as it is. But our collective refusal to face up to it makes it so much more terrifying than it need be that we retreat ever deeper into denial, and this doesn't bode well for how we'll cope with our dying when it comes. You can't really prepare for something you spend a lifetime avoiding.

Our forebears knew the importance of preparing for death. They made conscious efforts to learn how to die well, and even wrote and read guidebooks on how to go about doing it. Between the fifteenth and the seventeenth centuries especially, one of the most popular genres of Christian devotional literature was the *ars moriendi* or "art of dying." Its sole purpose was to tutor readers on how to die well. *Ars moriendi* manuals were anything but piously reassuring Sunday-school tracts. They refused to sugarcoat the bitterness of dying and sometimes actually exaggerated its terrors, presumably to shock readers into taking their mortality seriously. But, exaggerated or not, their candor about human mortality and the experience of dying is in marked contrast with our present-day silence.

Many of the *ars moriendi* books focused exclusively on how to prepare for death in order to avoid the postmortem fires of hell. The recommendations were predictable: resist despair, confess sins, show genuine contrition, make reparation, and throw yourself on the mercy of God. Texts were often illustrated with hair-raising woodcuts of leering demons huddled around a dying person's bed, eagerly waiting for him to slip up in his final moments so they could drag him to hell.

But other *ars moriendi* manuals took a broader view. Instead of limiting themselves to deathbed counsel, they stressed that an adequate preparation for death needed to begin long before the final illness struck. The best way to prepare for death, they advised, is to live a good life. The success with which we face death, the supreme challenge to our faith in God and our trust that existence is ultimately meaningful, depends on how virtuously we've lived during our healthy years. So learning how to die doesn't just improve our prospects of a good death. It simultaneously gives us guidelines, an *ars vivendi,* for a fulfilled life.

During the months I worked the hospital wards I often wished that my patients and I had our own *ars moriendi* to instruct us in living toward a good death. The approach and language of the fifteenth-, sixteenth-, and seventeenth-century texts don't really speak to us anymore, and even though there are plenty of books about death on the market today, most of them explore bioethical issues such as euthanasia or offer therapeutic counseling to dying persons and their families. Such books are helpful and important. But I wanted something else: a book that underscored the deep connection between living well and dying well, recognizing that the skills necessary for achieving the first *(ars vivendi)* are also vital for the second *(ars moriendi)*. I wanted an art of dying which was also an art of living, and I wanted it to speak to twenty-first century sensibilities.

This book is my attempt at such a contemporary *ars moriendi*. It's based on the conviction that the manner in which we die very much depends on and reflects the manner in which we have lived. A good death requires preparation that needs to begin long before we enter the final stage of life. Waiting until then is generally too late.

The best kind of preparation, I think, is habituation to those virtues or character traits that enable us to live well. Life is a seamless garment. It stands to reason that habits picked up in life color not only how we see ourselves, relate to God, and interact with others but also how we think about death and are likely to comport ourselves when we enter the dying process. If we cultivate destructive traits (or vices) such as selfishness, cowardice, impatience, or distrustfulness, we impoverish our inner life and foul our chances for meaningful relationships with others both while we're hale and hearty and when our final illness overtakes us. Habituating ourselves throughout life to positive traits (or virtues) such as love, gratitude, patience, or trust does the opposite. Such traits make our living richly meaningful and discipline us to ways of thinking and behaving that will stand us in good stead at life's end.

The best way to learn how to be virtuous is by observing and emulating virtuous persons as they go about the business of living and dying. But we moderns are handicapped in that regard in ways that our ancestors weren't. They were accustomed to witnessing the deaths of loved ones. Dying was typically done at home and closely witnessed by spouses, children, grandchildren, and friends. The lessons they learned from close observations of good deaths accumulated and were passed on by word of mouth from generation to generation in a sort of unwritten *ars moriendi*. Stories about exemplary deaths of family elders not only consoled grieving survivors. They also helped them deal with their own death-fear, gave them pointers on how to die well, and provided an example for them to follow when their own day came.

But today in the United States, Canada, the UK, and Western Europe, the odds are that most people will die in hospitals or treatment centers surrounded by gently humming medical equipment instead of family and friends. So even though there's still an opportunity to observe virtuous *living* in family members, friends, colleagues, and public figures, most of us are unlikely to have much occasion to actually watch them die. We get only half the picture, and the connection between how we live and how we deal with death remains an abstraction rather than a witnessed truth.

What I've tried to do in this book is offer the next best thing: an opportunity for secondhand observation and emulation through the stories of how seven different people lived and died well. Each of the stories focuses on a concrete, particular person. Each spotlights a virtue essential for living well and dying well. And each demonstrates the profound influence that living exerts upon dying. Reading the stories, we're able to follow the subjects through their life's journey to its end. We observe how they lived, how they coped with their mortality, and how their final days were fitting culminations of their entire lives. We get the whole picture rather than just a detached piece of it.

In order of appearance, our tutors in the art of living and dying well are Joseph Bernardin, Thea Bowman, Etty Hillesum, Jonathan Daniels, Dietrich Bonhoeffer, Pope John Paul II, and Caryll Houselander. The seven virtues they exemplify are trust, love, gratitude, obedience, courage, patience, and christing. Except, perhaps, for the final one, none of these virtues is unfamiliar. But too often our conventional understanding of them, while not necessarily incorrect, doesn't plumb deeply enough. So in exploring them, I try to move beyond their everyday sense to recover their hidden significance. Recollecting what we've forgotten about them revitalizes virtues which have grown, for many of us, a bit stale and uninspiring.

All of the people profiled here are modern figures—even the two eldest, Bonhoeffer and Houselander, are still within living memory—and they come from different backgrounds and life experience. Three are Americans—one is African American—another is British, and the rest are European. They include women and men, clerics and laypersons. Some died violently, others died in their beds. Some of them are familiar figures while others are less known. In telling their stories, I've let them speak for themselves as much as possible because their words are as rich and wise as their living and dying were fruitful. I've been especially generous in quoting Caryll Houselander, probably the least familiar of any of them.

I don't want to imply that the persons whose stories I tell here are the only ones who can teach us something valuable about living and dying. Good teachers abound, and most of them are "ordinary" people who never make it into the history books. Similarly, I don't want to give the impression that the seven virtues discussed in this book exhaust the range of positive character traits, although I think they *are* absolutely essential for a good life and death. The absence of any of them drastically diminishes our odds of living and dying well.

Finally, I don't want to suggest that living and dying well can be pulled off by cultivating only a single virtue. As we'll see in chapter 1, virtues are necessarily interconnected. The people profiled here each cultivated and practiced all of the seven (and more!) virtues. It's just that the one I specifically link with each of them most stands out when their individual stories are thoughtfully examined.

Although this book is written from a Christian perspective, I hope that readers from other faith traditions find it helpful. That there's no explicit discussion here of Buddhist, Hindu, or Muslim perspectives on living and dying well doesn't mean that I don't value these traditions, but simply that I feel unqualified to do them justice. I also hope that people of no faith might find something of value in this book. Non-religious folks are just as invested as religious ones in living and dying well, and the thoughtful cultivation of virtues can help them realize that goal. None of the virtues explored in this book, with the exception of the final one of christing, are exclusively Christian (although my own belief is that a Christian commitment brings them to fulfillment) or practicable only for Christians. Virtues belong to everyone, and so do the examples of people, religious or otherwise, who model for us how to live and die well.

CHAPTER ONE

LIVING TOWARD
A GOOD DEATH

Keep death and judgment always in your eye;
None's fit to live but who is fit to die.

The Night at Arzamas

A single terrifying night in the late summer of 1869 utterly changed the direction of Leo Tolstoy's life.

It was the last thing any of Tolstoy's acquaintances would've expected. He was at the top of his form. After seven long years, he'd finally put the finishing touches on his masterpiece *War and Peace*. His health was robust, he loved his wife and children, he was famous and wealthy, and he felt the deep satisfaction that comes from wrapping up a demanding creative project. As a treat to himself, he decided to travel several hundred miles from his estate to look at some land he was thinking of buying.

Three days into his journey, weary but in a holiday mood, Tolstoy stopped for the night in a small town in the middle of nowhere called Arzamas. He got a room at the local inn, ate dinner, crawled into bed, and quickly dropped off to sleep.

Around two o'clock the next morning he suddenly awoke, shuddering with a terror he could neither understand nor control. Staring into the darkness, struggling to quiet the panic that threatened to choke him, he tried to reason with himself. "This is ridiculous," he muttered. "What am I afraid of?" Then a voice came from the blackness. "Of me," it said. "*I* am here." And the voice belonged to Death. On hearing this terrible reply, Tolstoy tells us,

> A cold shudder ran over my skin. Yes, Death. It will come, it is already here, even though it has nothing to do with me now... My whole being ached with the need to live, the right to live, and, at the same moment, I felt death at work. And it was awful, being torn apart inside. I tried to shake off my terror. I found the stump of a candle in a brass candlestick and lighted it. The reddish flame, the candle, shorter than the candlestick, all told me the same story: there is nothing in life, nothing exists but death, and death should not be!"[1]

Although not a particularly religious man at this point in his life, Tolstoy got out of bed, knelt, and struggled to remember his prayers. But when he tried to say the Our Father, he was distracted by terrible images of Death seeping into him, infiltrating every organ of his body, and pulling him into the vacuum of non-existence. His despair gave way to fury. "I was in agony, but I felt dry and cold and mean. There was not one drop of goodness in me. Only a hard, calm anger against myself and what had made me."[2]

At some point during that long night, Tolstoy, restless with dread, left his room. As he paced up and down the inn's long corridor, he heard the rhythmic snores of sleeping guests and was bewildered by their indifference to the presence of Death. How could they sleep so peacefully when every breath they drew might be their last? How was it possible that other humans didn't feel the fragility of life as horribly as he did?

The dawn found Tolstoy a changed man. Utterly shaken by his encounter with Death, he forgot about the land deal and immediately set out for home. For the rest of his life—and he had forty-one more years left—Tolstoy searched for something, for *anything*, that could help him cope with the death-fear that felled him in Arzamas.

Death-fear and Death-denial

Tolstoy's experience led him to conclude that humans respond to death in one of two ways: terror (his reaction at Arzamas) or denial (the one he attributed to the sleepers at the inn). Either we quake with panic at the prospect of our own death or we try to avoid thinking about it. But denial, of course, is a coping mechanism, and we feel the need to cope only when we're threatened by something. So fear is the more basic response. Typically it smolders beneath the surface, tamped down by denial. But it's always there and can erupt at any moment.

Death-fear isn't cut from the same cloth as our other fears. Usually what we fear is straightforward enough and at least potentially avoidable or preventable. We fear being mugged or coming down with lung cancer. We have a good understanding of what each of these misadventures would be like—getting punched and robbed or wasting away—and we also know what steps to take—avoid risky neighborhoods, stop smoking—to minimize their likelihood. Getting mugged and being diagnosed with cancer are genuinely bad things that warrant our fear. But at least we understand them. They're not uncanny.

It's different with death. There's nothing straightforward about it at all. In fact, it's hugely paradoxical, because death at one and the same time is absolutely certain and absolutely uncertain. It's certain in the sense that it's inevitable. All living things die. One day you and I will die too. There's no getting around it, no means of escape. It's this no-appeal finality of death, this sense of being trapped, that so infuriated Tolstoy.

But death is also uncertain in the sense that, inevitable as we know it to be, we never know exactly *when* it will come for us. So we live in a state of chronic anxiety, waiting for the sword dangling over our heads to finally drop. Furthermore, death is uncertain in the sense that we don't have a clear-cut notion of *what* it is. True, we're able to define it medically. But subjectively, the prospect of our own death is chillingly surreal. How can it possibly be that my body, which feels so alive right now, will one day be stiff and cold? How can my consciousness, my sense of self, my *me,* just vanish as if I never was? The non-being with which death threatens us is unimaginable and dreadful. There's no possible way for us to get a handle on it. It simply lies beyond the scope of our experience. This is the aspect of death that paralyzed Tolstoy with terror.

It's unbearable to go through life constantly feeling the weight of death-fear. So denial mechanisms at both the personal and cultural levels kick in early on to help us cope. They're not failsafe, of course. Nearly everyone will experience an Arzamas breakdown some time or another. But, for the most part, our denial strategies do manage to get us through the day—and, more important, through the long dark nights.

Death-denial often expresses itself in whirlwind activity aimed at keeping us too preoccupied to think about the certain-uncertain fate which awaits us. We throw ourselves into our professions, hobbies, relationships, or pleasures, working each of them with such intense single-mindedness that there's no time or energy left over for "morbid" thoughts of death.

Many of us use religion to stave off death-fear. While it's not the case that all religious faith is motivated solely or even mostly by death-fear, it would be foolish to deny that it plays a significant role. Typically, religion promises that physical death isn't the end of *us,* but only of our *bodies.* That which is most vitally us—soul, spirit, personal identity—somehow endures. But even for people whose faith assures them of an afterlife, death remains frighteningly uncanny. How, for example, can I possibly remain myself in the absence of a body? Significantly, a 2009 British study discovered that dying patients with strong religious convictions were three times more likely than non-religious ones to ask for life-prolonging medical treatment.[3] So religion (not to mention the pious platitudes that often pass themselves off as religion) isn't much more likely than secular strategies to alleviate death-fear. As Henri Nouwen once wisely observed, "it somehow doesn't take death seriously enough to say to a dying person, 'Don't be afraid. After your death you will be resurrected as Jesus was, meet all your friends again, and be forever happy in the presence of God.'"[4]

Another denial strategy that safeguards us against unwelcome reminders of death is safely sequestering the dying in medical or long-term care facilities. Today, more than three out of four people in the United States die in hospitals and another 17 percent in nursing homes. In earlier times, relatives typically died at home surrounded by their loved ones. Today, we tuck dying people away in professional buildings and surround them with all the gizmos medical technology has to offer. We prefer that their dying be kept at a distance—and their death too. Funerals in which the bodies of the dead are actually present are increasingly unfashionable. We much prefer a tastefully impersonal urn of ashes to the sight of a corpse.

Ultimately, it's not just the dying and deaths of others from which we hope to distance ourselves. We wish to be absent at our own dying and death too. If we must die, we want it to come unannounced and unanticipated: a sudden heart attack or stroke, an accident while doing something we love, or—best of all—just slipping away one night in our sleep. (Wasn't it Woody Allen who said that he didn't fear death, but didn't want to be around for it either?) For us, a good death is one at which we're not present. As one commentator notes, "The only hope for a Good Death that you ever hear is the common one of, 'I don't want to know anything about it...' The only report we value is 'It was instantaneous, he can't have known anything.'"[5] The irony is that modern medicine's success at keeping ill and aged people alive suggests that chances for the quick and painless end we desire are slim.

Our Neighbor Death

The ancient philosopher Epicurus taught his followers that death is no cause for anxiety. "Where *I* am," he reasoned, "death is not. And where *death* is, I am not. So what is there to fear?"[6]

This is a clever argument, but there's something patently fishy about it. Life and death don't exclude one another. Death is always where we are, because to be human is to be a creature whose life trajectory arches toward death and who is aware of the fact. So an anxious sense of the permanent possibility of death is an essential feature of who we are. Death, as the German philosopher Martin Heidegger once put it, is our "ownmost possibility."[7] Without the awareness of it we would be something less than human. That's why our efforts to deny death are futile. Try as we might, awareness of our mortality always haunts us.

Given that, a more reasonable option than death-denial is a forthright acknowledgment of the fact that the course of our life ultimately leads to death. Much better than Epicurus's advice is the seventeenth-century counsel of Sir Thomas Browne: "Conceive that near which may be far off; approximate thy last times by present apprehensions of them: live like a neighbor unto Death, and that there is but little time to come."[8] Or as the essayist Lewis Thomas put it in our own day, "We had better face up to and speak about death—there's an awful lot of it going around these days."[9]

But still something in us balks. Why *should* we live "like a neighbor unto death"? What's the point? Perhaps we can't totally deny death, but must we live so intimately with it? Surely we're better off avoiding the topic until old age or illness forces it upon us.

This protest is understandable, but there are several good responses to it. In the first place, there's the matter of honesty. Pretending that death isn't real means that one lives a lie—or, even worse, that one deliberately courts delusion. As much as we may wish at times that we didn't have to die, none of us would really prefer to go through life with blinkered eyes. The good life isn't a pain- or anxiety-free one, nor is it a permanent state of childlike innocence. Truth is important to us, even if the truth sometimes hurts.

In the second place, facing our death-fear is actually a better way to cope with mortality than death-denial. As I said earlier, we'll never be able to totally get out from under death-fear. But what we can do is accustom ourselves to some extent to it so that it gradually becomes a more familiar although still uncanny part of our landscape. We need not sleep in our shrouds, as the poet John Donne is reported to have done, to get used to the idea that we're going to die. But we can certainly try to remember that death is an inseparable part of who we. If we do that, it just may be that we can lessen the frequency and intensity of our own Arzamas nights, even if we can't expect to avoid them altogether.

Once we face up to the inevitability of death, we discover a third good reason to make death our neighbor. Honestly acknowledging our mortality allows us to make choices that realistically take into account the brevity of life. Awareness of our own finitude sharpens our powers of discrimination, allowing us to dismiss the unimportant and focus instead on life-possibilities that promise genuine fulfillment within the timeframe given us. In a very real way, acceptance of mortality liberates us to make the most of every moment we have. Appreciation of the goodness of humans, the beauty of nature, and the comforts of the everyday is enhanced. So is the realization of how silly it is to waste time nursing grudges, clinging to resentments, and stoking anger.

Getting to the point where we can forthrightly acknowledge the inescapable fact of our mortality and turn what might otherwise be a paralyzing death-fear into a motivation for fruitful life choices isn't easy. It calls for disciplined resolve on our parts, and this in turn requires strength of character. A person of character is someone who has cultivated traits that enhance the richness of life and serve as a moral compass. These traits not only improve the quality of our living. They also necessarily affect the way in which we die, because the strength of character we cultivate for the sake of a fulfilling life also helps us cope when our time to die comes. We die as we live: this is the steadfast rule of human existence.

Virtues for Living Well

The traits that build strength of character and lay the foundation for resolutely facing mortality are traditionally called "virtues." When we cultivate them, we increase our chances of a good life and a good death. But to appreciate this claim, we need to get clear on what virtues are.

One of the most basic facts about humans is that we want good lives. By "good" we generally mean two things, one descriptive and the other prescriptive. Descriptively, the good life is one in which fundamental needs are met, talents are brought to fruition, and happiness is attained. Prescriptively, the good life is one in which we behave in morally decent ways that promote the well-being of others and ourselves. There's an intimate connection between the two meanings. Genuine happiness is impossible in the absence of moral decency. I can't be happy if I'm morally indifferent to the fundamental well-being of others, nor can I attain the good life if I nurture secret vices that blemish my character, even if my public image is above reproach.

But wanting a good life doesn't necessarily mean that we wisely pursue it. As St. Paul observed (Rom 7:18), we may long for a fulfilled, decent life, but often wind up behaving in ways that bring misery to ourselves and others. A desire for the good isn't enough. We must also discipline ourselves to the good, so that our attitude and behavior are consistent with our desire for it.

One reason a simple desire for the good isn't enough is that it's so easy to become confused about what the good actually is. Like many other creatures, we possess appetites and will. We know all too well from everyday experience that our appetites are insatiable, incessantly clamoring for immediate gratification regardless of the cost, and that our will easily inflates to the point where it insists that the entire world bend to its demands. Unchecked, the cravings of appetite and will insidiously re-define the contours of the good life. The appetites persuade us that happiness is identical to immediate gratification. The will slowly but surely promotes what it sees as self-interest over moral concern for others. Sometimes its rationalization for jettisoning morality is blatantly self-serving: *my* talent, *my* genius, *my* good looks, and *my* specialness justify bending the rules in *my* favor. More commonly, though, the will simply grows myopic to the needs of others. It's hard to get perspective if the center of your universe is yourself.

When the appetites and will sit unsupervised in the driver's seat, they don't chauffeur us to the good life. Instead, they hijack us, steering us toward behavior that both enslaves us and is ultimately unsatisfying. Whether the appetites lead us to gluttony or sloth or manic consumerism, the outcome is the same: we become addicts no longer in control of our lives. Similarly, when the will steers us in the direction of arrogant self-centeredness, we progressively exile ourselves to a desolate land that has no room for other people because it's filled to overflowing with our self-absorption. This is anything but the good life, even if in our confusion we think otherwise.

It's clear that something is needed to keep the appetites and will from going hog-wild and ruining our chances of a genuinely good life. This is where the virtues come in. Virtues are traits that enable us to regulate our desires and wills so that we may wisely pursue the good. In the Christian tradition, they're sometimes called "habits of the heart," an acknowledgment first of the biblical understanding of the *heart* as the seat of integrity, and second of the fact that virtue is a matter of disciplined *habituation* rather than on-again, off-again whim. The appetites and the will never cease pushing and prodding. Habituating ourselves to virtues that channel their energy in fruitful directions is the effective counterweight to them. Good intentions or the study of moral philosophy alone won't do. We become virtuous by acting virtuously, not merely by wanting to be virtuous or by thinking abstractly about virtue.

The most famous analysis of how virtues build character and promote the good life comes from Aristotle, who sees the virtues as balancing points between deficiency and excess. Take the virtue of courage, for example. Our appetite for personal safety may drive us toward the deficiency of cowardice, or our will for glory and fame may drive us toward the excess of foolhardiness. Either of these passions damages our characters, potentially harms others, and lessens our chance of happiness. By contrast, genuine courage neither runs away from danger nor underestimates it. The courageous person accurately sizes up the threat and judges what the proper response to it is. She doesn't allow her spontaneous impulse to flee or fight to have the final word.[10]

As with courage, so with all the virtues. Each of them tempers our excesses and deficiencies, educates our desires, disciplines our will, and accustoms us to a pattern of behavior that builds strength of character. The more successful we are at cultivating the virtues, the better our odds of living the good life.

Aiming as they do at a common goal, virtues are interconnected with one another. To become more practiced in the virtue of courage most likely means that complementary virtues such as patience or trust are also being cultivated. It may well be that one's personal temperament and talents make some virtues easier than others. But no virtue can thrive in isolation from the others. Possessing the virtue of love, for instance, and no other (if it were even possible to do so) wouldn't bring a fulfilled, enriched life, even though love undoubtedly is virtuous. Instead, it would give us a life seriously out of alignment and doomed to any number of inevitable frustrations and failings. Love in the absence of other virtues—prudence or honesty come immediately to mind—is dangerously blind and thus destructively unpredictable. Contrary to the Beatles song, love *isn't* all we need. So strength of character isn't a matter of excelling in one virtue to the neglect of others but rather of the harmonious cultivation of many virtues, even if no single one is ever brought to perfection.

Habituation to virtues loosens the grip of our natural appetites and nudges our will in genuinely beneficial directions. It strengthens our character by training us to avoid extreme courses of behavior that may seem immediately pleasurable but are actually destructive, and it creates in us an integrity or wholeness in which our values are consistent with one another and our behavior compatible with our desires. This absence of conflict and turmoil in turn promote the good life in both the descriptive and prescriptive sense. A happy and fulfilling life is the reward of virtue.

Virtues for Dying Well

We've seen that death, contrary to Epicurus, is always present in the midst of our living. Consequently, everything we do that helps us to live well also prepares us for dying well. Taming impulses and egoism by disciplining ourselves to virtue while we're hale and hearty can't but serve us when our time to die arrives. Make no mistake about it: even the best of deaths is an ordeal for which we will need to call up all the years of habituation to virtue that we've managed to accumulate. If a good life requires character traits that strengthen resolve, shield us from despair, and sustain our integrity, a good dying needs them even more.

Once we begin to die we become strangers in a strange land who can never turn back and return to the more familiar one we've left. The border closes behind us, separating us from those who still dwell in the land of the healthy. That's why friends and family often find themselves perplexed, embarrassed, and tongue-tied in the presence of a dying loved one. By the same token, most of the everyday concerns and interests of the healthy strike the dying as trivial or insipid. Who cares about which team wins the World Series, whether or not to trade in the old car for a newer model, or office gossip? All that becomes utterly unimportant when looked at from the strange land's new vantage point, and the dying person who tries to pretend otherwise soon discovers that her efforts are both foolish and frustrating.

Because dying removes her from the reassuring routine of work, socializing, bill-paying, child-minding, and all the other aspects of ordinary life, the dying person is forced to call upon her own inner resources to sustain her in the final stage of her life. This isn't to say she becomes totally indifferent to the things of the world or the people who matter to her. But what it *does* mean is that she's more on her own than she's ever been, and if she's not to sink into a quagmire of fear, sadness, and loneliness, character traits like courage, trust, and love must be firmly in place. Courage can't be learned overnight, and love born of deathbed desperation is a fragile thing at best. To enter dying with an irresolute character weakened by selfishness, greed, or rancor is to have no provisions for the final journey. It's like heading off into the wilderness with no backpack—or, worse, with one loaded down with rocks and briars.

The cultivation of virtues during our lifetime not only helps us cope with dying; it may also make our experience of dying a rich opportunity for learning some final truths about life and ourselves. This doubtlessly sounds bizarre to many ears. After all, we typically fear dying so much that it's hard for us to see how anything about it could possibly be valuable. Moreover, even if dying *does* have something to teach us, who cares? We learn, and then we take what we've learned to the silent grave. It seems futile at best, cruel at worst.

But think about it for a moment. Dying is surely a landmark experience in any person's life, and such experiences, if heeded, shed light on the nature of life and reality. Consider the landmark experience of love. Whenever I love another person and allow myself to be mindful of what the experience can tell me, I gain new insight into myself as well as a deeper appreciation of the nature of a world that allows for the possibility of love. Grave illness or a serious accident on the one hand or moments of sheer joy and beauty on the other can be landmark experiences that pluck me out of my everyday rut and toss me into the deep waters of somber reflection or delighted wonderment. What defines a landmark experience isn't whether it's pleasant or unpleasant, but whether it reveals new dimensions of reality.

If we're able to get beyond the panicked terror or black despair that can paralyze us when we enter the dying process, we may discover that dying is one of these opportunities for clarity and insight. As we've already seen, the concerns that consumed our attention in healthy days tend to fall off our radar when we begin dying. Looked at one way, this can be a cause of regret and sadness. But looked at another way, our loss of interest in these things can be a gift that clears our minds and hearts for more significant concerns. Dying can give us the leisure to reflect deeply on our lives, our values, our successes and our failures, our faith or lack of it, and in the process come to a better understanding of who we are and what life is about. And, while a cynic may find little value in enhanced self-understanding that soon ends in death, surely the value of what enriches or fulfills a life shouldn't be measured by longevity, but rather by how well it enhances character and awakens wisdom.

The possibility that our dying can become a final opportunity for discovery and insight depends on our possessing the inner resources to quiet our appetites' terrified scramble to flee death and our will's bull-headed insistence on an energy-squandering fight against the inevitable. If we've developed strength of character during our lifetime by cultivating virtue, we're prepared, or at least as prepared as we can be, to be present to our dying and to hear what it has to say to us. If we haven't prepared, the likelihood that we'll be able to heed any final lessons that come from dying is slim to none.

Being mindful of our own dying can transform the experience into a meaningful and enriching finale to life regardless of whether or not we have faith. But for Christians, there's an additional dimension: the mindfulness is also an act of devotion. Followers of Christ believe that dying is a participation in his suffering and death. Of course, Christians symbolically die and are reborn in the sacrament of baptism. But at life's actual end, symbols and reality converge. Like their Lord, the dying endure physical pain and emotional agony. Like him, they suffer anguished moments in which they feel abandoned and even betrayed. But their hope is that they can surmount the pain and despair of dying to re-affirm, as Christ did, faith in God and in the goodness of God's plans. Death cannot have the final word when it is embraced as a final opportunity in this life to affirm loyalty to the convictions of a lifetime. As theologian Christopher Vogt puts it,

> Taking Jesus as a model, it is necessary for Christians to come to see their own dying as a venue where the possibility exists to find deepened self-understanding and to bear witness to God. In other words, dying must be made a part of living in the sense that one's efforts at discipleship persist through this stage of life. Dying is not a time or a task that is devoid of meaning, divorced from God's presence.[11]

Vogt's claim that dying can be an occasion for bearing witness is a reminder that our dying, besides being personally enriching, can also be fruitful for others. The example of a good death is one of the most profound gifts the dying can offer the living, particularly when it helps the latter realize that dying well is inseparable from living well. Observation of a good death not only defuses some of the terrors death may hold for survivors; it can also inspire them to take stock of their own lives and resolve to begin disciplining themselves to virtues that will enrich them both now and in the future. In this context, as in so many others, deeds speak louder than words. The example of a good death as the culmination of a good life is likely to have more impact on observers than the reading of any number of books (including this one) on the art of dying and living well.

Henri Nouwen was so impressed with the great gift to others which dying can be that he properly viewed it as a recapitulation of Christ's "dying for others."

> Not only the death of Jesus, but our death, too, is destined to be good for others. Not only the death of Jesus, but our death, too, is meant to bear fruit in other people's lives. Not only the death of Jesus, but our death, too, will bring the Spirit of God to those we leave behind ... Thus God's Spirit of love continues to be sent to us, and Jesus' death continues to bear fruit through all whose death is like his death, a death for others.[12]

Viewed in this light, dying, and hence living, take on a significance that pushes through any sadness, fears, and doubts that may arise when we think about our mortality. Although it won't be pleasant, dying needn't be thought of as a senseless termination of life. Instead, it can be seen as the capstone to a life well lived, a final act of virtue, and a participation in the mystery of Christ's cosmic victory over death and decay. In viewing death this way, concludes Nouwen, we can "liberate" it from what otherwise appears to be its "absurdity."[13]

From the Abstract to the Concrete

To some extent, this chapter has done precisely what we ought to be cautious about doing when thinking and speaking of death: it has approached the topic a bit abstractly. But I'm not too worried. A certain amount of abstraction is necessary at the beginning of our inquiry. It builds a conceptual grid that helps us better appreciate the more concrete discussions that begin in the next chapter. Opening an exploration of living and dying on an abstract note is a forgivable fault, if fault it be. But ending abstractly isn't.

In the chapters that follow, this grid is fleshed out with the stories of seven people who died well because they lived well, and who lived well because they lived virtuously. We begin with Joseph Bernardin, who exemplifies trust, because trust grounds all the other virtues. We end with Caryll Houselander, who exemplifies christing, because christing is their culmination.

The stories of dying and living offered here are sometimes harrowing. Although death can be fruitful and even holy, it's never pleasant, and we would do well to be alert to the denial strategy of romanticizing it. But, painful though it sometimes will be, exploring how these persons lived and died teaches us valuable lessons about appreciating life, building relationships, arriving at self-knowledge, loving God, and dying with grace. Their stories *do* offer consolation to those of us who, still in the land of the living, gaze westward toward our destiny. But, much more importantly, they show us how our dying can befit a life dedicated to the cultivation of character. None of us could ask for more than this from living and dying.

CHAPTER TWO

TRUST

Joseph Bernardin

*"...from the very beginning of this illness,
I placed my life totally in God's hands..."*

A Somber Press Conference

The press room in the cardinal's residence was uncomfortably packed with television, radio, and newspaper reporters. Late summer in Chicago is steamy, the heat broken only occasionally by breezes blowing off the lake, and most of the reporters were in shirtsleeves and sipping from water bottles.

Anticipation was high. No one quite knew why Cardinal Joseph Bernardin had called the press conference. But, given the events of the past three years, everyone was braced for another big story. First, in November 1993, there had been the charge of sexual abuse leveled against Bernardin by an ex-seminarian. The ordeal had lasted for six months until the accuser confessed that the story was false. Then, just over a year after the nightmare ended, the cardinal was diagnosed with pancreatic cancer and underwent major surgery. That was in June 1995. Post-op therapy lasted several months before Bernardin was declared cancer-free.

Bernardin had called in the press when he was accused of sexual misconduct, when he was exonerated, when he was diagnosed with cancer, and when his oncologists gave him a clean bill of health. His policy when it came to the media was always total openness.

And now, on August 30, 1996, he was holding another press conference.

The cardinal and a few of his aides entered the press room. Bernardin walked over to the podium. Cameras flashed, illuminating his gaunt face and gentle smile. The buzz in the room ceased. And then the announcement: "On Wednesday of this week, examinations conducted at Loyola Medical Center indicated that the cancer has returned, this time in the liver. I have been told that it is terminal and my life expectancy is one year or less."[1]

The reporters sat in stunned silence. Several of them later admitted to tearing up when they heard the cardinal's announcement. Bernardin was much loved in Chicago, even by the hard-bitten press corps.

"Over the past year," he continued, "I have counseled the cancer patients with whom I have been in touch to place themselves entirely in the hands of the Lord. I have personally always tried to do that; now I have done so with greater conviction and trust than ever before. While I know that, humanly speaking, I will have to deal with difficult moments, I can say in all sincerity that I am at peace. I consider this as God's special gift to me at this moment in my life."[2]

And that was that. Bernardin said a few more words, calmly answered a handful of questions, waved a farewell to the reporters, and stepped away from the podium. One of the journalists shouted: "Why are you telling us this now?"

"Because you're part of my family," replied Bernardin, smiling. The journalists applauded as he left the room.[3]

Two and a half months later, Joseph Bernardin was dead.
It was the end of a meteoric career in the Church. He was the
youngest American bishop at the time of his appointment,
and was the senior active American bishop at the time of his
death. As one of the most influential voices in the National
Conference of Catholic Bishops, he led the way in writing
pastoral letters on peace-making and economic justice that
shaped the direction of Catholic moral discourse in the
United States. He tirelessly defended a "seamless garment"
ethic that extended pro-life concerns beyond abortion to include capital punishment, euthanasia, and poverty. Appointed
archbishop of Cincinnati in 1972, he was installed ten years
later as cardinal archbishop of Chicago. He was the first Ital-
ian-American to lead a major archdiocese. During his tenure,
the Chicago archdiocese was spread over 1,400 square miles
with 378 parishes, 277 elementary schools, 48 high schools,
6 colleges, 3 seminaries, 19 hospitals, and 2.3 million
Catholics. The archdiocese had the largest parochial school
system in the nation and employed nearly 20,000 priests,
nuns, and laypersons. Word on the street was that Bernardin
had a good chance of becoming the first American pope.

But despite these very real accomplishments, Cardinal
Bernardin's true greatness—and his most profound gift to
the rest of us—was his ability to trust even in the midst of
calumny, illness, and death. Throughout his entire life, Bernardin exemplified the importance of trust for coping with
the fragility of existence and the inevitability of death. Without trust, the likelihood of a good life and a good death diminishes almost to the point of impossibility.

In his public sermons and pastoral letters as well as his
private retreat journals, Bernardin returned to the theme of
trust time and again, and it was the core of his message in his
final press conference. For him, trusting God, trusting one's
fellow humans, and being a trustworthy person were valu-

able and proper ends of a Christian. But he was under no illusion about how difficult they are to attain. Cultivating the virtue of trust is the work of a lifetime, and the final proof of how well we've succeeded is the manner in which we die.

The Virtue of Trust

Bernardin often remarked, especially in his final three years, on how highly he valued the virtue of trust. His intuitions were good. No virtue is more essential for living and dying well. It takes pride of place over all the other habits of the heart explored in this book. Without the soil of trust, it becomes impossible for love, gratitude, obedience, courage, patience, or christing to thrive. Each in its own way rests on a foundation of trust.

Trust and Dependence

Some evolutionary biologists believe that we're hardwired for trust.[4] Given the inability of hominid children to make it on their own for years after their birth, a talent for trusting elders enough to heed their instructions and obey their commands is essential for survival. The theory is that primordial children who possessed a "trust gene" survived longer than those lacking it, and in turn passed the disposition on to their own offspring. We, their distant descendants, don't typically face the harsh, life-threatening conditions they did. But trust of parents and other adult authority figures remains.

Their willingness to trust diminishes as children grow into adolescents and adults. Everyone is familiar with the exercise in which participants are supposed to fall backwards into the waiting arms of another person. Children have no problem with this, especially if the person assigned to catch them is a grown-up. But adults are notoriously bad at letting themselves go, even when the person waiting to catch them is a spouse or close friend. The thought of placing our fate in the hands of others chills us because we distrust their willingness or ability to protect us.

If the biologists are correct, adults don't actually lose the ability to trust so much as repress it. The reason isn't difficult to figure out. Trust implies dependency: whenever I trust another, I confess that I'm not self-sufficient. It's perfectly appropriate for a child to be dependent on his or her parents. But, as we grow older, we naturally move away from our need for parental protection and assert our autonomy. We transit from being dependent to being in control, first over our own lives and then over the lives of others (as, for example, when we have our own children). There's nothing inherently bad about this. Self-assertion is a sign of developmental maturity, and the ability and willingness to take control of certain aspects of one's life is essential for a healthy adulthood. In its absence, neither psychological nor moral health is possible.

The problem is that the need to assert control gets out of hand in many of us. It becomes a driving force in our lives, and sometimes an obsession. Most of us aren't domineering bullies or control freaks. But most of us *do* associate dependence with weakness. To be dependent, we believe, is humiliating, displaying as it does an inability to take care of oneself. It's also risky, because it means relying upon someone who may let us down. Those of us who live in the United States put an especially low premium on dependence. For us, *in*dependence, self-reliance, and individuality are supreme cultural values. We typically feel pity for anyone who can't "stand on his or her own two feet."

But refusing to trust in order to maintain control is a short-sighted strategy. When our time to die comes, the cul-

tural values we've absorbed and lived by—self-reliance, independence, and control—will let us down. We'll necessarily
revert to a dependency very much like the one that defined
our situation when we were children. If we've resisted dependence all of our adult lives and ceased to nurture our intrinsic ability to trust, we'll be ill-prepared for our final
weeks or months. As Henri Nouwen once astutely observed,
"becoming a child—entering a second childhood—is essential to dying a good death . . . What characterizes this second
childhood? . . . A new dependence."[5] And dependence requires trust.

Nouwen's point is that dying is a stark reminder of the
utter dependency of our existence. We *are* only in and through
and by God. Not for a single instant in our lives have we
been independent of this divine grounding. The control and
self-sufficiency we painstakingly and jealously try to maxi-
mize during our healthy days is, ultimately, illusory.

It's easy to forget all this in the hustle and bustle of a
healthy, self-confident life. But when a final illness strikes and
the stamina we've always relied on begins to wane, our physical frailty can remind us of our total dependence on God, a
dependence just like that of a helpless child who is totally dependent upon her parents. Then each of us has an ultimate
choice to make: to accept our dependence or to rebel against
it.[6] Acceptance is difficult if we've shied away from cultivating the virtue necessary for it: trust. To acknowledge our
utter helplessness in the face of death is either a bleak act of
despair over losing control and a panicked refusal to enter
into the second childhood of dying or a trusting affirmation,
albeit one certainly tinctured with anxiety and sadness, that
the Ground of being which *has* sustained will *continue* to
sustain. As we'll see shortly, Cardinal Bernardin's lifelong
journey toward trust prepared him well for his own ultimate
choice of affirmation.

There's another factor to consider as well: dying makes us progressively dependent on care-givers. As our bodies weaken and our strength erodes, we're able to do less for ourselves and so inevitably must rely more on others. Even before we reach the end stage of our final illness, we may find ourselves needing help when it comes to transportation, housekeeping, and shopping. Eventually we might need others to wash and groom us, feed us, put us to bed, manage our medications, and comfort us when we're gripped with death-fear. Like it or not, dying does indeed return us to a child-like state of dependence on others. For many of us, this will be a humbling and perhaps even humiliating time of life. But it's a necessary one, and unless we've disciplined ourselves to trust others enough to ask and receive help from them, we're not likely to be able to at the end of our lives.

Letting Go, Letting Be, and Cleaving To

Remember the falling backwards exercise that tests our ability to trust others? It's a perfect metaphor for what might be described as trust's initial movement: relinquishment or letting go. When I let go, I give up my need to be in control by acknowledging life's uncertainty as well as my own vulnerability. But instead of sinking into despair, I resolve to trust, difficult and frightening as it sometimes is to do, that all will be well. In letting go, I fall backwards into God's waiting arms.

Dying is the most radical letting go any of us will ever face. When we begin to die, our hold on life slips through our fingers. Normalcy shears away from us as we confront the necessity to say farewell to everything we love: persons, beautiful landscapes, falling snow, the fragrance of freshly-brewed coffee, books, music. The trauma of letting go of everything is simply too overwhelming to deal with unless we've prepared for its inevitability before the dying process actually begins. By practicing trust throughout life, by letting go of the need to control, to clutch, to hang onto, we will be in a better psychological and spiritual condition to face the ultimate giving up of life.

When I start to let go, I'm also able to let be, the second movement of trust. Since I no longer feel the compulsion to manipulate the course of events, I can open myself to it without feeling unduly threatened. The same goes for my relating to other people. When I let go of my distrustful, adversarial attitude toward them, I can celebrate what they do rather than deplore it as a risk to my control or autonomy. I can let them be who they are, rather than struggling to remake them to suit my own needs. Letting be in this sense doesn't at all mean "letting alone" or "refraining from interfering." It isn't a kind of passivity or fatalism. Instead, as one commentator points out, letting be "is something much more positive and active, as enabling to be, empowering to be, or bringing into being."[7] When I let be, I actively invite forth the other, trusting him—and thereby liberating him—to be who he is. As we'll see, one of the reasons Joseph Bernardin was such an able and beloved diocesan administrator was his nurturance of initiative in his priests and his willingness to grant them a great deal of autonomy. His trust in them empowered them to be better pastors.

In cultivating the letting be aspect of trust, I also liberate God. Too many of us think of God as a divine Santa Claus who can fix any problem we have if only we pray hard enough. After all, God is "almighty," and almightiness means that God can do anything—right? But this way of relating to God as the Great Fixer is wishful thinking, not too far off from the foolish belief that wanting to win the lottery badly enough will somehow influence the numbers that come up. At worst, it's a cynical manipulation of God, much like the way that we seek to control people and events.

When we let go of our need to control, we're able to let God be who God is. We recognize that divine almightiness doesn't mean that God is the Great Fixer, but rather, as Archbishop of Canterbury Rowan Williams says, that "there is no situation in which God is not to be relied upon." Letting God be entails trusting that God "always has the capacity to do something fresh and different, to bring something new out of a situation."[8] God cannot "fix" the fact of our bodily frailty. All mortals die. But in letting God be, we come to trust that God is present even in the midst of death.

Finally, trust means that we're also better able to let death be what *it* is: the predictable and natural terminus of life which comes to everyone. In letting death be, we put it in perspective, at least as best we can. We acknowledge that even though our life is precious to us, we are, after all, no more privileged than any other human who has lived. What we endure now, others have endured before. Accepting death for what it is allows us to meet it without panic and terror. We will still regret leaving life. But we won't fight the departure as something unnatural or sinister.

Cleaving to is trust's third movement. The Hebrew word for "cleaving," *devekut,* is used by Jewish mystics to denote a radical fidelity to the divine Ground of our existence. It's not a frightened clinging to God in the way that a traumatized child latches onto her mother's hand. Instead, cleaving to God in the midst of bewilderment and pain, especially the bewilderment and pain of dying, is an affirmation that God's creation is purposeful and that death is neither arbitrary nor meaningless. From a Christian perspective, of course, cleaving to means faith that death is a new beginning, not an end. But the nature of that new beginning is so shrouded in mystery that it defies the imagination. All we can do is admit our utter ignorance of it and reaffirm our fidelity to God, who is equally mysterious. And this, too, is an act of trust.

At first glance, letting go and letting be might seem in-compatible with cleaving to. But they're not. We can let God be what God is and devote ourselves to God only when we've shed our devotion to lesser objects of attraction that get in the way. Moreover, once we cease pretending that we're in control, we naturally recognize our radical depend-ence on God and open ourselves up to it. When it comes to trust, it's a matter of proportion and balance, just as with all the virtues. Knowing what to give up and what to embrace is the key.

"God was calling me, and I had to listen"

Joseph Bernardin became acquainted with the dynamics of trust when he was still a youngster. He was the first child of Catholic immigrant parents who left their northern Italy mountain town of Tonadico di Primiero for a better life in the New World. His father Giuseppi, a stonecutter by trade, lived in the United States for a few years before returning to his village to claim his bride, Maria Simion, Bernardin's mother. It was during this trip home that the cancer which eventually killed him was diagnosed. Following a painful sur-gery, Giuseppi returned to America with his wife and settled in Columbia, South Carolina. Bernardin was born in 1928, and his sister Elaine four years later. At the time, more than 98 percent of Columbia's population was Protestant and fiercely xenophobic.

It wasn't long before Giuseppi's cancer returned, re-quiring additional surgeries. (As an adult, Bernardin recalled how his father once bled through his shirt while carrying him on his shoulders.) Doctors were unable to halt the ma-lignancy, and Giuseppi died in 1934 at the height of the Depression. He left behind a small insurance policy, but

Maria earmarked it for the children's education and refused to draw from it for everyday expenses. Instead, she took in work as a seamstress and was eventually hired by the Works Progress Administration (WPA) to make army uniforms. Before he was ten years old, Bernardin had learned something about letting go. Social standing in a southern city suspicious of Catholics and foreigners, a beloved father, economic security: all of these were absent. But he also learned about cleaving to. The death of his father brought him especially close to his mother and sister, and his religious faith was a steady and sustaining force during his early years.

Just how strong his trust in God was became clear when Bernardin declined a scholarship to the University of South Carolina, scrapping plans to become a doctor (influenced, perhaps, by his father's ordeal with cancer) to enter seminary. As he told the story, a couple of priests convinced him that he was better suited for ministering to ailing souls than bodies. Maria wasn't enthusiastic about her son's change of plans and tried to talk him out of giving up the scholarship. But Bernardin characteristically trusted that God was looking out for him. "I decided to go anyway," he later recalled. "God was calling me, and I had to listen."[9]

The next few years were devoted to education and priestly training. Wearing a cassock sewn by his mother, Bernardin studied at Saint Mary's College (Kentucky) and Saint Mary's Seminary (Baltimore), earning a BA in philosophy in 1948. One of his fellow seminarians remembered him as a down-to-earth youngster with a "terrible southern accent" who worried about grades even though he eventually graduated *summa cum laude*.[10] Four years later Bernardin received an MA in education from Catholic University. His superiors wanted to send him to Rome for further study, but he asked to be excused. He didn't want to be that far away from his mother and sister.

Bernardin was ordained in April 1952 and assigned to parish and teaching duties in Charleston, South Carolina. For the next fourteen years he performed priestly functions, taught high school, served as a hospital chaplain, and ably filled various diocesan offices. His administrative skills and conscientious work habits caught the attention of his superiors, and it was soon obvious to everyone that young Father Bernardin was on the fast track. In 1966, Pope Paul VI appointed him auxiliary bishop of Atlanta. He was only thirty-seven.

After that, things moved even more swiftly. Within two years Bernardin became the first secretary general of the National Conference of Catholic Bishops and moved to Washington DC. In November 1972, he was named archbishop of Cincinnati. While there, he also served for three years as president of the National Conference. Giuseppi Bernardin's little boy had arrived.

A Mid-life Conversion

But Bernardin's swift rise up the ecclesiastical ladder nearly derailed him spiritually. As the years passed and success followed success, his focus on administration began to take precedence over his interior life. The trust that had sustained him in his childhood, youth, and early manhood was in danger of being pushed aside by his steadily growing administrative duties and ecclesial authority. He found himself grasping instead of letting go, manipulating rather than letting be, and clinging to the trappings of office instead of cleaving to God. By the mid-1970s, he later recalled, "I was giving a higher priority to good works than to prayer. I was telling

others—seminarians, priests, lay people, and religious—
about the importance of prayer, emphasizing that they could
not really be connected with the Lord unless they prayed.
But...I was not setting aside adequate time for personal
prayer...I was very busy."[11]

Then, a few years into his time in Cincinnati, Bernardin
experienced a mid-life conversion to which he would always
refer as "a turning point in my life." Dining one night with
three young priests, two of whom he'd ordained, he confessed that he was having difficulty praying. They rather fear-
lessly took him to task, all but accusing their bishop of
hypocrisy and warning him that his life was more bureau-
cracy-centered than Christ-centered. Taking their words to
heart, Bernardin resolved "to give God the first hour of my
day, no matter what, to be with him in prayer and meditation where I would try to open the door even wider to his
entrance."[12] Moreover, he radically changed his lifestyle. He
lost weight—up to that point, he was in danger of becoming
the caricature of a soft and well-fed prelate—closed out his
bank accounts, donated the money to charity, and then
began getting rid of his personal possessions. According to
St. Petersburg, Florida, Bishop Robert Lynch, Bernardin
"gave away money, objects of art and other things he felt
were concerns that were more materialistic than spiritual."[13]
In the process of letting go and putting himself more faith-
fully than ever in the hands of God, he began to rediscover
the deep trust he'd known as a child and young man.

Few conversions change the habits of a lifetime overnight.
So, even after his own conversion experience, Bernardin wrestled with the difficulty of trusting God completely enough to
let go and let be. In a retreat journal he kept in mid-life, he
wrote frequently of the struggle. On the one hand, he observed, "I want desperately to open the door to let the Lord
in so he can take over my soul completely." But, on the other

hand, "I seem unable to do so. I let him come in partway. I talk with him but I am afraid to let him take over."[14]

Bernardin had a pretty good idea of why he stopped short of giving himself completely to God. "I want to succeed. I want to be acknowledged as one who succeeds... This drive causes me to want to control things, make them come out 'right.' For this reason, I tend not to put full confidence in people until they have proved their competence ... I deal with the Lord the same way." He also knew himself well enough to sense why he balked at letting God be God. "Do I refuse to let the Lord come in all the way because I am afraid he will insist on certain things (in terms of my personal life) that I am reluctant or unwilling to do or give up?"[15]

Bernardin admired Zacchaeus, the tax collector in Luke's gospel (19:1–10), for his open-hearted willingness to cleave to the Lord. "I have desperately wanted to open the door of my soul as Zacchaeus opened the door of his house."[16] But to do so, he realized, "requires that I truly love the Lord, more than anything/one else—trust him, really trust him as he accompanies me on his journey—'let myself go,' which can only be done if there is a lot of love and trust."[17]

If his actions after becoming archbishop of Chicago in August 1982 and cardinal six months later are any indication, Bernardin was more open to the virtue of trust than he suspected. The archdiocese he inherited was in bad shape. Bernardin's predecessor, John Cardinal Cody, had been an old-school bishop who never really accepted the reforms of Vatican II. He governed in an autocratic style that sought little counsel and tolerated no dissent. On top of that, his thirteen-year tenure was plagued by financial scandals. Under his leadership, over a million dollars of diocesan funds disappeared. By the time he died, lay Catholics in the archdiocese were cynical and the clergy alienated and discouraged.

Knowing that he was facing an uphill struggle to earn the trust of his new archdiocese, Bernardin hit the ground running. Upon arriving in Chicago, he presided over a huge Mass in Grant Park and heralded a new style of leadership by telling the faithful: "Today we celebrate the unity of us all."[18] In his installation sermon at Chicago's Holy Name Cathedral, he promised those assembled that they had "my service and leadership, my energies, my gifts, my mind, my heart, my strength, and, yes, my limitations."[19] He reassured the diocese's priests by letting them know that his management style was different from his predecessor's top-down one. "I am Joseph, your brother," he told them.[20]

In the years to come, Bernardin put his money where his mouth was. He demonstrated his trust in his priests by consulting them on a regular basis and involving them to an unprecedented extent in the administration of the archdiocese; he visited parish after parish, driving his own car, arriving unostentatiously, celebrating Mass, and leaving quietly; he always turned to mediation when disputes arose, avoiding adversarial confrontation; he let his clergy be by allowing them wide latitude in their own parishes; he proved consistent, reliable, and trustworthy to everyone who had dealings with him; and he cleaved to God in daily prayer and regular retreats. Bernardin had his detractors, but they were few and far between. For the most part, both laity and clergy loved and respected him.

And then the bottom fell out.

"I never felt more alone"

On November 11, 1993, Bernardin received the worst phone call of his life. It was from a reporter who warned him that Steven Cook, a thirty-four year old man, intended to file sexual abuse charges against Bernardin the following day. Apparently, Cook had been a seminarian in Cincinnati when Bernardin was archbishop there. Bernardin was stunned. He knew he'd never broken his vow of chastity, and he didn't even recognize Cook's name.

The next morning the story was splashed across the front pages of the nation's major newspapers, and interview-hungry reporters began ringing Bernardin's residence at the crack of dawn. Bernardin announced he would hold a press conference at one o'clock that afternoon. He was determined to answer the media's questions with candor and trust that his innocence would be proven as the facts came to light. But the night before had been sheer agony. "As I prayed the rosary early in the morning," he recalled, "I meditated on the first of the sorrowful mysteries, the Agony in the Garden. I said to the Lord, 'In all my sixty-five years, this is the first time that I have really understood the pain and agony you felt that night.' And I also asked, 'Why did you let this happen?' I had never felt more alone."[21]

The sexual abuse scandal that rocked the Catholic Church in the closing decade of the twentieth century and continues to this day was already well under way when Cardinal Bernardin was accused. Between 1984 and 1992, four hundred priests across the country were charged with sexual improprieties. In 1985, aware that the public accusations would likely increase, Bernardin became the second bishop in the nation (after Seattle's Raymond Hunthausen) to create a diocesan fitness review board charged with investigating sexual complaints against clergy. Even before the press conference, Bernardin made sure that Cook's allegations against him were submitted to the board.

In the early days of the sex scandal, the first response of many in the Church was to fight back by attacking the credibility of the accusers. Some of Bernardin's advisors counseled him to take this route, but he adamantly refused. He knew that he needed to defend himself, but he wanted no countersuit or scorched-earth approach. "The reason was that I did not want to deter persons who had really been abused from coming forward."[22] As he said at the press conference on November 12, he was also concerned about the effect the accusation and investigation would have on the people of his archdiocese, "the people whom I love, the people I shepherd."[23] Would they continue to trust him, or any other priest, after this?

At that initial press conference, and in many more during the next one hundred days, Bernardin steadfastly and calmly insisted on his innocence and compassionately expressed concern for Steven Cook, whom he believed was being manipulated by persons with axes to grind against the Church. As police, church officials, and journalists scrutinized the evidence, Cook's case began to disintegrate. Finally, on February 28, 1994, Cook, who by that time had been diagnosed with AIDS, recanted. Bernardin was vindicated. Ten months later, he flew to Cook's residence in Philadelphia to meet and reconcile with his accuser.

Shortly before he died, Bernardin reflected on the months he lived under the cloud of scandal and suspicion. "I was humiliated," he said. "It was total humiliation."[24] He went on to say that the ordeal was more horrible than the cancer that was taking his life. There's no doubt that the episode was the most painful one Bernardin ever endured. Ever since his ordination, and especially since his second conversion experience in Cincinnati, Bernardin had believed that trustworthiness was one of the most important virtues a priest could possess. He loved the story about what happened when the actor Alec Guinness was filming G. K. Chesterton's *Father Brown* on location in France. When the day's shooting ended, Guinness, still dressed in his character's black cassock, left the set to walk back to his hotel. Along the way, a small boy greeted him, confidently took his hand, walked with him a while, and then left him with an *"Au revoir, mon père!"* This was the kind of innocent trust Bernardin wanted to earn and inspire by his own ministry. That's why Steven Cook's claim that he'd betrayed his priestly vows wounded him so deeply.

But Bernardin also came to see the ordeal of the false accusation as a rehearsal for dying. Looking back on it, he realized that "the entire matter really served as scenes in the final act of a three-part play that I now believe constitutes my spiritual pilgrimage over the past three years."[25] The accusation left him feeling helpless and forlorn. But his years of disciplining himself to the three movements of trust gave him the strength to let go of rancor and pride and to let God be by putting himself totally in God's hands. The morning that Cook's accusation made national headlines, Bernardin told a friend that a long and hard night of prayer had revealed to him what he had to do. "I have to trust in God, who has allowed this for some purpose, and I have to put my trust in the truth."[26] It was a letting go and cleaving to that, under the circumstances, didn't come easily. But it would have been impossible had Bernardin not cultivated the virtue of trust in the years leading up to this.

Cancer

Life got back on track for Bernardin after his vindication, although friends and acquaintances noticed that he seemed more introspective than he had before the ordeal. But the normalcy was short-lived. In early June 1995, six months after his reconciliation with Steven Cook, Bernardin noticed that his urine was discolored. Not especially worried, he called his physician, who immediately sent him to Loyola University Medical Center for tests. The results stunned

Bernardin: pancreatic cancer. His doctors told him that the outlook was bleak. Pancreatic cancer is an unforgiving malignancy, with a five-year survival rate of less than 5 percent.

Bernardin's initial reaction, he wrote, was one of "disorientation, isolation, a feeling of not being 'at home' anymore."[27] For the first time in his life, he "had to face directly the prospect of a premature death. In one brief moment, all the plans for my future had to be put on hold; *everything* in my life had to be reevaluated from a new perspective."[28]

Feelings of anger and powerlessness sharpened Bernardin's sense of disorientation. He'd just gone through the worst period in his life battling Steven Cook's accusation, a period during which he had felt totally helpless at times, only to be thrown once more into a situation that threatened to rob him of his autonomy. "I had regained control of my life after the false accusation and here I was asking somebody else [his physicians] to tell me about *my* life, *my* body."[29] It was almost too much to bear, and at first Bernardin couldn't help feeling abandoned by God. "Why me? After all, Lord, wasn't the humiliation of the false allegation of sexual abuse brought against me enough?"[30]

Bernardin opted for something known as the Whipple procedure, a type of surgery often used in cases of pancreatic cancer. It involves the removal of pancreatic tumors as well as parts of the stomach, duodenum, bile duct, gall bladder, and lymph nodes. Virtually everything surrounding the pancreas that's expendable is taken out. Bernardin came through the brutal procedure and was out of hospital in seven days. While recuperating from the surgery—he would soon start six full weeks of chemotherapy and radiation, followed by a year of maintenance therapy—he came to the conclusion that his illness was another opportunity to exercise the trust he had always valued so highly. "I had to let go of everything. Again. God was teaching me yet again just how little control we really have and how important it is to trust in him."[31]

Bernardin's realization that his illness was an opportunity to be honest about his desire for control and his reluctance to let go needs to be approached cautiously. It's too easy to transform him into a plaster saint by imagining that it was easy for him to give everything up to God when faced with a deadly cancer. If we make that move, we trivialize his experience to the point where his example can offer us nothing in our own preparations for life-threatening sickness. Even after acknowledging that the cancer was another way God had of coaxing him toward a deeper letting go and cleaving to, Bernardin still endured, as do all patients, bouts of despair, anger, resistance, and self-pity. The nights he found "especially long...I sometimes found myself weeping, something I seldom did before."[32]

Bernardin neither repressed his upsurges of fear and doubt nor allowed them to carry him away. He was able to recognize that midnight bouts of fear and occasional doubts didn't mean he'd lost his faith. He still trusted in God, and that trust enabled him to live with the conviction that even though God isn't a Great Fixer, God does have the capacity, as Rowan Williams noted, to infuse any situation with new possibilities. Bernardin put it this way: trust isn't "an expectation that something [like a cure] will happen." Instead, it's "an attitude about life and living in God's loving care...It comforts us with the knowledge that, whatever is happening to us, we are loved by God through Christ."[33]

This trust got Bernardin through the bad moments when the darkness closed in and all seemed hopeless. As he told a gathering of priests the September following his surgery, he was "one who struggles each day—sometimes with little obvious success—to decrease so that the Lord can increase in him, a man whose life is full of crooked lines but who is willing to let the Lord write straight with them."[34]

Something else got him through the darkness and helped him remember what truly was in his control and what was not. While still in the hospital recuperating from the surgery, Bernardin received a handwritten letter from an eleven-year-old girl named Kelly Noone asking him to pray for her grandfather who was a patient at Loyola just down the hall from Bernardin's room. This was the beginning for Bernardin of a brand new ministry to the terminally ill. In the next few months, he cut down on his administrative duties to spend more and more time praying for the sick and visiting or writing to them. Toward the end of his life, there were more than six hundred names on his prayer list.

In ministering to the seriously ill, Bernardin especially wanted to help them avoid self-absorbed withdrawal from the world. "One of the things I have noticed most about illness is that it draws you inside yourself. When we are ill, we tend to focus on our own pain and suffering. We may feel sorry for ourselves or become depressed."[35] But he saw no inevitability to this withdrawal, recognizing that illness can also create its own community, "the community of those who suffer from cancer and other serious illnesses," a community whose members "see things differently"[36] and are bound together precisely by their new shift in focus. For them, life takes on a clarity that makes it "easier to separate the essential from the peripheral." When we're ill, we "need not close in on ourselves or remove ourselves from others. Instead, it is during these times when we need people the most."[37]

Bernardin's newly found hospital ministry was an act of trust on his part in at least three ways. First, it indicated that even though his illness required him to let go of some ways of serving, he trusted that God would help him find others—and God certainly did. As Bernardin observed of his year of working with patients, "I have never felt more like a priest."[38] Second, it indicated that he was willing to expose himself to fellow sufferers in order to hold their pain and in turn share his, both acts of radical trust. Finally, it attested to his trustful willingness to take seriously Jesus' message "that through suffering we empty ourselves and are filled with God's grace and love"—a fulfillment that in turn allows us "to think of other people and their needs."[39]

The End of the Play

When Cardinal Bernardin held the press conference on August 30, 1996 to announce that his malignancy had returned and that this time it spelled a death sentence, he had been cancer-free for months. Two days earlier he'd had a routine MRI in preparation for surgery to ease some of the pain of spinal stenosis, a condition that increasingly bothered him and frequently forced him to use a cane. That's when the liver cancer was spotted.

Even though he'd always known that his chances of beating the cancer were marginal, the news came as a blow to Bernardin. But he was grateful for his post-surgical year of relatively good health because it opened up a whole new ministry for him, deepened his trust in God, and nudged him toward the conclusion that "death is my friend."[40]

Two days later, at the press conference, Bernardin returned to the theme.

> We can look at death as an enemy or a friend. If we see it as an enemy, death causes anxiety and fear. We tend to go into a state of denial. But if we see it as a friend, our attitude is truly different. As a person of faith, I see death as a friend, as the transition from earthly life to life eternal.[41]

Bernardin came to think of death as a friend through the influence of Henri Nouwen, a long-time acquaintance who had visited the cardinal shortly after the first surgery. Nouwen's advice to Bernardin was to radically alter his attitude to death

by seeing it as something worthy of befriending, primarily because it's the doorway to eternal life but also because it liberates us from bodily suffering.

Nouwen's counsel seems extreme, and at least one Catholic moral theologian rejects it as unscriptural.[42] Death is such
an uncanny and total rupture of our embodied relation to the
world—such an utter letting go—that it's difficult to see how
we ever could or should look upon it as a friend. Even if we
manage an abstract, philosophical appreciation of the claim
that *death* is more friend than foe (as, for example, when it
relieves us of great suffering), it borders on a denial of reality
to think of the *process of dying,* especially when it brings pain
and debility, in a similar way. It may be the case, as we noted
in the previous chapter, that the experience of dying can give
us new perspective on ourselves, the world, and God. If this
happens, it's not inappropriate to feel gratitude for the insight. But it's a stretch to presume that this is a befriending of
death. For most of us, that's taking things too far.

Even Bernardin entered his final days with an ambivalent
attitude to what was happening to him. In a prayer service
with fellow priests held just a few weeks before his death, he
shared his mixed feelings about leaving the world. "My
brothers, I am in the midst of letting go. It is like the Cross:
sometimes it is sweet and easy; sometimes it is very difficult."[43] And in his memoir *The Gift of Peace,* finished only
days before the end, he still referred to death as a friend, but
also as a burden.

> Perhaps, the ultimate burden is death itself. It is
> often preceded by pain and suffering, sometimes ex-
> treme hardships . . . But notice that Jesus did not
> promise to take away our burdens. He promised to
> help us carry them. And if we let go of ourselves —
> and our own resources—and allow the Lord to help

us, we will be able to see death not as an enemy or a threat but as a friend.[44]

Bernardin was honest enough with himself and others to acknowledge his ambivalence as well as his occasional bouts of depression. "Jesus [in Gethsemane] was very lonely," he wrote after one particularly bleak night, "as was I."[45] But he remained convinced of two things. The first was that dying and living mean acknowledging our dependence and placing our life "totally in God's hands, confident of his abiding love,"[46] and that nurturing the kind of trust that enables us to do this is a "lifelong process" of ridding ourselves "of everything that keeps the Lord from finding greater hospitality in [our] soul or interferes with [our] surrender to what God asks."[47]

Bernardin's second conviction was that his final days invited one last pastoral act: "the most important thing I could do for the people of the Archdiocese—and everyone of good will—would be the way I prepare for death."[48] And he prepared well. The example he set for his people was commendable. After several weeks he opted to cease all chemotherapy and to let the disease run its course. He tied up loose administrative ends so that he could spend as much time as his waning energy permitted with his priests, fellow-patients, old friends, and sister Elaine. He worked hard on the manuscript that became his last book. And he entered ever more deeply into the dynamics of trust: embracing his dependence, letting go of life, letting death be what it is—both a burden and a friend—and cleaving to God.

By late autumn, Bernardin was clearly entering his final days. When Eugene Kennedy, an old friend and later biographer, visited him on November 8, Bernardin was barely able to speak. Sitting upright in a chair because his spinal stenosis made lying down painful, gasping for breath, and having trouble raising his head to greet his guest, the cardinal seemed to Kennedy to be participating in Christ's passion.[49]

On Monday, November 11, Dr. Gaynor, noting an abrupt downturn in Bernardin's condition, told him that the end was very near. Bernardin managed to reply that he was ready. By Tuesday night he was too weak to sit upright and took to his bed. On Wednesday, Pope John Paul II and President Bill Clinton called him and Cardinal Roger Mahony of Los Angeles flew into Chicago and said Mass at Bernardin's bedside. Shortly afterwards, Bernardin fell into a coma and died at 1:33 on Thursday morning, November 14. It was his mother's ninety-second birthday and sixty-two years to the day since his father's death from cancer. One week later, at Bernardin's funeral Mass, his close friend and assistant Msgr. Kenneth Velo ended his homily with these words: "Cardinal. Eminence. You're home. You're home."[50]

Bernardin's Legacy

Suspended from the highest point of the domed apse in Chicago's Holy Name Cathedral are five *galeri,* the broad-brimmed, tasseled hats worn by cardinals. The crimson *galeri* are given only to princes of the Church as a sign of great authority.

When a cardinal dies, the custom is to suspend his *galero* from the ceiling of his cathedral. It stays there until it eventually decays, shreds, and disintegrates. This is to symbolize the fleetingness of time, the frailty of life, and the vanity of power, and to remind living cardinals that even princes of the Church must one day return to dust. Tradition has it that the soul of a cardinal at last makes its way to heaven when his *galero* falls.

Joseph Bernardin's *galero* was hung in mid-December 1996, one month after his death, joining those of his four predecessors, Cardinals Mundelein, Stritch, Meyer, and Cody. The heavenward raising of it evoked, for those who knew Bernardin, one of his most characteristic virtues: upward-reaching trust even in the midst of calumny, illness, and death. Throughout his entire life, but especially in his final three years, Bernardin exemplified the importance of trust for coping with the fragility of life and the inevitability of death.

The manner of Bernardin's living and dying gifts us with valuable lessons about what it means to trust. He showed us that in letting go, we liberate ourselves to enter into relationship with God and our fellow humans, trusting them and in turn becoming trustworthy ourselves. We also liberate *them* because, no longer needing to be in control, we allow them to be who and what they are. And in letting God be God instead of a magical Great Fixer, we discover God as the certain and benevolent ground of our existence and are able to cleave to God in devotion and gratitude.

All of these qualities make for a good life. But they also enable us to die, when our time comes, with grace, patience, and good will. Trust doesn't eliminate the fear and sadness and pain of dying, nor does it necessarily help us look upon death as a friend. But it does help us realize, as Bernardin discovered, that God "accompanies us on our [final] journey."[51]

CHAPTER THREE

LOVE

Thea Bowman

"I want to take you back to where you first believed. I want to take you back to where you were loved and nurtured and sheltered. I want you to remember the people who taught you faith and hope and love and joy; people who taught you to love yourself and to believe in yourself. Who taught you to love your family, to love justice, to love sisterhood and brotherhood and fatherhood and motherhood and world harmony."

A Born Troubadour

Just a few months before she died, Thea Bowman, a nun of the Franciscan Sisters of Perpetual Adoration for nearly thirty-five years, spoke of her love of Franciscan spirituality. "There's a kind of craziness that is Franciscan," she laughingly declared, born of being wildly in love with God and God's creation. Only a crazy man like Francis would strip naked before the townspeople of Assisi, joyfully kiss lepers, sing a love song to Sister Death, or gleefully dance while sawing two sticks together as if they were bow and fiddle. It was exactly this kind of light-hearted, joyful craziness that immediately appealed to the troubadours and minstrels of Francis's day. It appealed to Sister Thea too. "Somebody like me," she said, "was made to be a minstrel and troubadour."[1]

Thea was right. She *was* born to sing and dance and laugh, and to infect others with her gaiety. She was crazy with love of God, of creation—she was so fond of birds that, like Francis, she frequently sang along with them—and of people in all their ethnic, cultural, and religious diversity. Nor was it just her peers whom she loved. She honored and celebrated generations that had come before her and generations that would come afterwards. Her love enabled her to bridge time and space, pulling the once-was and the not-yet into the here-and-now. For Thea, love truly had no boundaries.

It would have been understandable if Sister Thea had been less loving. As an African-American born into a totally segregated community in the deep South, she learned from an early age about hatred and suspicion. Later, as the only black novice in a northern convent, she experienced loneliness, homesickness, and occasional racism. Before finishing her novitiate, she was diagnosed with tuberculosis and endured a year of convalescence in a sanatorium. A large part of her adult ministry was spent trying to persuade a frequently clueless and predominantly white Church to be more hospitable to black Catholics. The cancer that eventually killed her struck in 1984 when she was only forty-seven. With only a brief thirty months of remission, she endured it and the brutal effects of surgery, chemotherapy, and radiation therapy until she died in 1990 at the still young age of fifty-two. Before the end came, she suffered horribly.

But Thea weathered the storms that might have bewildered and embittered another person. Like everyone else, she had her moments of despair and anger, particularly as the cancer began to get the upper hand. What got her through the bad times was the same thing that fueled her joyful Franciscan craziness: the power of love. From an early age, Thea had been reared in the virtue of love, and as she grew to maturity she continued cultivating it. The abandonment with which she loved both enlightened and lightened her life. It's not surprising that she took as her signature song "This little light of mine, I'm gonna let it shine," and that love's light was a comfort and source of strength when Sister Death finally came for her.

Thea once said that her only prayer after she came down with cancer was "Let me live until I die." This is a good prayer, and it's one whispered by many people diagnosed with fatal illnesses. But Thea had another prayer as well—"Let me *love* until I die"—because living made sense to her only as an opportunity for loving. Her living and dying, both exemplars of her commitment to the virtue of love, can help the rest of us learn how to live and love until Sister Death calls for us too.

The Virtue of Love

If trust is the foundation of the virtues, love is their driving force. Given its importance to Christians (for whom God *is* love), you'd think that we'd be pretty clear about just what love is. Surprisingly, we're not. So before we can begin to appreciate the richness of love, its importance for a good life and a good death, and the ways in which Sister Thea exemplified it, we need to get clear on what love isn't and what it is.

What Love Isn't

Perhaps the most common misconception about love comes from thinking about it mainly in terms of romantic passion. Love is what happens when we fall for another person. It's a "drifting mooniness in thought and behavior, the mad conceit that the entire universe has rolled itself up into the person of the beloved, a conviction that no one on earth has ever felt so torrentially about a fellow creature before"[2] that we associate with "falling in love."

It's not hard to see why we so effortlessly think of romance when we hear the word "love." We live in a culture that celebrates romance at every turn in popular songs, films, novels, and television shows. Additionally, some of the most intense experiences in life revolve around falling in love, and it's only predictable that memories of them spring to mind whenever the subject of love comes up.

But there are big problems with assuming that love is identical to the mooniness, madness, and emotional highs associated with romantic love. The most obvious of these is that the conflation ignores the different contexts in which we appropriately use the word "love": the love between parents and children, between friends, and between humans and God.[3]

A less obvious but serious difficulty with the conflation is that it implies love is present only when we experience the seething torrent of emotion that comes with romantic love. But anyone who's ever fallen head over heels in love knows that the intensity is transient. We can and often do fall *out* of love as quickly as we fell *in* love. Even if our love endures, chances are good that its initial ardor will give way to an intimacy that blazes less but sustains more. If we conflate love with romance, we paint ourselves into the absurd corner of denying that this long-term intimacy counts as love.

Finally, reducing love to romance turns love into something that takes us captive, controls our will and behavior, and makes us utterly passive (hence the expression "romantic passion"). "Falling in love" is a perfect metaphor for this understanding of love. In the throes of romantic passion, we lose our equilibrium and tumble, powerless to control our trajectory and completely at the mercy of our yearning for the beloved. This kind of passion makes us giddy with excitement but also enslaves our reason and will. That's why the Greeks called romantic love *theia mania,* the "divine madness," and warned that it can drive us in directions that harm ourselves and others. But if romantic passion is so potentially destructive—and world literature as well as the daily tabloids testify that it certainly can be—it's surely a mistake to equate love and romance. As Sister Thea knew, genuine love builds up and connects us with an expanding circle of others. It doesn't destroy or enslave.

There's another common error in thinking about love: the belief that whatever else it may or may not be, it's ultimately a pleasant feeling or emotion. Admittedly, there's something to be said for this understanding of love. When we love, we often *do* feel emotionally pleased or satisfied. But even though love can be *accompanied* by pleasant emotion, it's a leap to assume that love is *identical* to the emotion. If we make that assumption, we're forced to conclude that love is absent when the feeling we associate with it is absent. I love my son when I experience feel-good emotions about him, but don't love him when I'm angry with him or, less dramatically, when I'm simply so focused on mowing the lawn or battling rush hour traffic that I'm not even thinking about him. This turns love into a bizarre on-again-off-again affair that pops in and out in a rather unpredictable way, violating the commonly held intuition that genuine love abides, even when it isn't consciously experienced.

There's another difficulty as well: the very obvious fact that love frequently *doesn't* make us feel good, warm, and satisfied. Father Zossima, the wise and holy priest in Fyodor Dostoevsky's novel *The Brothers Karamazov,* observes that love is often a "harsh and dreadful thing." What he has in mind is "love in action" as opposed to "love in dreams."[4] The latter is an abstract and effortless fantasizing about love which we frequently mistake for the real thing. We imagine ourselves loving suffering humanity, for example, and our concern makes us feel nice and warm inside. We may even shed a tear or two over the plight of those millions of hungry and poor people for whom life is a burden. But our feel-good love stops at the point where we actually have to perform demanding and quite possibly unpleasant tasks in the real world to help them. Dream love is neat and clean and sentimental. Real love is frequently messy and smelly and painful. It requires that we expose ourselves to unpleasant situations, enter into the suffering of others, and sometimes sacrifice our own well-being and comfort for their sake. *This* is real love. The feel-good variety is an immature sentimentality that can quickly degenerate into indifference if not outright callousness.

What Love Is

Back in the thirteenth century, Thomas Aquinas offered a definition of love that avoids the errors we've just examined. Love, he said, is a virtue that consists in willing the beloved's good for the sake of the beloved without any expectation or desire of recompense.[5] It isn't a romantic passion over which we have no control or an inevitably pleasant emotion that befalls us and over which we have no control. Rather, it's a disposition and mode of comportment to which we consciously discipline ourselves. We can habituate ourselves to love by disciplining our intellect, emotions, and imagination, but this often demands hard work on our part. Love isn't the easy and sentimental fantasizing that Zossima calls "love in dreams." But, when done right, it *is* the human activity that most reveals our Godlikeness.

Obviously a requirement for properly loving another is knowledge of what's truly in the other's good. What the beloved may desire isn't necessarily what anyone who wishes her well should desire for her, because her desires may be harmful to herself or to others. Knowing what's genuinely good for her involves a certain degree of abstract reflection on the nature of virtue, the purpose of human existence, and the contours of the good life. But just as importantly, it demands knowing the beloved as a concrete person with a unique life history and identifiable strengths, talents, dispositions, and weaknesses, because willing her good requires entering into the context that makes her who she is. In order to lovingly will the beloved's good, we must enter her world, even if it means leaving our own comfort zone. We must make ourselves totally "available" to her. To be unreservedly available is to love.[6]

When I make myself available to another, I place all of my material, emotional, intellectual, and spiritual resources at her disposal. I hold nothing back, keep nothing of myself in reserve. My only thought is the well-being of the person to whom I'm making myself available, and I'm utterly dedicated to maximizing it. Questions of whether she deserves my availability or of my recompense for bestowing it don't enter into the picture; the relationship isn't a contractual one. When I contract with someone, the relationship is external: two humans co-existing alongside one another for the purpose of pursuing a shared interest. The relationship is purely instrumental. We use one another as means to an end. But when I make myself available to someone, the relationship moves from an external mode of relating to an intimate "being-with,"[7] something along the lines of what the Jewish philosopher Martin Buber calls "thou-ing." He argues that the appropriate way to relate to a fellow human is to see him as a "thou" rather than an "it." Treating others as "thou"s means honoring them as concrete subjects possessing freedom and subjectivity, and refraining from using them as if they were inert, dumb objects.[8] From a Christian perspective, treating others as "thou"s means recognizing and celebrating the Christ-presence that radiates from them, a point we'll return to in the final chapter when we explore the virtue of christing. In honoring the other as a thou, I also honor the Thou.

We too frequently ghettoize love by specially designating a tiny handful of our relationships as loving ones and throwing all the others into the broader category of casual or contractual acquaintance. (This move, by the way, is encouraged by popular culture's reduction of love to romance or feel-good emotions. After all, we can't feel passionately or pleasantly about everyone.) But if love is putting oneself at the disposal of another for his or her sake with no expectation of recompense, there's no justification for being so selective. Like God, whose love rains indiscriminately upon everyone, I'm free to be available to all. It's not necessary for me to feel emotional warmth for someone as a pre-condition for "being-with" him or her.

By its very nature, love isn't doled out on the basis of what is deserved but is given unconditionally out of a desire to enhance the beloved's good (that's why scripture tells us that God's love falls on saint and sinner alike). As we cultivate a spirit of availability, everyone we encounter—even our enemy—becomes the beloved. This new way of relating to others isn't naïve. Their faults aren't whitewashed. Genuine love, contrary to the popular sound bite, isn't blind. Indeed, in some cases, willing the beloved's good may demand helping her to become more mindful of her shortcomings, especially if they harm herself or others, and that entails an awareness of them on the part of the lover. But familiarity with the beloved's faults doesn't inhibit or destroy love for her, any more than God's awareness of human weaknesses diminishes God's love for us. In making myself available to another—in relating to her as a thou—I accept her as she is, not who I think she ought to be.

Love, then, is willing the beloved's good, and the only way to do that is to put oneself freely and unreservedly at her disposal. Doing so means more than just knowing what the good in general is. It also means connecting with the beloved so that she, in all her rich and sometimes confusing particularity, can open up to me if she wishes. Self-gifting, total availability, "being-with," connecting: these are the qualities of genuine love. All of them can be cultivated and, so far as humanly possible, perfected. They're exactly the qualities that Thea Bowman was taught as a child, nurtured all her years, and passed on to others in her living and her dying.

An Old Folks' Child

In the nineteen forties and fifties, Thea Bowman's hometown of Canton, Mississippi was a sleepy agricultural center where local farmers brokered their harvests. Like all other pre–Civil Rights towns of the deep South, Canton was rigidly segregated. Thea remembered that the color line was so entrenched that she never really knew any white people during her childhood.[9] Whites were always vaguely threatening and never trustworthy. "I learned survival," she recalled. "You learn very early on how to wear the mask so that if I had to work with [a white racist], I learned to guard my manner, to guard my speech, even to guard my thoughts, my feelings, my passions, and emotions."[10]

For a naturally outgoing person like Thea, this early need to muzzle herself—to be unavailable to others—must have been terribly frustrating. That it didn't embitter or inhibit her is a testimony to the loving environment nurtured by her parents and the wider black community of Canton. Thea grew up knowing that she was loved, and that the connections established by that love linked her not only with living kin and family but also with those who had come before her. From an early age, she felt a deep intimacy with the black spiritual tradition passed on from her ancestors. They rooted her in something larger than herself and significantly shaped her identity. As an adult, she was fond of saying "I am an old folks' child." In part, she was referring to the fact that she was born late: at her birth, her mother was thirty-five and her father forty-three. "My parents were o-o-old when I was born," she frequently joked.[11] But, more significantly, she was also expressing her sense of gratitude, indebtedness, and affection for the ancestral "old folks" who had bequeathed to her the spirituality that sustained her throughout her life. It was a tradition that placed a high premium on establishing "being-with" relationships and practicing active love.

Bertha Elizabeth Bowman (Thea was the name she chose when she became a nun) was born in 1937 to Theon and Mary Esther Bowman. Her father was one of two black physicians in Canton and practiced medicine there for over sixty years. Her mother had been a teacher before marriage, and prepared Bertha so well for school that she was able to skip the first grade.

For as far back as she could remember, Bertha was a spiritually hungry child who loved to go to church. It was there that she learned "what [her elders] called the 'old-time religion,'" and she grew up wanting to be a preacher.[12] The faith she absorbed was joyful, deeply communal, musically expressive, and intimately connected with the past through the "old ones" who served as her first spiritual teachers.

I grew up in a community where the teaching of religion was a treasured role of the elders—grandparents,

old uncles and aunts, but also parents, big brothers
and sisters, family friends, and church members.
Many of the best teachers were not formally educated. But they knew Scripture, and they believed the
Living Word must be celebrated and shared.[13]

Bertha's parents weren't deeply religious, but they recognized the spiritual streak in their daughter and encouraged
her to explore it. By the time she was ten years old, Bertha
had "tried," as she later wrote, "the Methodist, Baptist, Epis-
copalian, Adventist, A.M.E., and A.M.E. Zion churches." She
appreciated them all. But "once I went to the Catholic
Church, my wanderings ceased. I knew I had found that for
which I had been seeking."[14] With her Protestant parents'
blessing, Bertha became a Catholic in the summer of 1947.

What immediately drew Bertha to the Catholic Church
was the dedication and love—the radically available love in
action—she observed in the clergy at Canton's Holy Child
Jesus Mission. "I had witnessed so many Catholic priests,
brothers and sisters, who made a difference that was far
reaching. I wanted to be part of the effort to help feed the
hungry, find shelter for the homeless, and teach the children."[15] A year later, when she enrolled in the school affili-
ated with the Mission, she discovered to her delight that the
sisters who taught in it worked hard to create a learning environment that exemplified that same love. Bertha's years at
the school shaped the contours of her adult life.

The nuns who taught Bertha, members of the Wisconsin-
based Franciscan Sisters of Perpetual Adoration (FSPA), had
been invited by the priests of the Holy Child Jesus Mission to
travel south and open the school. Somewhat to the priests'
surprise, the sisters jumped at the opportunity, and the first
class matriculated in 1948. The school, housed in an old

army barracks, turned no student away. Students too poor to afford the monthly $2 tuition had the fee waived. Skin color and religious affiliation were completely unimportant.

Partly because the school operated on a shoe-string budget, but mainly because the sisters wanted to teach more than just book-learning, students from the very first learned collaboration and the importance of community. Working together, they fashioned bookshelves out of wooden crates, sanded desks, cut grass, and painted walls. They made flash cards, helped cook school lunches, and wrote personal thank-you notes to donors of money and goods. Under the nuns' guidance, older students tutored younger ones in their studies, and students talented in a particular subject worked with those who needed a bit of help. "I was poor in math," Thea recalled, "so someone had to coach me. I was good in reading, so I had to help someone else. We didn't realize it, but we were learning to cooperate and to build our community."[16]

The Franciscan sisters' availability wasn't restricted to their students. They also reached out to Canton's townspeople, offering first aid classes for pregnant women, regularly organizing sales where clothing and other items donated to the school could be bought at rock-bottom prices, and working to ease the tension between Canton's white and black communities. None of this was lost on a perceptive and precocious Bertha. She was fifteen when she announced to her parents that she wanted to journey to the FSPA motherhouse in La Crosse, Wisconsin, complete high school there, and enter the order.

Theon and Mary Esther, understandably upset at the thought of losing their only child and worried that Bertha would face discrimination in the all-white FSPA, said no. Bertha, used to getting her way, dug in her heels and went on a hunger strike, quickly losing more weight than her already thin frame could afford. Seeing that there was nothing they could do to change their headstrong daughter's mind, her parents gave in. But they weren't happy about it. Just before Bertha took the train to La Crosse, her father took her aside. "They're not going to like you up there," he warned, "the only black in the middle of all the whites." Bertha's reply was typical. "I'm going to *make* them like me," she said.[17]

Confident though she was, Bertha's move to La Crosse wasn't easy. "I was the only 'convert,' the only Southerner, the only Black in a totally white, Northern, Catholic school environment," she later wrote. "I met high school students, young adults, even teachers who had never worked, played, prayed or even talked with persons of other faiths."[18] Whether out of overt bigotry or a parochialism that seems incredible to us today, one of the older sisters told sixteen-year-old Bertha that black people "go to nigger heaven together with the dogs and other animals."[19] Even those students and teachers who worked hard to accept Bertha found the southern black spirituality that had formed her off-putting. "I was loved and accepted," she later said of her initial experience in La Crosse. "Still," she ruefully added, "secretly, I felt very much the outsider."[20] Without quite realizing what she was doing, Bertha began to downplay her black cultural background in an effort to fit into the white, German-American culture she'd entered.

Despite her culture shock, Bertha was usually happy at the convent and excelled in her studies. But in April 1955, after she'd been in Wisconsin for nearly a year and a half, she came down with tuberculosis and was shipped off to a sanatorium one hundred miles north of La Crosse. She stayed there for nearly a year, enduring drug and diet therapies and chaffing at the almost continuous bed rest prescribed for her. During her exile in the far north, Bertha wrote a touching essay that gave voice to her homesickness and sense of isolation. Written in black southern dialect and entitled "Away f'om Home," the piece captures her longing for warm weather, southern cooking, and the black community that had nurtured her when she was a child. "I lies abed an' dreams that I 'as stranded in the sno', an' I can heah the old folks callin', but I jes can't move along. Sometimes I think as if I'll never git t' see that old bayou no mo'. Sometimes I think as if I'll never make it home." "I ain't complainin'," the essay concluded, "but you all can see that thisyere ain't at all like home. Nossuh! I ain't complainin', but thisyere ain't like home a'tall."[21]

Well enough to leave the sanatorium in March 1956, Bertha returned to La Crosse and worked hard to make up the year of schooling she'd missed during her convalescence. That fall she was formally received into the FSPA as a novice and took Thea as her religious name. Thea was a fourth-century saint. But Bertha probably chose the name because it was a feminine version of Theon, her father's name, and because she resonated with its meaning: "of God." She enrolled as a student at Viterbo College (now University), an institution founded in 1890 by her religious order, and threw herself into her studies. Once again, she proved to be an excellent student, shining especially in English literature and Latin. Taking an action that was not unusual for the time, Sister Thea's superiors gave her a a teaching assignment before she had completed all the requirements for graduation. Three years into her college studies, she was sent to Blessed Sacrament School in La Crosse, where she taught fifth and sixth grades until 1961.

Thea took summer classes at Viterbo to finish up her undergraduate degree requirements, and eventually earned her BA, *magna cum laude,* in 1965. But by then she'd left Wisconsin and been back in Canton, Mississippi, for four years. Reassigned after her stint at Blessed Sacrament to teach in

her alma mater, Holy Child Jesus School, Thea returned joyfully to the South she knew and loved.

Becoming Fully Functional

Her years as a student at Holy Child Jesus School had been
crucial ones for Thea. They helped her grow in her faith,
continued her training in the ways of availability, and inspired her to become a nun. The time she spent at Holy
Child Jesus when she returned as a teacher was just as important. In the seven years (1961–1968) during which she
taught there, Thea rediscovered the black spirituality she'd
suppressed at La Crosse. She loved the Catholic liturgy, and
her fidelity to both the teachings of the Church and her own
vocation (she took final vows in 1963) was unwavering. But
her earliest experiences of church as a child in Canton had
instilled in her a love for less formal, more spontaneous expressions of joy, celebration, and thanksgiving than she
found in the all-white Catholic congregations of her day.

Back in Canton as a teacher, she began to encourage students and fellow nuns to explore ways of worshiping God
that incorporated the spiritual style she had known as a girl,
one in which "people participate—sing, pray, clap, sway, raise
their hands, nod their heads."[22] Thea's vision of black spirituality was holistic and embodied, engaging the "mind, imagination, memory, feeling, emotion, voice, [and] body."[23]
During the 1960s, she began to sense that many blacks were
alienated from an American Catholicism which they perceived
as buttoned-down, overly-cerebral, and relentlessly white.
Catholic African Americans, she concluded, needed to be encouraged by the Church to connect with their traditional
spiritual roots and to incorporate them into their identity as

faithful Catholics. "If we as blacks are going to answer to the call to be truly Christian Catholics," Thea observed, "we have to be truly ourselves."[24]

One crucial way for the Church to become more welcoming to blacks was through song and music. Thea had always loved music, and some of her favorite hours as a child had been spent learning traditional black gospels from the "old folks." For Thea, these spirituals were "a living repository of the thoughts, feelings, and will of Black Spirituality."[25] They connected the present generation with previous ones for whom the songs had been a way of maintaining black identity in a dominantly white culture. "Those songs helped my people to survive. They let them express themselves, their joys, their pain, their grief, their longing, their frustrations, their love of God, and their love of each other."[26] To connect with them was to touch the heart of the African American Christian experience.

> Black sacred song is soulful song—holistic: challenging the full engagement of mind, imagination, feeling, emotion, voice, and body; participatory: inviting the worshipping community to join in contemplation, in celebration and in prayer; real: celebrating the immediate concrete reality of the worshipping community—grief or separation, struggle or oppression, determination or joy—bringing that reality to prayer within the community of believers; spirit-filled: energetic, engrossing, intense; life-giving: refreshing, encouraging, consoling, invigorating, sustaining.[27]

At Holy Child Jesus School, Thea taught English and vocal music, and used both subjects to introduce her students to black spirituals. It wasn't long before she'd put together a fifty-member high school choir that eventually cut an LP album called *The Voice of Negro America*. The record, dedicated to "the promotion of brotherhood and universal peace," featured black spirituals such as "Go Down, Moses" and "Deep River" that spoke to the African American experience of deep spiritual longing. In between the record's songs, Thea spoke a message that expressed her growing embrace of her black heritage.

> Listen! Hear us! While the world is full of hate, strife, vengeance, we sing songs of love, laughter, worship, wisdom, justice, and peace because we are free. Though our forefathers bent to bear the heat of the sun, the strike of the lash, the chain of slavery, we are free. No man can enslave us. We are too strong, too unafraid. America needs our strength, our voices to drown out her sorrows, the clatter of war. Listen! Hear us! We are the voice of Negro America.[28]

In addition to helping her reconnect with black spirituality, the Canton years were also the period in which Sister Thea became more aware of the social and political dimensions of what it meant to be black in America. While studying at Viterbo College in the summers, she began taking classes in black history, culture, and literature. Southern hostility to nuns in general and to a black one in particular— "when I was riding with the white nuns," Thea recalled, "I would duck down in the car when we passed white people"[29]— as well as the general turmoil of the struggle for Civil Rights, encouraged Thea to think deeply about the racial divide that alienated and damaged blacks as well as whites. She became convinced of the need for actively cultivating a reconciliatory spirit of "being-with" instead of "standing-against."

After graduating from Viterbo, Thea began taking graduate courses—initially in the summer but, starting in 1969, full time—at Washington, DC's Catholic University. While there, she became a founding member of the National Black Sisters Conference and was soon on the lecture circuit speaking about black music, poetry, oral tradition, and history. By the time she earned her PhD in English literature in 1972, she was in wide demand as a lecturer and preacher. Thea skillfully wove song into her presentations, often breaking out into a verse from one of her beloved spirituals before returning to her spoken text. She also began wearing traditional African caftans and turbans. To white Catholic audiences, she came across as exotic, a bit baffling, and sometimes even threatening. To black ones, she was a breath of fresh air.

So far as Thea was concerned, the years at Canton and Catholic University reawakened her to what it meant to be African American. By the time she took her next assignment, returning to Viterbo College to teach English, she considered herself a "fully functioning" black *and* Catholic woman. "What does it mean to be black and Catholic? It means that I come to my church fully functioning . . . I bring myself, my black self, all that I am, all that I have . . . my African-American song and dance and gesture and movement and teaching and preaching and healing and responsibility as gift to the church."[30]

When Thea took up her teaching duties at Viterbo, she had less than two decades to live. But the amount of work that she crammed into those years is staggering. She quickly became one of the most popular professors on campus. She loved the literature she taught, and her enthusiasm for the works of St. Thomas More, Shakespeare, Faulkner, Eudora Welty, and an assortment of African American authors was infectious. Students flocked to her classes, drawn by her personal charisma and expertise, the obvious affection she felt for them, and the fact that she regularly led study trips to Mississippi to show students the places that inspired Faulkner and Welty. As a teacher, Thea was demanding and pulled no punches when it came to evaluating her students—"More Hemingway, less Henry James" she sometimes wrote on wordy essays—but students adored her.[31]

Thea stayed at Viterbo for six years, ultimately serving as chair of the English Department. But in the summer of 1978 she made a decision that ushered in what would be the last and most fruitful period of her life. She returned to Canton to be with her aged and frail parents. As soon as she settled in, she went straight to Mississippi's bishop, Joseph Brunini, and asked for a job. Brunini jumped at the chance to welcome Thea to his diocesan team and immediately appointed her Diocesan Consultant (later Director) for Intercultural Awareness. Her charge was daunting: to build interracial relations between white and black Catholics, find ways to improve black student performance in the diocese's Catholic schools, and encourage black vocations.

Using her position as a springboard, Thea devoted her final twelve years to a thriving ministry of intercultural awareness and reconciliation. In 1980 she became a charter faculty member of the Institute for Black Catholic Studies at Xavier University in New Orleans, teaching summer courses in black literature and music until 1988. In the 1980s she traveled to Africa twice and crisscrossed the United States several times to speak at universities, churches, and community centers. It seemed to her friends that Sister Thea was always on the go, running from one engagement to the next.

As she had from the very start of her public speaking, Thea continued to make the black spirituals she loved essential ingredients in her presentations. For her, preaching and lecturing were always opportunities to "be-with" the members of her audience, and music was one way to build the intimacy she wanted. As a reporter covering one of her lectures noted, "She's not embarrassed to kick off her shoes in front of an audience and walk around in her stocking feet, to sing at the top of her voice or to boast about her hundred-year-old Uncle Harvey, who earned his high school diploma at age ninety-four."[32] Some people were put off by Thea's style, dismissing her as a showboat or a buffoon. One observer uncomfortably admitted that she thought Thea came across at times like a performer in a minstrel show.[33] But her critics were clearly in the minority. Most people responded positively to the exuberance with which Thea delivered her message. When Mike Wallace interviewed her in 1987 for *60 Minutes*, giving her a wider audience than she'd ever had before, viewer response was wildly enthusiastic. Overnight, Sister Thea moved from being a Catholic to being a national celebrity.

Practicing Love

What accounted for Thea's widespread appeal? Two factors that surely played a part were novelty and context. Catholics and non-Catholics alike were intrigued by this black Franciscan nun who dressed in colorful African robes, sang and danced during her sermons, and was just as comfortable delivering a scholarly paper on Faulkner as she was rhythmically clapping her hands and shouting hallelujah during Mass. Thea, in short, was a character.

More significantly, Thea brought her message to America at the right time. After the Civil Rights struggles of the 1960s, conditions were ripe for her celebration of black spirituality. African American Catholics in particular, alienated as

many of them were from the Church, found her message liberating. But Thea wasn't content to reach out only to black
audiences. The United States, she recognized, was a multi-
cultural society in which every ethnic and religious group
brought something of value to the table, and she made sure
that her lectures and sermons spoke to all of them.

But neither novelty nor context is decisive in accounting
for Thea's popularity. What attracted people first and foremost to her was her message. And that message, voiced by
her words and embodied in her life, was love. The core of
her ministry was "building the Kingdom—in other words, to
love the Lord your God with your whole heart, with your
whole soul, with your whole mind, and to love your neighbor as yourself."[34] This message of total availability is as old
as Christ's earthly ministry, but Thea gave it a freshness that
touched the minds and hearts of thousands.

For Thea, one of the primary characteristics of the Kingdom is "being-with" connectedness: first with God, the
supreme Love and Lover, then with God's world. In good
Franciscan fashion, she saw everything in creation as qualified
to be the beloved for her. Fellow humans, ancestors, future
generations, nature and wildlife: all were kindred through the
sharing of one and the same loving Parent. "The very word
'catholic,'" she said, "means 'all.' Jesus loved all men—and
true love always tends to bring people together."[35] But it was
clear that for Thea, the word "catholic" encompassed not just
people but all of creation. In her world, there were only
"thou"s. Nothing was merely an "it."

The interconnectedness of creation served and celebrated
by Thea shouldn't be thought of as a blending together that
dissolves individual identity. Thea was convinced that we can
love only particulars, not abstractions. We can manipulate,
enjoy, or even exult in an idea. But we can only "be-with," be

available to, a concrete thou. The Kingdom she wanted to help build doesn't drown diversity and idiosyncrasy in abstract principles. Instead, it's a loving community in which all of us, in and through our own tangible contexts and unique personalities, are I's to the other's thou and "thou"s to the other's I.

Thea's celebration of particularity shone through in her lectures and sermons to both African American and mixed audiences. She had come into her own as a "fully functioning" black Catholic woman by embracing her own cultural identity, and she encouraged others to claim theirs too. "Black is beautiful!" she proclaimed. But in addition, "White is beautiful! Brown is beautiful! Red is beautiful! Yellow is beautiful! All the colors and hues in between that God made us are beautiful! Straight hair is beautiful! Kinky hair is beautiful! Bald is beautiful!"[36] Differences need not be alienating or in any way diminish the underlying truth of the interconnectedness of all creation. When viewed through the prism of love, they enrich our experience of the world.

Efforts to dissolve cultural, ethnic and spiritual diversity into the proverbial American melting pot might be well-intentioned, Thea believed, but pointed to an underlying fear of unfamiliar particularity that prompts us to invent artificial abstractions like "the American personality" or "the typical Catholic." Ultimately this is a refusal to be present to people (not to mention non-human creation) different from one's own group. People who endorse the melting-pot model, she said,

> profess to be free of prejudice, but at the same time they show little appreciation for the qualities that make people different. It is through this lack of respect for unique qualities that people miss out. It

means that you're deprived of my experience and I'm deprived of yours, and we're both probably hurting.[37]

A melting-pot attitude impoverishes by shutting us off from one another's experiences. Instead of stubbornly insisting that others conform to my own inevitably narrow point of view, how much richer my spiritual life is if I make myself available to others who have different angles of vision. In opening myself to them, I retain my own identity and culture without demanding that they conform to it. Indeed, my hope is that their "being-with" me is a catalyst for deeper exploration on their part of their own identities and traditions, just as my "being-with" them has given me new insight into my own. Sister Thea had a special gift for practicing and nurturing this kind of love in action. As one of her fellow nuns said of her, "She could reconnect you with your own spirituality rather than have you try to duplicate somebody else's spirituality."[38] And what else is this but an expression of the willing and acting for the beloved's well-being which Thomas Aquinas and Father Zossima called love?

Thea believed that the practice of love—"being-with" the other as thou, making oneself totally available to him, willing and working for his best interests, being comfortable enough with oneself to celebrate his uniqueness instead of feeling threatened by it—is our natural inclination. We are made for love by a loving Creator. But she knew that fear of the other, of intimacy, and of self-exposure can inhibit our practice of love. Equally destructive of our natural talent for loving is the lack of self-love that afflicts too many people, especially those who have been devalued by the society in which they live.

Self-love is not narcissism, even though we frequently use the terms interchangeably. Instead, self-love is the recognition that we are worthy of love because we're made by an all-loving and all-good God who creates nothing that *isn't* lovable. In order to appreciate this, we need to discern and "be-with" that which is best in us. We certainly oughtn't to turn a blind eye to our faults and weaknesses, but neither should we lose sight of the fact that we're created in the divine likeness and hence eminently lovable and capable of goodness. As Thea said, "let us not be so awed by the gifts of others"—nor by our own weaknesses, she could have added—"that we forget to marvel at the gift of ourselves."[39]

Failure to appreciate our own goodness can blind us to the goodness of other people and, indeed, of all creation. We become trapped in a whirlpool of self-doubt, self-recrimination, and even self-loathing that encourages us to obsess in a poisonously unfruitful way on our personal failings and to suspect that the same faults we despise in ourselves are also present in others. The entire world becomes contaminated.

The single most powerful cause of this kind of self-loathing, Thea was convinced, was the horrible sense of being unloved. Thea herself was fortunate. She grew up in an incredibly nurturing, loving environment. But she knew that many people are less fortunate. Their childhoods are blighted by unhappy and unsupportive families, or they possess qualities or hold stations in life sneered at by conventional society. Enduring these situations day in and day out weighs them down with a heavy burden of self-recrimination. Eventually they come to believe that they're so ridden with faults that they're neither loved nor lovable. What they require, but what they can't find, is self-forgiveness for their real and imagined faults. As Thea observed, "An amazing number of people are looking for forgiveness. They are looking to forgive themselves. They are looking for ways to let go of the mistakes of the past and the realization that no matter where I come from or what I have done, I am still a good person, and I can still move forward."[40]

Practicing love means that we naturally *want* to help someone trapped in self-loathing move toward a level of spiritual health where the process of self-forgiveness can begin. This was certainly Thea's goal. "I want to be good news for other people," she said. "I want to feel good about myself. I want you to feel good about me. I want to help you feel good about yourself."[41] In making ourselves available to broken and suffering people, we help them recognize that they're intrinsically sound and lovable, gently nurturing them to the point where they can affirm their gifts as much as we do.

As they acquire a new self-image by coming to know that they're loved, they also begin to look at other people with less cynical eyes—an essential step toward full availability. The process of internal reconciliation they experience is paralleled by external reconciliation with others. Connections that were broken by self-loathing are re-established, and the Kingdom comes a bit closer. "Loving ground becomes holy ground; holy ground becomes Kingdom ground."[42] The result is that all of us, lover and beloved, enter more deeply into the mutual support we were made for. "If we trust in humanity, if we teach, help, and reconcile with each other, we can love one another into life."[43]

"I want to love until I die"

Nineteen eighty-four was a bad year for Thea. Even though she didn't know it at the time, it signaled the beginning of the end of her life. That March she was diagnosed with breast cancer. During surgery for a modified radical mastectomy, physicians discovered that the cancer had metastasized.

She began a grueling course of chemotherapy that lasted for months. Then, toward the end of 1984, both her parents died within weeks of one another. In one sense, she was relieved that they had been spared further worry over her health. On learning of her illness, her first concern had been for her parents. "How could I keep them from being traumatized by what was happening to me?"[44] But of course she missed them terribly.

In February 1985 Thea decided to end the chemotherapy. Its after-effects had simply been too horrible. Besides, her doctors had told her there was only a 20 percent chance that it would lead to a remission. Sure enough, more cancer was discovered a month later and the nightmares of surgery and post-operative treatment were replayed. This time Thea opted for radiation instead of chemotherapy, enduring so many treatments that she was soon calling herself a "certified radiant woman."[45] She also began a regimen of a special diet and megavitamins which she continued until her death.

By mid-1985, Thea resumed her busy schedule. For the next two and a half years, she felt relatively well. Friends hoped that the cancer was gone for good. But Thea knew better. She sensed she was living on borrowed time. Even though she'd always imagined herself growing old, she realized this wasn't to be. But she was determined to do as much as she could in the time left to her.

For Thea, this meant expanding the orbit of love. She began assuring audiences that "we need to tell one another in our homes, in our church and even in our world, I really really love you,"[46] and friends and associates noticed that she was even more available to them than she'd been before the cancer. Many people who find themselves seriously ill shrink inwards, burrowing deeper and deeper into their own anxious misery and shutting out the world. It's as if their sickness saps their ability to love along with their physical vitality.

But Thea blossomed outwardly in her illness to embrace as many people as she could.

Thea's intuition that cancer wasn't finished with her was confirmed in January 1988 when tests revealed that it not only had returned but had spread to her spine and bones. More chemotherapy was endured, this time with a loss of her hair—"grooming is surely easier," she quipped, "one swipe with a damp washcloth and a touch of oil for sheen"[47]—and until she died she suffered increasingly from nausea, dizziness, weakness, thrush, and pain. Eventually her bones became so brittle that she had to rely on a wheelchair to get around.

The African American spirituals that had been sources of inspiration all her life were especially important to Thea during her final months. When the pain became unbearable and the fatigue overwhelming, she fell back on them as forms of prayer. And when even singing took more energy than she could muster, she moaned in a musical, rhythmic way. The "old people" had moaned when they couldn't pray, she remembered. So,

> Yes, I too, moan sometimes and I sing sometimes. When I'm sick and don't have the internal resources to pray as I would like, I sing or moan or hum. Because the songs are so familiar, it is an easy way to pray, to unite myself with God. When I have pain, I find it goes away when I hum or sing. When I concentrate on the song I forget the pain . . . It's a lesson I learned from my people and my heritage.[48]

Her one regret was that she wasn't able any longer to dance along with the spirituals. "The body says, 'I like you, I love you, I want to be in solidarity with you.'"[49] But her body was long past the point of capering with Franciscan exuberance.

The heritage passed on to Thea by the old folks as well as her years of schooling in love helped her endure her suffering. But they also enabled her to make her dying a gift to those around her. "Old people in the black community taught us that we should serve the Lord until we die. We can even serve the Lord on our deathbeds or in any circumstances in life. If we have faith, hope and love we can pass it on."[50] To the very end, Thea focused on demonstrating by example the power of love in action. She taught those around her that although death is the final act, it needn't have the last word, that we can still "be-with" those whom we love through the way in which we die. As Thea said just weeks before the end, "There is an urgency about my life. I know I have not got long ... My role in life is to open people up to life ... I want to love until I die." Characteristically, she laughingly added: "And, as I've always said, I want to have a good time!"[51]

By December 1989, Thea was too ill to leave her bed. She suffered for another four months, finally dying on March 30, 1990. When she was buried the following week, her white tombstone was engraved with an epitaph she had written herself: "She tried."

As Strong as Death

Love, the Song of Songs tells us (8:6), is as strong as death. Thea's life and dying testify to this ancient insight. She was, as one of her admirers put it, a women "deeply in love with God—and as a result, in love with people,"[52] and the strength of that love continued to sustain her and those who loved her in her final months. Thea never stopped building the Kingdom while she drew breath, and her example continues to inspire years after her passing.

Each of us will experience utter helplessness when our time to die arrives. Dying is the one experience in our life when no one—not family member, nor friend, nor priest, nor doctor—can rescue us. When death comes for us, it breaks down all resistance. It commands, and we are helpless not to die. But this doesn't mean that we need die alone. The more we habituate to love during our lifetime, the more we make ourselves available to others for the sake of their well-being, the more we love others into a fuller life, the more "thou"s we will find ourselves surrounded by, both in our healthy years and in our final ones of sickness and weakness. For the person who practices love, the universe becomes a progressively friendlier place, saturated through and through not only with the presence of God—the ultimate Thou—but with a multitude of beloveds as well. The strength of their love surrounds us when we die, comforting us on our dark journey. In turn, our manner of dying can strengthen them to face their own ends with courage. Even in the face of death, love continues to connect and sustain people.

But the great lesson—and warning—that Thea passes on to us is that love, although something for which God hardwires us, isn't something that most of us can do without training and discipline. It doesn't come as automatically as breathing. An eagerness to "be-with" others in a totally available way demands honest self-scrutiny, cultivation of a healthy self-love, willingness to enter into the beloved's context without demanding that she conform to ours, and a devotion to the beloved's well-being that stretches even to the point of sacrifice. These are qualities of character that must be self-consciously and methodically nurtured, especially since love in action is sometimes a harsh and dreadful thing.

If we fail or refuse to open ourselves lovingly to others during our lifetime, we can scarcely expect to know how to do so when, at life's end, our resources and energy begin to ebb. Then we not only will die helplessly, as everyone does. We'll also die alone, surrounded not by "thou"s but by the silent and impersonal "it"s to which our manner of living has reduced everyone. Theologian Dorothee Soelle put it like this: "It is not the final departure that is death. It is that purposeless, empty existence devoid of genuine human relationships and filled with anxiety, silence and loneliness."[53] Sister Thea would've shouted a hearty "AMEN!"

CHAPTER FOUR

GRATITUDE

Etty Hillesum

> *"I continue to praise your creation, God,*
> *despite everything."*

"We left the camp singing"

Every Tuesday a convoy of railroad cattle cars crammed with a thousand or more Jews left the transit camp of Westerbork in northeastern Holland, headed for the death factory of Auschwitz. The camp held thousands of Dutch Jews, rounded up with chilling efficiency from every corner of the German-occupied Netherlands. Because Westerbork was built on a patch of heath no larger than a half square kilometer, it was vital, if new arrivals were to be accommodated, for the transports to Auschwitz to roll out with clockwork regularity. And so they did, ninety-three trains in all between 1942 and 1945. Nearly 110,000 Jews passed through Westerbork on their way eastward. Barely 5,200 of them survived the war.

On September 7, 1943, as the day's transport pulled past Westerbork's gates, a postcard was pushed through the slats in one of the cattle cars. On it, scrawled in pencil, was a message whose calm tone, under the circumstances, was extraordinary. "Opening the Bible at random I find this: 'The Lord is my high tower.' I am sitting on my rucksack in the middle of a full freight car. Father, Mother, and Mischa are a few cars away. In the end, the departure came without warning. On sudden special orders from The Hague. We left the camp singing . . ."[1]

The postcard, found later by Dutch farmers, was written by Etty Hillesum, a twenty-nine year old woman held for a few months at Westerbork and killed at Auschwitz on November 30, 1943. The world knows about Etty's Amsterdam neighbor Anne Frank, who herself spent a month at Westerbork before being shipped to Auschwitz. But Etty is less familiar to most people. This is unfortunate, because the diaries and letters she left behind are an "exceptional witness," in the words of Archbishop of Canterbury Rowan Williams, "to the dawning of God in someone's awareness." To read Etty Hillesum is to discover "a real and completely, powerfully transforming divine faithfulness, present even in the depths of the nightmare of totalitarian inhumanity."[2]

The overriding theme that emerges in Etty's writings is, astonishingly, gratitude. Time and again she expresses thanks for the beauty she encounters in the world—the warm colors of flowers, the poetry of Rilke, the sun sparkling off the water of an Amsterdam canal—and the heart-warming goodness displayed by people. Not especially religious in her earlier years, and never religious in any institutional sense of the word, her war experiences convinced her that God was real and that the world—"despite everything," as she writes at one point—is saturated with divine presence. Life under the Nazis was hellish and cruel. Etty never indulged in denial about the horrors that surrounded her. But because she knew that God *is*, she saw life as a meaningful and good gift which continuously elicited her gratitude.

Before her internment at Westerbork, Etty's gratitude for the simple, ordinary things of life had already blossomed. Writing in November 1941 about her lodgings, she noted the welling up of "gratitude, fully conscious deep gratitude suddenly for this bright, spacious room with the wide divan, the desk and books..."[3] Nearly two years later, shortly before she and her parents and brother made the final journey to Auschwitz, Etty's sense of thankfulness had broadened and deepened. "My life," she wrote from Westerbork, "has become an uninterrupted dialogue with You, oh God, one great dialogue. Sometimes when I stand in some corner of the camp, my feet planted on Your earth, my eyes raised towards Your heaven, sometimes tears run down my face, tears of deep emotion and gratitude."[4]

The spirit of gratitude that Etty discovered and cultivated during the final years of her life is a habit of the heart as vital for living and dying well as it is rare. Familiarity need not breed contempt, but it *can* breed a complacency that encourages us to take things for granted. Too often, we fail to appreciate the people and experiences that enrich our daily lives. Their proximity to us dulls our sensitivity to their beauty and uniqueness, and they start to come across as unremarkable landmarks in our everyday geography. Perhaps, too, the busyness of modern life keeps us too distracted to take notice of just how special they really are. At any rate, it's typically when our lives are turned upside down by their loss that we consciously sense their importance, and even then our response is more often one of petulance for what's no longer ours than gratitude for what once was.

The virtue of gratitude keeps us focused both on the things in life that really count and on the fact that there is an underlying God-given goodness and beauty to reality discernible even in the darkest of moments. Habituating ourselves to gratitude also nurtures a healthy sense of humility by reminding us that life and creation are gifts rather than rewards. For these reasons, our lives are enriched if our sense of gratitude becomes a constant presence rather than sporadic and spontaneous episodes that puncture our everyday complacency. And our dying can be enriched as well, because those of us who have habituated ourselves to gratitude will know, even in our darkest moments, even when our lives are coming to an end, that we've been blessed to feel the warmth of sunshine, the laughter of children, and the fragrance of freshly baked bread. A person who dies with grateful memories dies well.

The Virtue of Gratitude

Thanking Is Confessing

We are grateful when we receive a boon or gift, something that is good, unearned, and pleasing. Gratitude's target is generally the gift itself. We may *thank* the giver for her generosity, but we are *grateful* for the gift. That's why it's perfectly appropriate to experience gratitude for the aroma of a flower or the colors of a sunset, even though there's no immediately obvious gift-giver to thank.

Whenever we experience and express gratitude, we simultaneously acknowledge that what we're grateful for is of value to us. In fact, the Old Testament's *yadha,* usually translated as "to thank," frequently means something more like "to confess." Psalm 136 is a typical example of the close connection between thanking and confessing, avowing, or acknowledging the goodness of that for which one is grateful. The psalmist tells us to "give thanks to the Lord" for God's enduring love, goodness, wisdom, power, providence, and care. To give thanks to God is necessarily to *proclaim* what God is and, moreover, to *confess* one's fidelity to God. Gratitude, in one way or another, is always creedal.

Ultimately, the creed on which biblical gratitude is founded is the conviction that God's creation is both good and beautiful (*tov,* as we're told in Genesis), and that humans, despite the wickedness we're capable of, are made in God's likeness and so share in the divine qualities praised in Psalm 136. Bad things can and do happen to innocent people, and the natural world can be cruel as well as beautiful. But divine goodness and beauty, two of God's greatest gifts to us, shimmer through all of reality. They are outpourings of the Deity's nature, and when we experience gratitude for them we also proclaim the majesty and loving-kindness of the Giver.

One of the consequences of the Fall is a coarsening of our sensitivity to the God-given goodness and beauty found in the world and in ourselves. And because thanking is confessing, this coarsening also diminishes our relationship with God. A complacency that takes the good things of life for granted is also spiritually tepid. That's one of the reasons why the spirituality preached by the first followers of Christ so stressed the importance of gratitude. St. James reminds followers of Christ of the connection between gratitude and confession when he proclaims that "every good thing given and every perfect gift is from above, coming down from the Father of lights" (James 1:17). St. Paul begins no fewer than nine of his letters with expressions of thanks to the Lord and perfectly captures the essence of creedal gratitude when he urges Christians to "rejoice evermore. Pray without ceasing. In everything give thanks" (1 Thes 5:16–18). Rejoicing is an appropriate response to the God-given gifts of beauty and goodness. Prayer is a form of confession. And there is nothing that comes to us in life that isn't touched by God and hence worthy of our deepest gratitude. As St. Irenaeus noted in the second century, "Nothing is a vacuum in the face of God. Everything is a sign of God."[5]

Thinking Is Thanking

The German philosopher Martin Heidegger once wrote that the "most thought-provoking [thing] in our thought-

provoking time is that we are still not thinking."⁶ At first
glance, his remark seems absurd. Of course we think! How
else could we put rockets into space, cure diseases, or create
wealth? If we didn't think, how could I write, and you read,
this book?

But this objection misses Heidegger's point. He doesn't
deny that we humans are skilled in the calculative reasoning
that makes science, practical know-how, and communication
possible. Such thinking is an essential tool for survival, and it
oughtn't to be downplayed. But neither should its underlying motive: the urge to control the world. When we calcu-
late, we look at natural objects, events, people, and human
interactions as if they were problems waiting to be solved.
How do we extract precious metals from the earth? How do
we put a space station on Mars? How do we reduce crime?
How do we fix the leaky faucet? How do we cure a patient's
psychological anxiety? Taken too far, this way of thinking insidiously encourages an adversarial attitude toward reality.
The world becomes something to be conquered by intellect
and force of will; witness the belligerence of slogans such as
"war on poverty," "war against cancer," "war against drugs."

In contrast to calculative reasoning, Heidegger argues
that genuine thinking is an act of receptivity in which the
subject observes and appreciates without trying to dominate
or control. It requires an alert attentiveness in which we put
aside our prejudgments, habits of thought, and urges to control long enough to be mindfully receptive to the present
moment.

By cultivating genuine thinking—something that doesn't
come easily to most of us, given our culture's obsession with
calculative reasoning—we begin to take notice of objects and
events usually dismissed as too commonplace to bother with.
And when this happens, we realize that they're actually quite
extraordinary. A drop of dew dangling from a blade of grass
blazes forth with luminous beauty. A smile on a stranger's

face and the touch of a child's hand become objects of won-der. The song of a bird or the moaning of the wind in a pine forest reveal a depth to existence that suggests holiness. We dive beneath the surface of our usual calculative way of look-ing at the world to touch the deep-down nature of things, and when we do we necessarily experience both awe and gratitude: awe at the shimmering beauty of existence, grati-tude for its gracious presence in our life.

Heidegger is so convinced that true thinking inevitably evokes gratitude that he sees them as inseparable. *Denken* is *danken,* he says. All proper thinking is really thanking. This is exactly the insight that Etty Hillesum reached in the final months of her life.

Gratitude as Discipline and Ethic

When most of us think of gratitude, what naturally comes to mind is the spontaneous surge we experience in response to a gift. Someone gives us a pretty object or a badly needed helping hand, a smile or a loving word, and we feel aglow with thankfulness.

But, strange though it may sound on a first hearing, we can also discipline ourselves to gratitude so that what was once spontaneous response becomes abiding attitude. If we settle for only the first, we let external events determine our inner states, making ourselves hostages to whatever happens around us. But if we cultivate the second, we actively bring to the world an interior disposition, a thinking that is also a thanking, that's both revelatory and liberating.

Henri Nouwen, for one, urges us toward a discipline of gratitude. Like many of us, he started out thinking of grati-tude as simply a response. But it gradually dawned on him that gratitude can be a state of mind rather than just an occa-sional experience. "The discipline of gratitude," he came to believe, "is the explicit effort to acknowledge that all I am and have is given to me as a gift of love, a gift to be celebrated with joy."[7]

The opposite of gratitude is resentment. A grateful person experiences life as a gift that prompts astonishment and joy. The resentful person experiences it as unfair and is convinced that he never gets a break, never receives what he rightfully deserves. There's always someone or something holding him back and taking what ought to be his.

All of us experience resentment at times, and it's not always misplaced. Occasionally we *are* treated unfairly or unkindly. But if we've disciplined ourselves to the attitude of gratitude, we can choose to temper our resentment by remembering that life is a grace-gift the beauty and goodness of which outshine whatever darkness we run up against. As Nouwen puts it,

> Gratitude as a discipline involves a conscious choice. I can choose to be grateful even when my emotions and feelings are still steeped in hurt and resentment. It is amazing how many occasions present themselves in which I can choose gratitude instead of a complaint. I can choose to be grateful when I am criticized, even when my heart still responds in bitterness. I can choose to speak about goodness and beauty, even when my inner eye still looks for someone to accuse or something to call ugly. I can choose to listen to the voices that forgive and to look at the faces that smile, even while I still hear words of revenge and see grimaces of hatred.[8]

Obviously the choice that Nouwen recommends requires great effort on our part, at least initially. But, like all virtues, gratitude becomes a habit after a while and what was originally a burdensome task becomes both second nature and joy. Gratitude is a virtue that's especially easy to cultivate because the payoff is so pleasing. To respond to existence with gratitude rather than resentment, to think deeply enough about each present moment to discern its beauty and goodness, to regularly experience life as a plenitude of blessings rather than a hamster wheel of frustrated desire and unfulfilled ambition, is surely how all of us want to live.

Someone who takes this attitude to heart is more likely to treat other people, even those who are cruel or violent, with gratitude and compassion: gratitude because they, like everything else in life, can be sheer gifts to her, even if the gifts they bring are accompanied by pain and suffering; compassion because their wickedness is born from their fall into poisonous lives of miserable resentment. Moreover, she realizes that it's good to midwife gratitude in others. Too many people live stunted existences which cause them, as they age and grow resigned to their own quiet desperation, to shut down to beauty, goodness, and joy. A person of gratitude naturally wants to help awaken these somnolent souls.

It's not that we owe something to others in repayment of the gift of existence God has given us. A gift, after all, doesn't oblige the recipient to repay the giver or pass on the gift to someone else. That's the wonderful thing about a gift: it's bestowed out of sheer beneficence, with no other desire on the part of the giver than to please the person for whom the gift is intended. But once having received and appreciated the gift for what it is, there's a natural urge both to praise the giver and to share the gift with others. The discipline of gratitude flows naturally into an ethical lifestyle that desires to encourage others to see life as worthy of grateful praise and celebration. A person grateful for the generosity shown her is generous in her dealings with others. It's as simple—and as rich—as that.

The Family Madhouse

In 1931, shortly before the eldest child Etty went away to university, the Hillesum family sat for a group photograph. It's an unsettling portrait. No one smiles. Instead, Etty, her parents, and her two younger brothers stare at the camera with stony faces. Louis, the father, hunched in a chair, looks owl-like and withdrawn. Mischa, the baby of the family, has his arm slung around the neck of Riva, his mother. But there's nothing intimate about the gesture. Mother and son look, in fact, distinctly uncomfortable. Jaap, the tall, bespectacled brother two years younger than Etty, is aloof and slightly disdainful. Etty, seated behind her mother, looks sullen and rather flushed, as if the photographer interrupted a family squabble. And he could well have. Etty once called the household in which she grew up a "remarkable mixture of barbarism and culture" both "depressing and tragicomic." "I don't know what kind of madhouse this really is," she sighed. "But I know that no human being can flourish here."[9]

The Hillesum madhouse was mobile. By the time Etty reached her mid-teens, her family had moved four times, eventually landing in Deventer, a city in east central Holland. The moves were connected to father Louis's career. A gymnasium teacher of Greek and Latin, he relocated from school to school until winding up as a headmaster at Deventer. Louis wasn't a popular teacher. Reclusive, scholarly, and partially deaf, he had a hard time maintaining order in his classes and compensated by being overly strict. But outside the classroom he was noted for his dry humor and stoical patience.

Louis married Riva in 1912. She had been born in Russia, but fled to Amsterdam in the aftermath of a pogrom in her hometown. By all accounts, Riva was her husband's temperamental opposite. She was extroverted, tended to be domineering and occasionally even something of a bully, and was prone to extreme emotional ups and downs. Not surprisingly, their marriage was stormy.

Etty, their first child, was born in January 1914, Jaap almost exactly two years later, and Mischa, the youngest, in 1920. Jaap was a scientific genius. By the time he went to university to study medicine, he had published several articles in scientific journals. Mischa was a musical prodigy. He performed his first public concert when he was six years old and was immediately acclaimed as one of Holland's up-and-coming artistic stars. But both brothers were afflicted with what Etty would later call the family "taint." Jaap suffered severely from depression and had to be hospitalized on several occasions. Mischa was diagnosed with schizophrenia in his teens and institutionalized for a period shortly before the outbreak of World War II. His instability was worsened by the brutal Nazi occupation of his country. The mental illness of her two brothers as well as the occasionally erratic behavior of her mother convinced Etty that her family was "riddled with hereditary disease,"[10] and she swore to remain childless.

The word that Etty used most often to describe her household is "chaos." She learned at an early age that to survive she needed to hold her dysfunctional family at arm's length and disassociate from them as much as possible. "It is that very chaos that also threatens me, that I must make my life's task to shake off."[11] But she wasn't particularly good at remaining aloof. She adored her brothers, especially Mischa, although she was frightened and occasionally angered by their instability. She fought nonstop with her mother, frequently accusing her in furious diary entries of irrational irritability, greediness, and selfishness. Her resentment sometimes exploded at the slightest provocation—such as, once, watching her mother eat. "She revolted me, sitting there, and at the same time I was filled with incredible pity for her. I really can't explain it. Her gluttony gave her the air of being terrified of missing out on anything. There was something pathetic about her as well as something bestially repulsive."[12]

Etty was intrigued by the fact that she felt compelled to observe her mother so closely, especially when she so disliked what she saw. What dawned on her only slowly was that the attraction and repulsion probably stemmed in large part from the fact that she and Riva were so similar temperamentally. Like her mother, Etty was prone to sometimes startling mood swings. The chaos that she saw in the family and believed epitomized by her mother she also sensed within herself. Her resentment of her mother was at least in part a projection of what she disliked and resisted in herself. "Mother is a model of what I must never become!"[13]

Etty's relationship with her father was more tender, but just as complicated. She admired his intellect, but found his withdrawal—his "impersonality," as she once referred to it[14]—hard to take. Eventually, although she saw Louis as both lovable and in need of protection, she concluded that his stoicism was actually a form of cowardice. Her father, she decided, had "traded all his uncertainties, doubts, and probably also his physical inferiority complex, his insurmountable marriage problems, for philosophical ideas" that helped him "gloss over everything."[15] Books and abstract ideas were the weapons—ineffectual ones, Etty concluded—that Louis wielded against the chaos.

As Etty matured emotionally and spiritually, she achieved the distance from her parents she'd sought as an adolescent, and this helped her to grow more understanding and less unforgiving of them. "My parents," she eventually wrote, "always felt out of their depth and as life became more and more difficult they were gradually so overwhelmed that they became quite incapable of making up their minds about anything." Riva and Louis, their daughter concluded, "never established a foothold for themselves." They had "lost their way."[16] She determined not to follow in their footsteps.

"Something is happening to me"

Etty left the family madhouse in March 1932 to study law at her father's alma mater, the University of Amsterdam. Little is known about her next few years, but in all likelihood she felt wonderfully liberated, both by getting away from her dysfunctional household and by living a bohemian student's life in cosmopolitan Amsterdam. She seems to have made many friends and to have taken several lovers, and she regularly associated with left-wing student groups. But she was bored by the law, and immediately after earning her degree she enrolled in the Faculty of Slavonic Languages to study Russian language and literature. As a child, Etty had picked up a working knowledge of Russian and inherited from her mother a deep love of authors such as Dostoyevsky, Lermontov, and Pushkin. Her diary and letters are punctuated with references to them as well as to the German-language poet Rainer Maria Rilke. Rilke's poetry, especially the religious verse in his *Book of Hours,* was probably the greatest literary influence on Etty's thinking.

In 1937 Etty moved into the Amsterdam home of Han Wegerif, a sixty-two year old widower. Etty took up the rather loosely-defined duties of housekeeper for Wegerif's large home, where his twenty-one year old son, a couple of lodgers, and the family cook also lived. Etty had her own room on the third floor where she could read and write, luxuriate in her privacy, and receive the undergraduate students she tutored in Russian to make ends meet. She frequently and fondly describes the room in her diary and letters. The

Wegerif household gave her the domestic happiness and peace she'd never experienced in her family's home.

Etty also began an affair with Han, who was nearly forty years her senior. He appears to have been a gentle and undemanding lover who neither shared nor felt threatened by her intellectual interests. There was no fiery passion to their relationship, but Etty felt a deep affection for him and enjoyed their physical love-making. Perhaps significantly, she usually referred to him as "Papa Han."

As much as Etty tried to escape the chaos she'd come to know as a child, she still felt victimized by it. "At times," she wrote, "I am nothing more or less than a miserable, frightened creature despite the clarity with which I can express myself," and in many of her early diary entries she records with evident frustration her "inner chaos," "depression," and the "forces now at loggerheads within me."[17] At times she felt herself on an emotional rollercoaster.

The chaos within was matched by the chaos without. World War II began on September 1, 1939 with Hitler's invasion of Poland. Although the Netherlands tried to remain neutral, the German Wehrmacht invaded on May 10, 1940. There was fierce resistance on the part of the tiny Dutch army (infuriating Hitler, who had boasted that the Netherlands would be taken in a day), and equally fierce retaliation by the Germans, who reduced the heart of the port city of Rotterdam to rubble. Four days later, it was over. The country surrendered, Queen Wilhelmina fled to London to establish a government in exile, and the occupation began. The nation's Jews—many of them refugees from Germany—anticipated the worst.

One of those German Jewish refugees was Julius Spier. Born in Frankfurt in 1887, Spier was a psychochirologist, a therapist who claimed the ability to read his patients' personalities through the study of their hands. Spier abandoned a

career in business to train for two years with the psychologist
Carl Jung and then practiced his craft in Berlin for a decade
before fleeing in 1939 to the Netherlands. He was allowed to
leave Germany only after paying a huge bribe to Nazi officials.

Regardless of what one thinks of psychochirology, it's
clear that Spier was a skilled although utterly unconventional
therapist. Nearly everyone who met him fell under the spell
of his charisma. A physically large man with an outgoing
temperament, he took a holistic approach to treating his
clients, insisting that "body and soul are one."[18] Wrestling
bouts with his clients on his office floor were typical therapeutic exercises.

Etty met Spier in February 1941 at a social gathering
and shortly afterwards became one of his clients. The first
time they wrestled, Etty surprised both of them by pinning
Spier to the floor. She later wrote that in that moment, "all
my inner tensions, the bottled-up forces, broke free." This
may be something of an exaggeration, but there's little
doubt that her relationship with Spier, which would continue for the next eighteen months until his death, was the
most important one of her life. She described him as "the
one . . . who attended at the birth of my soul," and considered the day she met him to be her real birthdate.[19] Their relationship eventually evolved from a therapeutic to an
emotional and then a physical one. But Etty's friendship
with Spier wasn't just another sexual encounter. Instead, it
was an apprenticeship in personal and spiritual growth. As
she wrote a year after meeting him, "I only know that I love
him, a bit more every day, and that I ripen beside him into a
genuine and adult human being."[20] She considered him "the
first person to whom I have ever related inwardly,"[21] and
noted early on in their relationship that "by coming into
such very close contact with him over and over again, something is happening to me."[22]

Spier gave Etty the confidence to dig underneath the "inner chaos" bred by her family history to touch base with the deep and quiet places within her. On his advice, she began the diary in which she recorded the extraordinary spiritual growth of her final two and a half years. Under his steady guidance—"he is the unyielding rock and my moods lap around him"[23]—she became less impulsive and fragmented. She came to value solitude and introspection, and in the process arrived at a deeper appreciation of her friends and a greater compassion for her dysfunctional family. There were still moments in which she was depressed and others in which she felt overwhelmed by inner and outer conflicts. But with Spier's guidance, Etty discovered an identity which her sometimes stormy personality had concealed. Her newly acquired self-insight in turn opened her up in exhilarating ways to the beauty and goodness of creation.

In the process of this awakening, Etty also found God. As she wrote in her diary on the night of Spier's death in September 1942, "What energies I possess have been set free inside me. You [a reference to Spier] taught me to speak the name of God without embarrassment."[24] And with the discovery of self and God came a deep and enduring sense of gratitude.

The Girl Who Knelt

Etty came from a completely secular family. When she first began to use the word "God" in her diaries, it referred to the self which she was in the process of discovering. Five months after meeting Spier, she wrote "I regained contact with myself, with the deepest and best in me, which I call God."[25] Etty seems to be gesturing here at what's sometimes called the "true" or "authentic" self, an identity more stable and enduring than the fragmented and ever-restless ego.

Typically, the true self is seen as that interior still point where the individual human encounters God, and Etty didn't hesitate to use traditional religious language to describe her own experience of it. But it's clear that she didn't mean the word "God" to refer to an entity actually existing outside of her subjectivity.

Gradually, however, Etty dropped the identification of self and God. In her excavation of her interior depths, she discovered that the self she was just beginning to explore was accompanied by something that didn't feel as if it originated from within her. "There is a really deep well inside me," she wrote. "And in it dwells God. Sometimes I am there, too. But more often stones and grit block the well, and God is buried beneath. Then he must be dug out again."[26]

Then something happened which can only be described as a moment of conversion. In December 1941, four months after her discovery of the deep interior well, Etty found herself on her knees, "as if I were trying to seize peace by force."[27] Han unexpectedly walked in on her while she was on the floor and Etty, embarrassed, told him she was searching for a lost button. But it's obvious that Han's appearance wasn't the only thing that rattled Etty. She was just as startled by her sudden need to assume a worshipful position. After all, as she noted in her diary, she had the reputation among family and acquaintances as "the girl who could not kneel."[28]

In the following months, the kneeling which once had seemed so alien to Etty became second nature. Again and again, she spontaneously fell to her knees in what she now recognized to be a kind of prayer. Slowly she came to understand that her earlier embarrassment had been confused. When Han caught her kneeling, she thought the embarrassment sprang from getting caught in a ridiculously pious act. Now she recognized that she'd been embarrassed because the act of praying was "more intimate than sex . . . , as inti-

mate as gestures of love that cannot be put into words...
except by a poet."[29] Han had interrupted her in an act of
love.

What Etty was discovering under Spier's tutelage was
that the more she focused on the "really deep well" inside
her, the more skilled she became at moving away from the
inner chaos that had always distracted her. Sexual turmoil,
self-doubt, unhappy childhood memories, restlessness, jeal-
ousy, resentments: all these began to evaporate, leaving a
calm that allowed her for the first time in her life to be really
mindful of what was going on around her. Her vision grew
unclouded, and events and objects which earlier had been
overlooked or dismissed as commonplace were now seen in a
totally different light. Before her breakthrough, Etty wrote
that her ability to see the world—and God—was as ob-
structed as a well filled with stones and grit. Now the
metaphor she used to describe her spiritual state, "soul-landscape," evoked a wide open place. Prayer, or what she often
referred to as "meditation," became a ride "through the
landscape of my own soul."[30] Her goal in prayer was to turn
her "innermost being" into a "vast empty plain, with none
of that treacherous undergrowth to impede the view." Her
hope was that "something of 'God' can enter..., and something of 'Love' too."[31]

One of the most important discoveries she made while
standing on the vast plain of her soul-landscape was that she
was free, unfettered by anything that might have happened to
her in the past or that could happen to her in the future. This
was a breakthrough that opened her eyes to the fact that

> every moment gives birth to a new moment, full of
> fresh potential, and sometimes like an unexpected
> present. And that one must not cling to moments of
> malaise and prolong them needlessly, because in so
> doing one may prevent the birth of a new moment.

Life courses through one as a constant current in a
great series of moments.[32]

The uncluttering of her inner landscape allowed Etty to
begin to *think*, in Heidegger's sense of the word. As a student
she had been trained in the calculative reasoning and analysis
intended to help her master the law and achieve worldly success. But the new perspective attained in the landscape of her
soul called into question this way of relating to reality. "Why
do I have to achieve things?" Etty asked herself. "All I need is
to 'be,' to live and to try being a little bit human . . . Knowledge is power, and that's probably why I accumulate knowledge, out of a desire to be important."[33] But she was learning
that knowledge isn't the same as wisdom. The former encouraged a spirit of having, appropriating, and seizing; the
latter, a spirit of receiving and appreciating. Writing in her
diary about one of her increasingly frequent moments of receptivity, Etty compared it to the attitude with which she
once approached the world.

> Just now, when I was sitting on a dustbin in the sun
> out on our stony little terrace, with my head leaning
> against the washtub and with the sun on the strong,
> dark, still, leafless branches of the chestnut tree, I
> had a very clear sense of the difference between
> then and now . . . The sun on the dark branches, the
> chirping birds, and me on the dustbin in the sun
> . . . In the past, I took in the tree and the sun with
> my intellect. I wanted to put down in so many
> words why I found it so beautiful, I wanted to un-
> derstand how everything fitted together, I wanted
> to fathom that deep primitive feeling with my
> mind . . . In other words, I wanted to subject nature,
> everything, to myself. I felt obliged to interpret it.

And the quite simple fact is that now I just let it happen to me.[34]

Etty's resolve to become more receptive to the world around her—to "be," as she said, instead of perpetually doing—wasn't a repudiation of books or ideas. She remained a serious student of literature to the end of her days. But her scholarship was now complemented by an awed gratitude for what revealed itself when she quietly opened herself to creation. "I am filled with a sort of bountifulness," she characteristically exclaimed. "I am so grateful."[35] What once seemed mundane now became transfigured into the extraordinary, reminding Etty again and again of the wondrous gift existence is. And the more this realization became a part of her, the more the girl who could not kneel knelt. "Sometimes," she confessed, "in moments of deep gratitude, kneeling down becomes an overwhelming urge..., a gesture embedded in my body, needing to be expressed."[36]

The bountifulness with which Etty felt herself filled profoundly transformed her relationships with people. She began to sense that her fellow humans, like the rest of creation, were saturated with beauty—and also, because made in God's likeness, a kind of holiness. She grew more tolerant of human weakness, more forgiving of wrongs inflicted on her and on others.

Even her attitude to the Nazi occupiers underwent a change. In March 1942, she and dozens of other Jews were summoned to the Gestapo headquarters in Amsterdam to fulfill some administrative requirement. A young German officer in a dangerously surly mood stalked through the crowd yelling nonstop at the nervous Jews and singling out Etty for special verbal abuse. Afterwards, writing about the experience in her diary, she reflected on the surprising fact that she felt neither anger nor fear.

That was the real import of this morning: not that a
disgruntled young Gestapo officer yelled at me, but
that I felt no indignation, rather a real compassion,
and would have liked to ask, 'Did you have a very
unhappy childhood, has your girlfriend let you
down?' Yes, he looked harassed and driven, sullen
and weak. I should have liked to start treating him
there and then, for I know that pitiful young men
like that are dangerous as soon as they are let loose
on mankind. But all the blame must be put on the
system that uses such people. What needs eradicating
is the evil in man, not man himself.[37]

Westerbork

There is a cruel irony to Etty Hillesum's liberating discovery
of soul-landscape. Her awakening to gratitude coincided with
the steady erosion of the rights of Dutch Jews under the Nazi
regime. The registration of Jews and the mandatory public
display of the yellow Star of David had immediately followed
the German occupation of the Netherlands. So had the usual
anti-Semitic slogans on billboards and walls, not to mention
the press. The situation was tense, and Dutch Jews were
frightened by rumors of deportation and forced labor camps.

In the early summer of 1942, when Etty was twenty-
eight and Spier was already showing symptoms of the lung
cancer that would kill him in just a few months, the Nazi
pogrom began in earnest. New regulations designed to mar-
ginalize the Jews were posted in Amsterdam and other
Dutch cities. Jews were ordered to remain inside their homes
between 8 PM and 6 AM under penalty of death. Jews lodging
with non-Jews were to evacuate immediately. Jewish teachers
(including Etty's father) were removed from their posts.

Cabarets and music halls were declared off-limits to Jews, and Jews were also forbidden to visit the seashore. Jews were permitted in train stations or cafes for only two hours in the afternoon. Jews were denied the use of public telephones at all times. Jews owning bicycles were to turn them over to the Nazi authorities.

At about the same time, the Nazis launched a *Judenfrei* campaign, deporting Dutch Jews to the Polish death camps at Auschwitz and Sobibor. To facilitate the round-up, the Nazis commandeered Westerbork, a refugee camp that the Dutch government had built in 1939 to house Jews fleeing Hitler's Germany. Under Nazi management, Westerbork became a *Judendurchgangslager*, a transit camp into which Jews from all over Holland were funneled before being shipped off. The weekly transports started that summer.

Denial is a perfectly understandable psychological defense strategy in such a horrific situation, and many Dutch Jews adopted it. Those not yet sent to Westerbork tried to convince themselves that they wouldn't be. Those already there tried to pretend that their names would never come up for the weekly transport to Auschwitz. Even when being loaded onto the cattle cars, some Westerbork inmates persisted in believing that they were headed for labor camps in Germany instead of death in Poland.

But Etty knew better. From the very start of the *Judenfrei* program, she sensed that it spelled the end for her and most of the other Jews living in the Netherlands. Her uppermost thought wasn't how to escape, but rather how to retain clarity and gratitude in the face of the death sentence she was convinced she was facing.

Unavoidably, there were moments of despair. In July of that terrible summer she wrote, "sometimes I feel as if a layer of ashes were being sprinkled over my heart, as if my face were withering and decaying before my very eyes, and as if

everything were falling apart in front of me." Etty grieved for
the future that was being stolen from her, for the never-writ-
ten books, the never-met lovers, the unseen sunsets. Her
heart, she said, mourned all these losses and tried to "let
everything go."[38] But the deep conviction of the past year
and a half that the God who lovingly gifted humans with existence would continue to look after them endured. "Dear
God," she wrote. "What will happen to me? No, I shall not
ask You beforehand, I shall bear every moment, even the
most unimaginable."[39] Despite the Nazi horror, life was
worth living and God worth trusting. The grateful habit of
the heart that Etty had cultivated didn't blind her to the evil
and suffering surrounding her. But it did give her perspective.

Shortly after the crackdown began, Etty's brother Jaap
pulled strings to get her a position on Amsterdam's *Judenrat,* or Jewish Council. The Nazis established Councils in
every country they occupied that had a significant Jewish
population. The ostensible purpose of the Councils was to
let Jews police themselves. But in reality they were merely
administrative bodies tasked with guaranteeing that Nazi
rules and regulations were obeyed. The Councils were often
accused of collaboration. But the attitude of Council members was that cooperation bought concessions for Jews living
under occupation.

Etty, who shared the widespread suspicion of the Councils, disliked working for the Amsterdam *Judenrat.* She worried that its personnel couldn't resist the temptation to
finagle unfair advantages for themselves and their families.
So she soon requested a transfer from Amsterdam to Westerbork, where she worked in the department of Social Wel-
fare for People in Transit. Her task was herculean: helping
new camp arrivals correspond with relatives and friends on
the outside, coordinating sleeping arrangements and medical assistance for those in the camp, and generally being

available as a troubleshooter. The work was bittersweet. Etty knew that whatever help she gave was cruelly temporary. Sooner or later, everyone—even Council workers—was destined for Auschwitz. But she was spiritually and psychologically prepared for this inevitability. Shortly before going to Westerbork, she wrote, "An awful lot has happened inside me these last few days; something has crystallized. I have looked our destruction, our miserable end . . . , straight in the eye, and accepted it into my life. And my love of life has not been diminished."[40]

Etty's first stay at Westerbork lasted until December, with a week off to visit her parents in Deventer. The next six months saw her back in Amsterdam. From the end of 1942 to the beginning of June 1943 she was too ill to resume her work at the transit camp. It's not entirely clear what was wrong, but it's possible that Etty was physically exhausted from her work at Westerbork. She could also have been reacting to Spier's death in September 1942. Etty had grown steadily more independent of him as her familiarity with soul-landscape deepened, and part of her was genuinely relieved that Spier's death had rescued him from the horrors of Westerbork. (The Gestapo came knocking at his apartment door only days after he died.) But she never ceased loving him, and remained grateful for his midwifery of her. His passing was a blow.

By the time Etty returned to Westerbork in June 1943, the final round-up of Dutch Jews was under way. Toward the end of that month, Louis, Riva, and Mischa were sent to the camp. Life there was especially hard on Louis, who spent most of his time in the hospital withdrawn and ill. One month later, the special status exempting Jewish Council personnel from deportation to Auschwitz was revoked by the Nazis, and Etty, still working to assist new camp arrivals, became just as subject to the weekly transports as anyone else.

Westerbork was a study in surreality. On the one hand, the camp had a patina of normalcy. Except for the crowded conditions, it sometimes seemed like an ordinary town. It was administered almost entirely by German Jews, remnants of the refugees for whom the Dutch authorities had originally erected the camp. There were never more than thirty SS guards and personnel. Westerbork had a hospital with close to two thousand beds and over one hundred Jewish doctors, a post office, a school for children, and athletic playing fields. Because Jews from all walks of life eventually wound up in the camp, there was never a lack of talent for musical concerts, theatrical performances, or scholarly lectures.[41]

But the normalcy, of course, was an illusion. Westerbork was a Potemkin village whose residents were prisoners awaiting a cruel death. They lived from one Tuesday to the next, dreading the day when, called up for deportation to Poland, they would march to the railway station at the end of a street revealingly called the *Boulevard des Miseres.* One of the blackest ironies of the camp was the efficiency with which the Jewish authorities organized each week's transport. They hoped that their administrative skills would save them from Auschwitz. After all, what purpose could possibly be served by killing off such useful people? But their efficiency only prompted the Nazi authorities to ratchet up the weekly quota.

For Etty, the chief contrast wasn't between the veneer of normalcy and the underlying murderous purpose of the camp. Instead, she was struck by the sharp contrast between the suffering and squalor of the camp—"enough gloom here," she wrote, "to last a lifetime"—and the beauty and goodness that punctuated its bleakness. On the one hand, infants dying of pneumonia were piled on the Auschwitz-bound freight cars and people already in the cars stuck their hands through gaps in the planks "and waved as if they were drowning." On the other hand, there were always moments in which the beauty of nature or the fundamental decency of people shone through. "The sky is full of birds, the purple lupins stand up so regally and peacefully, two little old women have sat down on the box for a chat, the sun is shining on my face." Despite the fact that "right before our eyes, mass murder" was taking place, life was still a gift that inspired profound gratitude.[42]

In the final months of her life, expressions of Etty's gratitude for the beauty of existence cropped up again and again in her diary and letters. In July 1942, during her first stay at Westerbork, she wrote with some surprise that her experiences in the camp hadn't soured her conviction that life was a God-given gift. Safely back in Amsterdam, "surrounded by my writers and poets and the flowers on my desk, I loved life. And here among the barracks, full of hunted and persecuted people, I found confirmation of my love of life."[43] This confirmation was so important to her that at one point she even thanked God for "driving me from my peaceful desk into the midst of the cares and sufferings of this age."[44] It wasn't that Etty trivialized the suffering that surrounded her. It was just that even in the midst of the horror she was aware of the deep goodness of life. Looking into the frightened faces of young and old inmates, she felt the presence of God. Gazing upwards from the barbed wire into the sky, she also felt God's presence. "I can see gulls in the distance moving across the flat gray sky. They are like free thoughts in my mind."[45]

Later on, in the early fall, Etty wrote a passage in her diary that attested to how deeply ingrained in her the character trait of gratitude had become. "It all comes down to the same thing: life is beautiful. And I believe in God. And I want to be there right in the thick of what people call 'horror' and still be able to say: life is beautiful."[46] Despite everything, "I rejoice and exult time and again, Oh God: I am grateful to You for having given me this life."[47] *This* life, Etty wrote. *This* life in Westerbork, the one lived on borrowed time, the one awaiting the transport. She was grateful too for her previous life in Han's house, for her room with its flowers and books. But the extent of her gratitude stretched to embrace the bad as well as the good, the tragedies that unfold in life and settle like ash on one's spirit as well as the moments of sheer luminous grace that reveal deep meaning. That's why she could write a line that, unless read as an expression of the virtue of gratitude, seems bewildering. "I have learned," she confessed in September 1942, "to love Westerbork."[48]

In her final weeks at Westerbork, Etty spent the bulk of her time caring for patients in the camp hospital, writing about the drama unfolding around her, and praying. She wanted above all to be "the thinking heart of the barracks."[49]

Etty described some of the scenes she witnessed in one of her letters. The "wailing of the babies" awaiting transportation that reminded her of Herod's slaughter of the innocents; her conversation with a young girl just beginning to recover from paralysis who said "in a level, grey little voice, 'Such a pity, isn't it? That everything you have learned in life goes for nothing'"; a dying old man chanting the *Shema* on his way to the trains; a female inmate squatting beside a dying woman "who has swallowed some poison and who happens to be her mother"; and the camp guards whose presence challenges her to reaffirm her convictions that God is present everywhere, even in them.

> When I think of the faces of that squad of armed, green-uniformed guards—my God, those faces! I looked at them, each in turn, from behind the safety of a window, and I have never been so frightened of anything in my life. I sank to my knees with the

words that preside over human life: And God made man after His likeness. That passage spent a difficult morning with me.[50]

On Monday, September 6, 1943, Etty got word that she, her parents, and Mischa would be on the next day's transport. Apparently the order came from no less an authority than General Johann Rauter, commander of the SS in the Netherlands, to whom Riva had impulsively written pleading for privileges for her musical prodigy son Mischa. Rauter, a notorious anti-Semite, was furious that a Jew would have the effrontery to write him directly and commanded the commandant of Westerbork to put the entire family on the next transport. As the train pulled out of the station, Etty shoved her final message to the world through a slat in the cattle car she was riding. "We left the camp singing..."

The train reached Auschwitz three days later. According to Red Cross records, Louis and Riva died on September 10, suggesting that they either perished during transport or were gassed as soon as they arrived at Auschwitz. Etty died on November 30, and Mischa early the following year. Jaap was sent to Westerbork just a few weeks after his family was transported to Auschwitz. In February 1944, a month before Mischa's death, Jaap was sent to Bergen-Belsen. He lived to see the camp liberated by Russian soldiers, but died from disease and malnutrition a few days later.

In one of her last letters from Westerbork, Etty penned a prayer of praise that could serve as her life's epithet. "God ...That says everything, and there is no need for anything more...There are many miracles in a human life. My own is one long sequence of inner miracles...At night, when I lie in my bed and rest in You, oh God, tears of gratitude run down my face, and that is my prayer."[51]

Gratitude and Mortality

Most of us have a normal lifespan in which to discipline ourselves to the virtue of gratitude. Etty Hillesum had less than three years. Her "birth," as she said, dated from early February 1941, when she met Julius Spier and embarked on the exploration of soul-landscape that eventually led her to the discovery that genuine thinking is thanking. During those months, Etty's life grew enriched despite the death that surrounded her.

Etty's story not only teaches us that attuning to the present moment and becoming attentive to God's presence in it opens us to the beauty and goodness of life and the decency of our fellow humans. It also shows us that cultivating gratitude as a habit of the heart allows us to put our own dying (and the dying of loved ones) in perspective. Even death is powerless to rob life of its wonder. When our end comes, we can rejoice at just how splendid a gift life is, and even in our dying remain grateful to the God who gave it to us.

Etty once wrote that "all that really matters" is that we humans struggle to "safeguard that little piece of You, God, in ourselves. And perhaps in others as well."[52] One way of honoring that obligation is by cultivating the deep thinking that leads to deep thanking—a thanking that sustains even when life is hard and bitter, even during that final, bittersweet moment when we must return the gift of life to God with profound gratitude for the having of it as long as we did.

CHAPTER FIVE

OBEDIENCE

Jonathan Daniels

*"I believe very firmly... that my life is not my own but His—
which means that before anything else I am a servant
of Christ, however sinful I may also be—and that
consequently the possibility of death, whether immediate
or remote, cannot be a deciding factor for me."*

Murder in Alabama

In the final seconds of his life, Jonathan Daniels saw Tom
Coleman, a white deputy sheriff, level his shotgun at Ruby
Sales, a seventeen-year-old field secretary for the Student
Nonviolent Coordinating Committee (SNCC). Pushing her
away just as Coleman pulled the trigger, Jon took the blast
full in his chest. He died instantly. His body lay in the street
for nearly an hour before finally being taken to a Montgomery funeral home.

Ruby later told reporters what had happened on that hot
afternoon in August 1965. A week earlier, she'd been arrested with twenty-two others in Fort Deposit, Alabama, for
peacefully picketing for the right of black Alabamians to vote.
Most of the demonstrators were African American, but two
of them, "outside agitators" from up north, were white:
Jonathan Daniels, a twenty-six year old Episcopal seminarian,

and Richard Morrisroe, a young Roman Catholic priest from Chicago.

Jailed at the county seat of Hayneville just a few miles from Fort Deposit, the prisoners were released on the same sweltering day that Daniels was murdered. Ruby, Daniels, Father Morrisroe, and another SNCC volunteer named Joyce Bailey were heading down the street toward a wood-frame store to buy cold soft drinks.

"When we got to the store," Ruby remembered,

> I was in front, and Jon, Joyce, and Father Morrisroe were behind me. And when we got to the door—I think I had walked up a step or two—this man, standing in the doorway with a shotgun, said, "This store is closed." Then, as I remember, this [same] man Tom Coleman said, "If you don't get off this god-damned property I'm going to blow your damned brains out. And I mean get off." The next thing I knew someone pulled me from behind. I heard a shotgun blast and I looked and saw Jon falling.[1]

Ruby Sales would never forget the day that Jon Daniels saved her life. Neither would Martin Luther King Jr., a man Daniels admired and emulated. When he heard about the shooting, King called Daniels' sacrifice "one of the most heroic Christian deeds of which I have heard in my entire ministry... The meaning of his life was so fulfilled in his death that few people of our time will know such fulfillment or meaning if they live to be a hundred."[2]

King put it perfectly. Jonathan Daniels' manner of dying testified to the deep meaning in life he'd begun to discover, a meaning that focused on obedience to God's will. It had taken him most of his short life to come to the realization that the virtue of obedience is anything but the unimaginatively lockstep conformity to orders that most people think it is. He discovered that true obedience allowed him to enter ever more deeply into joyful service to God and humans and ultimately into the freedom to sacrifice for the sake of another. Daniels may have been young in years when he died, but he was wiser, as King observed, than most of us who live to a ripe old age.

The Meaning of Obedience

Unlearning false beliefs is pretty hard. But if we're to get clear on the real meaning of obedience, we need to unlearn our legalistic understanding of it as synonymous with "law-abiding," "rule-keeping," or "command-compliance." According to this understanding, an obedient person is one who follows instructions and conforms to orders, and this is probably why many of us find the thought of obedience so distasteful. It smacks of the imperious handing-down of commands on the one hand and lockstep conformity, subservience of the will, and even undignified servility on the other.

But the Judeo-Christian understanding of obedience is quite different. In the Old Testament, the Hebrew word usually translated as "to obey" literally means "to hear" or "to listen." Similarly, the New Testament Greek for "obedience" is a compound of two words meaning "to hear," and "under." To obey is to listen while seated at the feet of a master. The Latin *obedire*, "to hearken," suggests a similar sense of heeding sage counsel, and was clearly understood as such by St. Benedict when he advised novices in his monastic Rule to listen/obey "to the master's instructions."[3]

The notion of obedience that emerges from these older meanings is refreshingly different from our contemporary understanding. For our ancestors, as for us today, "to obey" certainly implied submission to proper authority. But the submission is a consequence rather than the essence of obedience. One submits because one first heeds or hears or attends to in a special way—"with the ear of the heart," as Benedict said. True obedience is a heart-listening, a yearning receptivity to the life-changing word. What gets attended to in obedience is wisdom, not a set of bureaucratic rules and regulations. Listening to the latter can be a mechanical act in which the hearer isn't at all invested, especially if the rules and regulations are resented. But attending to wisdom makes the heart leap for joy.

So, at its deepest level, obedience is an intensely focused kind of listening. As such, it has another feature that sets it apart from the way we think today: it presupposes trust. We only sit at the feet of someone we believe to be a genuine authority, an authentic guide. When we hearken to what she or he has to say, we do so as a disciple listens to a master, and this means putting ourselves in that person's hands. This is a far cry from a legalistic model of obedience based on fear of punishment for nonconformity. When it comes to obedience, the wrong questions to ask are: "What's in it for me if I follow this rule?" or "What will happen to me if I break this law?" The right questions are: "To whom am I attending?" and "What am I hearing?"

Jesus and Radical Obedience

Some Jews of Jesus' day, especially the Pharisees, had slipped into a legalistic piety. Rigid conformity to cultic laws had become the standard of religious and ethical purity for them. According to biblical scholar Rudolf Bultmann, they understood obedience to God as purely formal, "as an obedience which fulfills the letter of the law, obeying a law simply because it is commanded without asking the reason, the meaning, of its demand."[4]

Jesus taught a new "radical obedience" that protested against reducing the relationship between God and humans to a formal, legalistic one. God demands more than mere outward conformity to commands. Instead, God "claims man whole—and wholly."[5] But in order to respond to God's total claim, there must be an interior embrace, not merely an external conformity, of the demand God makes. This in turn requires that we sense and affirm the significance of the demand. "What counts before God is not simply the substantial, verifiable deed that is done, but how a man is disposed, what his intent is."[6]

Disposition and intent bring us back to what we've already seen is the core of authentic obedience: deep listening. To obey God's commands, we must first hear what they are, and we can do this only if we dispose ourselves to do so by being alert and attentive. Our intent is to receive wisdom from a trustworthy authority—in this case, the most trustworthy of them all—so that we can honor God, serve others, and enrich our own lives. Radical obedience is born out of a desire to commit totally to God, and this, not mechanical conformity to the Law, is precisely what God desires of us.

The most obvious example of the radical obedience taught by Jesus is the Sermon on the Mount. In it, Jesus proposes a number of antitheses: "You have heard it was said to the men of old . . . , but I say to you . . ." In contrast to a lockstep external conformity to the letter of the law, the obedience of which Jesus speaks involves interior conversion. Forswearing the act of adultery (which doesn't necessarily mean forswearing lustful thoughts) is obedience of the body to God's will. But forswearing the reduction of another person to a purely sexual object even in the privacy of one's

imagination is total obedience of the body *and* will. It's
heeding God's demand for the whole person.

Obedience and Freedom

Radical obedience is acquiescence to God's will prefaced by
discernment—the attending to—of what God wants us to do
and be. But won't it rob us of our freedom? After all, if our
will is the seat of decision-making, relinquishment of it
seems to be a surrender of the ability to choose for oneself.
If this is so, how is obedience to God any different than the
mindless, lockstep conformity demanded by demagogues,
cult leaders, and tyrants? And if there isn't any significant difference, how can obedience possibly be a virtue that helps us
live and die well?

The answer is that genuine obedience—the radical obedience taught by Jesus—actually enhances human freedom
in two ways.

When we obey God, our will fuses with God's in a
process St. Paul called "putting on Christ." Putting on
Christ *frees* us *from* the alienation that comes with any kind
of separation from God. Made as we are in the divine likeness, we have a natural affinity for God and God's ways.
When we listen deeply enough to discern those ways, we joyfully embrace them. Obedience becomes a fulfillment of our
potential, a freeing from everything that prevents us from
becoming what we are.

Moreover, obedience to God's will *frees* us *to* act less
fearfully and more creatively in the world. It expands our
horizons and offers us opportunities to recognize and use
our God-given talents. Sure of who we are and what's truly
in our best interest, we're liberated to throw ourselves into
the often wonderful, sometimes tragic, but always God-filled
business of living.

The freedom-from and freedom-to offered by obedience not only liberate us to live well. They free us to die well too. As mortal beings, we know that we must die one day. This is the conformity mortality demands: we're born, age, and eventually cease to be. But we're free to choose how we respond to our mortality. Habituating ourselves to radical obedience prepares us to listen and assent to God's final command to us, the command to die. This doesn't mean that the prospect of dying will be an occasion for rejoicing, but it does suggest that a lifetime of obedience, freely chosen in the confidence that what God wills is in our best interest, will take away some of death's sting.

Groping toward Obedience

Jonathan Daniels eventually understood that obedience was a heartfelt heeding of God's will rather than a mechanical compliance with the orders or expectations of superiors. He came to know that the authentic nature of obedience lay more in answering a call than in formal rule-keeping. But it took a few years for all the pieces to fall into place.

Jon was born in Keene, New Hampshire, in the late winter of 1939 to Philip and Connie Daniels. His father was a respected physician and decorated World War II veteran and his mother had been a public school teacher of French and Latin before her marriage. They were a solid, upper-middle-class couple. Jon was their first child. A second, Emily, was born four years later.

Dr. Daniels was away from home so often attending to patients that most of the parenting was left to Connie. Jon adored and venerated his father, but began clashing with his mother as soon as he hit adolescence. A relatively quiet although intense child who enjoyed reading and music, Jon went through a period in his early teens when he rebelled against family rules he found too constricting. The main bones of contention were innocent enough: smoking cigarettes, running around with kids Connie disliked, cutting up in school, earning mediocre grades. (Connie the ex-teacher was especially mortified when Jon failed ninth-grade Latin.) But the sparring between mother and son created tension in the Daniels household.

Jon's behavior, and probably his academic performance as well, were exacerbated by a period of depression immediately sparked by his failure in school sports. (The depression had deeper biological roots. Jon's sister Emily would later be hospitalized with the same illness.) Not much of an athlete, plagued by asthma, and too independent to be a good team player, Jon fell short in every sport he tried. He was torn between a ferocious desire for freedom and an equally strong need to fit in, and his parents and teachers found his mood swings taxing.

A life-threatening accident in November of his junior year helped steady Jon. One of his friends had bought an old jalopy and invited him to go joyriding in the dead of night after both sets of parents were asleep. The friend pulled up to his house around midnight, Jon climbed out of his second-story bedroom window, and the two cruised around in the car for an hour or two. It was when he returned and tried to sneak back into his bedroom that things went wrong. Jon slipped off the roof and hit the frozen ground hard. Reeling with pain from a broken leg and multiple sprains and bruises on his left side, he somehow managed to get back in the house. But he was in agony for the rest of the night, and the next morning wound up in the hospital. He stayed there for a full month, finally returning home only on Christmas Eve.

The recovery period, much of it spent in solitude, gave Jon time to think and read. Always introspective and bookish, he seems to have taken an honest look at himself and decided to direct his energies and ambitions away from school athletics to where his talents really lay. Music, which had always been an important part of his life, became even more central. (His tastes ran to classical rather than popular genres. He wrote with the snobbery of a precocious adolescent that he "detest[ed] much modern music, especially 'rock 'n roll' and the trash that Elvis Presley sings."[7]) He also began performing in school plays and summer stock.

Then there were his books. From an early age, Jon displayed a strong romantic streak, reveling especially in "exciting tales of knights and fair ladies" and dreaming "of myself as a great hero."[8] He continued to enjoy the Arthurian legends, but also began reading the likes of Eugene O'Neill, James Joyce, Dostoyevsky, and Kafka. He dipped into philosophy and theology as well as the Bible, and was so moved by John's Gospel that he believed it "changed my life and thought more than any other writing I know."[9]

A major consequence of Jon's accident and convalescence was his decision to leave the New England Congregationalism of his family to join the Episcopal Church. The rich liturgy of the Episcopal Church appealed to Jon's love of drama as well as his romantic attraction to ritual and pageantry. His mother initially opposed the move to the Episcopal Church, worrying that it might split the family. But Jon calmed the waters—and broke from his earlier confrontational style of dealing with his mother—by agreeing to wait until he graduated from high school.

After joining the Episcopal Church, Jon told family and friends that he was considering the priesthood as a career. So everyone was surprised when he decided to attend the Virginia Military Institute (VMI). His high school grades weren't good enough to get him into the Ivy League schools his parents preferred, although they certainly would've earned him a spot

at any good liberal arts college. But Jon chose to matriculate
at one of the toughest military schools in the country.

The reasons for his decision are complex, but three in
particular stand out. His love of stories about chivalry and
knightly courage fueled his pride in a long family tradition of
military service and prompted him to want to contribute to
it. Jon's ancestors fought in the Revolutionary and Civil
Wars, and his father fought and was wounded in the Second
World War. Jon also romanticized the Old South and the
Confederacy, and this was an additional draw to an institution whose faculty at one time had included both Stonewall
Jackson and Robert E. Lee. As he wrote shortly before heading to VMI, "I think of the South as my adopted home and
because of this, I cannot help but sympathize with her—in
fact I must confess that I have a great affection, I hope not
too disloyal to my country and heritage, for the gallant and
valorous but misguided Johnny Rebs."[10]

The same love of ritual that drew him to the Episcopal
Church also played a role in his decision to attend a military
academy opulently rich in tradition and ceremony. Jon came
to dislike most military aspects of his life as a VMI student.
But the institution's dramatic, quasi-religious pageantry—
not to mention the splendid uniforms worn by cadets—
weren't among them.

Finally, VMI's reputation for strict military discipline
appealed to Jon. Ever since his convalescent stock-taking,
he'd sensed a need for order in his life and feared that he
lacked the resolve to attain it on his own. So he went to
VMI looking for external constraints on his will and behavior. It's also possible that he felt the need to compensate for
his athletic failures in school by proving to himself and others that he could make it through VMI's rigorous physical
training. (He told the wife of one of his VMI professors that
he'd come to the academy to see if he "had the makings of

a man."[11]) At this point in his life, Jon wanted mental and physical discipline, and he thought that the best way to get it was in a regimented environment that stressed unquestioning conformity.

Not surprisingly, Jon's years at VMI were difficult. Neither his romantic fondness for tales about chivalry nor his pride in his soldierly lineage prepared him in the least for the brutal treatment endured by all first-year "Rats." Later, when he was an upperclassman, he became known as a "Rat Daddy" because he frequently came to the defense of first-year students when hazing went too far.

Jon's failure as an athlete had made him feel like an outsider in high school. He was an outsider at VMI too. According to one of his fellow cadets, "The Virginia Military Institute was not the kind of school where one would expect to find a man like Jon Daniels. He simply seemed out of place there. He spoke softly; he looked, and probably was, frail physically. He was 'intellectual.'" But Jon was more comfortable being a square peg in a round hole at VMI than he'd been in high school. Besides, there was something in him, despite his strangeness, that soon earned the respect of most of his fellow cadets. "Appearances deceive," the same classmate remembered, "and Jon's did. When you spoke with him you forgot his frailness, his seeming effeminacy and weakness. His words were strong; there was nothing frail about his ideas, nor—even more—about his willingness to admit his error if it were shown him in a clear debate."[12] The esteem in which his classmates came to hold this bookish, nonathletic Rat Daddy was demonstrated in his senior year when they elected him valedictorian. Jon Daniels may not have been career soldier material, but he'd shown in his own quiet way that he had the makings of a man. He'd learned discipline. He'd learned how to obey orders. Yet, at the same time, he'd remained his own person, demonstrating to himself that obedience wasn't the same thing as conformity.

From Harvard to the Magnificat

The unpleasant regimentation of daily life at VMI cured Jon of his tendency to glorify the military. The intensive reading he did there for his English major—a suspect course of studies at a place where most students majored in engineering or the sciences—also knocked the wind out of his Christian calling. Less than a year after his confirmation in the Episcopal Church, Jon, like many intelligent college students, found himself impatient with religion. He dropped his private nightly prayers and began to cut mandatory chapel as often as he could.

In hindsight, Jon's conversion in high school was an aesthetic attraction to High Church liturgy that couldn't compete with his new conviction, fueled by a heady reading of French existentialism, that life was absurdly devoid of intrinsic purpose. His lack of genuine commitment to Christianity at this point in his life surfaced in a revealing conversation he had with one of his VMI professors. Asked in his sophomore year about his career plans, Jon mechanically answered that he was thinking about the Episcopal ministry. When the professor wanted to hear the reasons for his choice, Jon ran through a singularly uninspired list. "First—well, people expected it of him—the folks back home in Keene. Secondly, he was basically afraid. He didn't trust himself in the world, he didn't think like the world, he hardly understood it, and he didn't trust its reaction to him or his to it . . . The ministry looked like a safe and quiet way to read, study, have congenial friends, etc."[13]

Apparently Jon's reasons sounded as unconvincing to him as they did to his professor. By the time the conversation ended, Jon "finally admitted to real qualms about the whole deal. He didn't know why he was thinking of the ministry. He didn't even know that he believed in anything. At any rate, he decided that the Episcopal Church game was not for him."[14]

Jon moved even further away from the game when his father died after a struggle with kidney disease in Jon's third year at VMI. Dr. Daniels was only in his mid-fifties, and his death was both emotionally traumatic and financially disastrous for the family. Connie Daniels was forced to return to work, and Emily, already beginning to show signs of depression, suffered a breakdown that put her in and out of hospitals over the next year. Her medical expenses were an unwelcome burden to a household already strapped for cash. For Jon, the untimely death of his beloved father—"the man who most influenced me"[15]—only confirmed the absurdity of existence. What meaning was there in life if a good man like his father could die so young? As Jon later wrote, "My father's death during my junior year in college precipitated an attack of anxiety which demanded intensive self-scrutiny and a thorough reconstruction of my life."[16]

Part of the reconstruction meant jettisoning any lingering thoughts of seminary after VMI and instead embarking on English graduate studies at Harvard in the fall of 1961. But almost from the very beginning the decision proved disastrous. Jon took an intense dislike to what he saw as the pedantically lifeless dissection of literature insisted on by his professors—a "shedding [of] false light on non-problems," he scornfully said.[17] Moreover, the anxiety that hit him when his father died apparently followed him to Harvard, and he sought psychological counseling to cope. In the meantime, his sister Emily was hospitalized again, and the family finances hit a new low. At the end of his first semester, Jon took incompletes in two of his four courses. By the time the spring semester began, both he and Harvard had come to the conclusion that he'd be better off elsewhere. Jon resolved to finish out the year and rethink his options.

Then the unexpected happened. The stress in his life had reawakened Jon's religious hunger and he'd started attending services at Boston's Episcopal Church of the Advent. On Easter Sunday, 1962, he experienced a second conversion there—this time, a deep and abiding one. He never went into details about what happened on that morning. But it proved a turning point for him. "I made a decision which radically changed my life. I decided to return to the church, having left her quite deliberately several years before. God followed that gift with another, as I felt his not so gentle nudge reminding me that I didn't belong in the graduate school. I decided then . . . in God's good time, to seek Holy Orders."[18]

At the end of the academic year, Jon shook the dust of Harvard off his feet, returned home to Keene, and applied for admission to the Episcopal Theological School (ETS; since renamed Episcopal Divinity School) in Cambridge, Massachusetts. He took a couple of jobs to help out his mother, read widely, and became active in his parish church of St. James. As part of his preparation as an aspirant for Holy Orders, Jon preached a guest sermon there one Sunday that expressed the vision of ministry he would carry with him to seminary and, eventually, to Alabama. Taking his text from the prophet Isaiah, Jon proclaimed that

> Somebody must visit the sick, and the lonely, and the frightened, and the sorrowing. Somebody must comfort the discouraged, and argue lovingly and convincingly with the anguished doubter. Somebody must remind the sick soul that healing is within his grasp and urge him to take the medicine when his disease seems more attractive. Then I heard

the voice of the Lord saying, "Whom shall I send? And who will go for us?" Then said I, "Here am I. Send me."[19]

When Jon began his studies at ETS in September 1963, he knew immediately that he'd made the right decision. Unlike his earlier experiences at VMI and Harvard, he felt totally at home. His biblical and theological studies stimulated him and he respected his professors and classmates. He was no longer an outsider.

Despite his disgust with what he saw as the nit-picking of Harvard professors, Jon went into seminary expecting that he would pursue graduate studies after ordination and then settle down somewhere to a cozy teaching position. He was a young man who lived very much in his head—on arriving at ETS he was giddy with delight at being surrounded by "millions of books!"[20]—and knew much more about the world of ideas than the one of politics and public policy. Although he was familiar with some of the social issues of his day—"I am repelled by the valuation of material acquisition in our life," he wrote. "I am appalled at the proportion of the gross national product devoted to military capability"[21]—he was shockingly naïve about others, especially the struggle for Civil Rights that was going on around him.

Jon's political awareness and his sense of Christian discipleship soon began to expand. He arrived in Cambridge in the middle of a highly visible NAACP campaign to integrate Boston's schools, and for the first time in his life he took serious notice of racial injustice. He may have attended a huge public rally held on Boston Common that fall in support of the campaign. At any rate, he joined the NAACP in October.

His sensitivity to the race problem soon grew exponentially. First-year students at ETS were required to perform

twelve hours of weekly field work. Jon and a classmate drew
assignments at Christ Episcopal Church, a black inner city
parish in Providence, Rhode Island. Every Saturday they
boarded a train to work as youth counselors to the kids in
the parish. His months there gave Jon firsthand experience
of the grinding poverty endured by urban blacks, and added
flesh to what hitherto had been a mainly abstract understanding of racial discrimination.

Jon found the work exhausting and frequently frustrating, but he came to see it as "crucial to my 'holy' history."
It totally "revised my preconceptions of my own ministry
and opened unexpected horizons." Instead of devoting
himself to a teaching ministry which "virtually exclud[ed]
either the challenge or the value of the parish priesthood,"
Jon now believed that "I could serve my Lord with a glad
heart in a slum."[22]

In keeping with his new sense of calling, Jon's understanding of the Church began to change as well. He still rel-
ished the rich pageantry, poetic liturgy, architectural beauty,
and scholarly tradition of the Episcopal Church. But he now
appreciated the danger of using the religious life as a retreat
from the very world that the Church is called to serve. "I
think sometimes," he wrote to a friend, "we are afraid to
admit that our religion is anything other than a (rather precarious) intellectual venture." Too often, the Church focused
narrowly on polity and internal squabbles and remained indifferent to poverty and injustice in the world. In doing so, Jon
feared, it shied away from shouldering the Cross Christ calls
it to bear. "The Church still needs priests and prophets, men
who through word and sacrament will wage the sword of
peace, who will proclaim with the totality of their lives that
the way of the Cross is ultimately the road of life and that the
ongoing sacrifice of the Cross is the only triumph of significant value . . . It is . . . easier to preach it than to live it."[23] Jon's

new understanding of discipleship as following the way of the Cross would become increasingly central to his thinking and his actions.

The summer after his first year at ETS found John working in a New York hospital as an intern chaplain. Once the fall term began he once again threw himself into course work at Cambridge and field work at Providence's Christ Church. That winter the parish bought a nearby tenement house and turned it into a homeless shelter. Jon, his commitment to Christ-centered social activism now firm, spent nearly every weekend there.

Curiously, however, he was still trying to work out what genuine obedience to God means. As racial unrest escalated in the southern states, the Episcopal bishop of Alabama made headlines in early 1965 when he announced that civil rights workers were unwelcome in his diocese. At an open meeting of ETS students and faculty, Jon vigorously defended the right of the bishop to lay down the law in his diocese and the obligation of outsiders to comply with his orders. Part of Jon recognized that obedience to the church hierarchy wasn't necessarily the sort of obedience Jesus had in mind for his disciples. But another part of him—the same part that had longed for acceptance by high-school athletes, VMI professors, and Harvard academics—still felt pulled toward authority-pleasing conformity.

Jon's ambivalence was resolved in early March. Frustrated by the South's stonewalling when it came to the Civil Rights Act signed by President Johnson the preceding summer—the favorite delaying tactic was to put hurdles in the way of blacks who tried to register to vote—Martin Luther King Jr. called for a peaceful march from Selma, Alabama (Selma was located in a county especially notorious for its refusal to register blacks) to the state capitol of Montgomery. On the morning of Sunday, March 7, some six hundred people began the trek. Following a church service, they processed through downtown Selma toward the Edmund Pettus Bridge (named after a general in the Confederacy that Jon had once romanticized) which spans the Alabama River. There, without warning, they were attacked by state troopers and county deputies with clubs, whips, nightsticks, and tear gas. Many were beaten as they knelt praying. Dozens wound up in hospital. In minutes the march was over, having proceeded only six blocks. The day became known as "Bloody Sunday."

That night, King announced a second march to take place two days later and called on clergy from all over the nation to participate. The next morning, Jon and his fellow students at ETS discussed the possibility of going down to Alabama. Jon reluctantly decided that he couldn't spare the time and "with a faintly tarnished feeling" decided instead to contribute funds to a Selma relief fund. But later on that day, the youth who two years earlier had invoked Isaiah's readiness to answer God's call as a model for ministry heard the call himself.

I had come to Evening Prayer as usual that evening, and as usual I was singing the Magnificat with the special love and reverence I have always felt for Mary's glad song. "He hath showed strength with his arm." As the lovely hymn of the God-bearer continued, I found myself peculiarly alert, suddenly straining toward the decisive, luminous, Spirit-filled "moment" that would, in retrospect, remind me of others—particularly of one at Easter three years ago [a reference to his conversion at the Church of the Advent]. Then it came. "He hath put down the mighty from their seat, and hath exalted the humble and meek. He hath filled the hungry with good things." I knew then that I must go to Selma. The Virgin's song was to grow more and more dear in the weeks ahead.[24]

The next morning, Jon and ten other ETS students headed south.

"That freedom which is holy obedience"

In 1965. Selma was a town of stark and typically southern contrasts. A sleepy rural community for most of its history, the place got an economic shot in the arm in 1940 when a new interstate highway opened it up as a transportation and distribution hub. By the time King called for the Selma-to-Montgomery march, the town boasted twenty-odd millionaires, an all-white country club, three hospitals, two golf courses, and the usual mix of schools and suburbs that went with them.

That was white Selma. Black Selma was something else altogether. In 1964, only 19 percent of Alabama's blacks were registered to vote. In Selma the figure shrank to scarcely 1 percent, even though blacks made up the majority of the city's population. The local sheriff was a hard-nosed character who made sure that blacks in his county stayed off the voting rolls.

When Jon and his classmates arrived in Selma on March 11, they immediately ran up against the southern way of doing things. Hundreds of people from all over the nation had answered King's call for a second march. But in spite of their numbers and the fact that dozens of nationally known celebrities, scholars, clergy, and activists were present, the marchers were stopped and turned back by state troopers, getting no further than their predecessors had on Bloody

Sunday. That night, James Reeb, a white Unitarian minister from Boston, was beaten to death by angry segregationists in downtown Selma. A protest march on the town courthouse the following morning was blocked by the local police, forcing the demonstrators to stand in place most of the day. "This symbolizes the progress of the Negro race in the last hundred years," Jon bitterly observed. "You stand around and wait and then you move forward an inch or two."[25]

That night, a good many of the clergy who'd come to Selma for the aborted march headed back home. But Jon and fellow ETS student Judy Upham, worried about the backlash Selma's blacks would suffer when both the demonstrators and the northern press left, decided to stay on a few more days. They lodged with a black family, organized an integrated prayer service outside an Episcopal Church that refused to receive blacks, took part in a second march on Selma's courthouse between a gauntlet of angry shotgun-toting whites, and eventually decided that God was calling them to remain in the South a little while longer to work for what Jon, following the example of Martin Luther King Jr. increasingly referred to as the "beloved community." The two students made a quick return to Cambridge to square their decision with the seminary and then returned to Alabama just in time for the launch of the third and successful Selma-to-Montgomery march.

The first few weeks of their return to Alabama were spent trying to convince the rector of St. Paul's Episcopal Church, in front of whose doors they'd held the prayer service, to integrate. Predictably, the congregation furiously resisted them. Once, when an enraged parishioner confronted him, Jon replied, "We're trying to live the gospel." But the snarling man told him to go to hell and stalked off.[26] After the bishop of Alabama defended the church's segregation, Jon and Judy wrote him a couple of heated letters that all but accused him of betraying Christ's teachings. Jon had come a long way from his ETS defense of episcopal authority a couple of months earlier.

Jon and Judy remained in Alabama until early May. They were sponsored and partly financed by ESCRU, the Episcopal Society for Cultural and Racial Unity, and tasked with teaching literacy, registering black voters, and integrating churches. The angry threats their presence provoked both bewildered and frightened them. Jon said on more than one occasion that he knew he was putting his life in danger by remaining in the South, and occasionally he couldn't help but burst into anger himself. "There are still moments," he confessed, "when I'd like to get a high-powered rifle and take to the woods, but more and more strongly I am beginning to feel that ultimately the revolution to which I am committed is the way of the Cross."[27]

For Jon, the "way of the Cross" first and foremost meant subordinating his own will to God's. As early as his Isaiah sermon in Keene, he'd sensed that a life dedicated to God meant carefully listening to God's will and heeding it. In April 1964 he returned to the theme, this time exploring the connection between obedience and Christian freedom. He was, he wrote, beginning to have "an uncomfortable, glorious glimpse now and then of what the Cross of Jesus Christ calls us to...: obedient service in which is our only perfect freedom."[28]

When Jon wrote this, he was still thinking his way through the exact relationship between obedience and freedom. But a year later, after being tear-gassed at a public demonstration in Camden, Alabama, the pieces fell together for him. The experience proved to be the third great insight of his life, every bit as important as his second conversion in the Church of the Advent and the Magnificat call to go to Alabama.

In describing the demonstration to a friend, Jon began by admitting that his anger had been growing over the weeks leading up to it: anger at bigoted white southerners, at a social system that condoned Jim Crow, at the cowardice of the Christians who failed to speak out against it. "My hostility lasted really until last week," he wrote in mid-April 1965.

> I think it was when I got tear-gassed leading a march in Camden that I began to change. I saw that the men who came at me were themselves not free: it was not that cruelty was so sweet to them (though I'm afraid it is), *but that they didn't know what else to do.* Even though they were white and hateful and my enemy, they were human beings, too.[29]

Jon went on to say that a month earlier he'd come to the realization that as a "soldier of the Cross" he was "totally free—at least free to give my life, if that had to be, with joy and thankfulness and eagerness for the Kingdom." But in Camden, he discovered a new depth to the freedom of obedience.

> Last week in Camden I began to discover a new freedom in the Cross: freedom to love the enemy. And in that freedom, the freedom (without hypocrisy) to will and to try to set him free...As I go about my primary business of attempting to negotiate with the white power structure..., there is a new factor—I rather think a new Presence—in our conversations: the "strategy of love."[30]

Judging from how often he returned to it in letters and essays during the final four months of his life, Jon's insight into the relationship between obedience and freedom was never far from his mind. In May, reflecting on his past weeks in Selma, he explicitly linked dying and rebirth to the new freedom he'd found in the way of the Cross. "The gospel is less and less a matter primarily of the intellect. And more and more a matter of living and dying and living anew."[31] There was a cost, he understood, to this new understanding of the gospel, and he suspected that he had only begun to pay it. "I have a hunch [that] I have a little more to learn of 'radical obedience' (and of poverty and chastity, too, for that matter). It is so hard to give oneself up. And yet so essential."[32] Later on that summer, he told a group of youngsters that surrendering in obedience to God was first and foremost a matter of quieting down long enough to hear what God wants. "One begins by listening," he said, "making sure that one is really *listening*."[33]

In a letter to a friend who had voiced concern about his safety, Jon discussed obedience in words that, while probably doing little to ease the friend's anxiety, clearly underscored the freedom—in this case, from fear—that listening to God's will gave him.

> I decided a long time ago that the Holy Spirit had brought me here [to Selma], that I believe very firmly in the gospel and its faith, that my life is not my own but His—which means that before anything else I am a servant of Christ, however sinful I may also be—and that consequently the possibility of death, whether immediate or remote, cannot be a deciding factor for me.[34]

A few weeks later, less than two months before his murder, Jon once again drew an explicit connection between obedience and freedom: "I am inclined to be a little skeptical about all the 'freedoms' which are not grounded in the

'slavery' of His service."[35] And in one of the last student essays he wrote for ETS, Jon again tied obedience and freedom to love. It is his most complete analysis of the great
insight that dawned on him as he coughed and gasped
through the tear gas at Camden.

> When the Christian first begins to answer with his
> own feeble love the overwhelming Love of God, he
> finds himself animated by an attitude that is equally
> "holy obedience" and "perfect freedom." In that
> freedom which is holy obedience, the Christian has
> only one principle, only one agenda. And that is the
> dynamic of life-in-response to the loving, judging,
> healing, merciful revelation by God Himself of His
> holy will.[36]

Obedience unto Death

Jon returned to Cambridge in May to take final exams and
then spent a few weeks back in Keene with his family. It was
the last time he would see his mother and sister. In July he
headed back to Selma.

Once there, he threw in his lot with the Student Nonviolent Coordinating Committee (SNCC), the civil rights organization that worked throughout the Deep South to
register black voters. That summer, SNCC coordinators in
Alabama, one of whom was Stokely Carmichael, were especially concentrating their efforts in Lowndes County.

In the mid-1960s, Lowndes County, which lies between
Selma and Montgomery, was one of the nation's poorest and
most segregated areas. It was known as "bloody Lowndes"
even by other Alabamians because the beating or killing of
blacks by the KKK was so commonplace. A black person

could be murdered simply for failing to step aside on the sidewalk for a white person.[37] Even Selma looked safe by comparison.

Economically, blacks in Lowndes were the poorest residents of an already dirt-poor county. The wage system hadn't taken hold there. Ninety percent of the farms were worked by sharecropping tenants, and ninety percent of the tenants were black. Chronically indebted to the county's few wealthy landowners, Lowndes blacks were still virtual plantation slaves a full century after the Civil War had ended.

Politically, Lowndes County blacks were utterly disenfranchised, despite the federal Voting Rights Act. Although 80 percent of the county's residents were black, county officials were so good at throwing up bureaucratic roadblocks that fewer than 4 percent of blacks were registered to vote. Needless to say, all the local authorities, from county supervisors to law officers, were white.

SNCC aimed to change things in Lowndes County and in the summer of 1965 launched a voter registration drive. Jon immediately volunteered to help out. Carmichael, worried that SNCC couldn't adequately protect him from whites who deeply resented the interference of northern outsiders with the "southern way of life," tried to talk him out of it. But Jon insisted, and was soon transporting SNCC field workers and speaking at registration drives in different towns throughout the county. One of the people he worked with was Father Richard Morrisroe, another white, northern "outside agitator."

On August 14, Jon and Morrisroe joined several SNCC field workers, including Stokely Carmichael and Ruby Sales, at the tiny town of Fort Deposit to organize a voting rights demonstration. The event had barely begun when local police arrested the participants and crammed them into the Fort Deposit jail. A half hour later, a flat-bellied garbage truck pulled up and the prisoners were loaded onto it for transportation to the larger jail at Hayneville, the county seat.

Conditions at the Hayneville jail were atrocious. The twenty-odd prisoners were packed into just three squalid cells. Toilets backed up, the food was nearly inedible, and the heat was killing. Bail was set at $100 per head, but the prisoners agreed that they would leave the jail together or not at all. When an official from ESCRU offered to get Jon out, he refused.

Six days later all the prisoners were released, their bail requirement suddenly dropped. To this day it's unknown if local authorities let the prisoners go because they were tired of looking after them or, given what happened shortly afterwards, if there was a more sinister motive. At any rate, Jon Daniels, obedient to the last, was gunned down by Deputy Sheriff Tom Coleman less than an hour later. Coleman, who a few years before had shot and killed a black man he claimed threatened him with a bottle, was charged with murder. At his trial, he perjured himself by testifying that Jon had lunged at him with a knife. The all-white male jury deliberated for all of two hours before acquitting him. After the verdict, an unremorseful Coleman boasted to reporters that he'd do the same thing all over again if he had the opportunity.[38]

"The mightiest Wind in the world at my back"

Jonathan Daniels always remembered what one of his New Testament professors at ETS once said: "When the call comes, you have to drop what you're doing and go. Sometimes the call comes at the least convenient moment you can imagine. But whenever it comes, you must go."[39] Jon recorded hearing the call three times in his life: once in the Church of the Advent, once at Evensong, and once in Camden. But he must've heard it at least one more time: when he pushed Ruby Sales out of the way and took the shotgun blast intended for her.

In describing the call, Jon wrote that it was as if "the Holy Spirit has picked me up by the scruff of the neck... Though I cannot guess precisely where I am being driven, I have the haunting feeling again and again that I am flying with the mightiest Wind in the world at my back."[40]

Words failed Jon when he tried to describe what it felt like to hear God's call and respond to it in radical obedience. When he wrote that he'd been picked up by the scruff of his neck and driven, he obviously didn't mean to say he was coerced. Jon's obedient receptivity to God's will was, as he knew, an exercise in freedom. He freely chose to obey, not sure where the obedience would take him but confident that it was where he needed to go.

And yet Jon's scruff-of-the-neck image is an appropriate metaphor, because to be radically obedient to God is to offer up one's freedom as freely and trustingly as a kitten that allows itself to be carried by its mother. The worldly understanding of freedom straightforwardly equates it with absolute individual autonomy and unhindered self-direction. But Christian freedom is paradoxical. Christians are subject to none but God, and even our subordination to God must be freely chosen. Once given, it is an unconditional commitment that accepts total subordination to divine will. But in obediently aligning our will with God's, we discover perfect freedom to flourish because we embrace an attitude and lifestyle in keeping with the divine plan. "It is for freedom that Christ has set us free," wrote St. Paul. "Stand firm, then, and do not let yourselves be burdened again by a yoke of slavery" (Gal 5:1). God's yoke, unlike slavery's, is a light and easy burden (see Matt 11:30). Even more, it's truly in our best interest, so freely choosing it not only honors God but also enriches our life—even, as Jonathan Daniels discovered, if the choice leads to martyrdom.

True, most of us won't die as martyrs. But we *will* die, and that is part of the spiritual journey to which we are called. It is our inescapable destiny, a command, as it were, which we must obey. How we obey it will be determined by how well we've cultivated obedience as a habit of the heart over our lifetime. We can resist the inevitability of our dying, refusing to go gently into that dark night. Or we can listen, *really* listen, to the meaning of death, recognizing it as a last call from God, a crossing-over to our final home, and embracing it as a Cross that leads to Resurrection. This doesn't mean cultivating a passive fatalism in the face of our mortality. Nor does it implausibly suggest seeing dying as a joyous or eagerly-awaited event. It does mean, however, that death, for all its sadness and mysterious fearfulness, is a summons. We may have no clear idea where the summons will take us, but we know that the mightiest Wind in the world will be at our backs.

CHAPTER SIX

COURAGE

Dietrich Bonhoeffer

*"The Bible, the Gospel, Christ, the Church, Faith, they
are all one great war cry against fear in the life of man.
Fear—that is somehow the original enemy himself. Fear
dwells in the hearts of men."*

A Death on the Gallows

The military doctor who witnessed Dietrich Bonhoeffer's execution on April 9, 1945 never forgot what he saw. That morning, Bonhoeffer and five of his fellow prisoners, all implicated
in a plot to kill Hitler, were led out of their Flossenburg
Prison cells and curtly informed that they'd been convicted of
treason and would be hanged within the hour. Shortly afterwards they were stripped naked and led to the place of execution. Bonhoeffer appeared calm as the noose was slipped
around his neck. "I was most deeply moved by the way this
lovable man prayed," recalled the doctor, "so devout and so
certain that God heard his prayer...He climbed to the steps
of the gallows, brave and composed...I have hardly ever seen
a man die so entirely submissive to the will of God."[1]

The calmness Bonhoeffer displayed at the moment of his
death had been hard-won. For most of his life—as schoolboy,
theology student, pastor, author, head of an underground

seminary in Nazi Germany and, finally, conspirator against
the Nazi state—Bonhoeffer had struggled with the fearful
ambiguities of free will as well as his personal anxieties about
who he was and what he was called to do. There were times
when the necessity to choose between competing courses of
action made him feel as if he were being torn apart. At such
moments, the burden of freedom felt too heavy too bear, the
perplexity of moral responsibility too dreadful to endure.
After he joined the German resistance, Bonhoeffer discovered
that the tension between his Christian pacifism and his conviction that Hitler needed killing was so painful that all he
could do was throw himself upon God's mercy.

There was another cause of anxiety as well. Always, lurk-
ing on the horizon, never far from Bonhoeffer's gaze, was
the specter of death, the final fate of all living things. Why
must we humans be deprived of the life we find so precious?
What sense can we make of who we are in light of our mortality? And how are we to reconcile the dreadfulness of death
with our faith in a good and loving God?

Bonhoeffer began to feel the weight of these questions
as a schoolboy, and he grappled with them the rest of his
days. In the process, he discovered a virtue essential to good
living and good dying: courage. Reflection on his inner life
as well as observation of the people around him convinced
Bonhoeffer that "fear dwells in the hearts of all men," and is
ineradicable.[2] The task isn't to find a way to live *without* fear,
but rather to live well and richly *despite* fear. Courage is facing up to the messy ambiguity of life, the burden of freedom, and the inevitability of death, and yet continuing to
affirm life and God rather than sinking under a weight of despair. This is the virtue that allowed Bonhoeffer to live with
integrity in his turbulent times and to meet his death with
such equanimity. It is a good habit of the heart for all of us
to cultivate. In all likelihood, our lives will be outwardly less

tumultuous than Bonhoeffer's. Few of us will have to confront an evil akin to Nazism. But in our own less dramatic ways, each of us must deal with the same anxieties that Bonhoeffer faced. And to do that, we need to be courageous.

The Virtue of Courage

Courage in the Face of Nothingness

There are different kinds of courage: physical bravery when risking bodily harm or death, moral courage when defending unpopular ideals or challenging authority, and spiritual fortitude when overwhelmed by a sense of meaninglessness or dread. What do they have in common that makes them all courage?

The theologian Paul Tillich famously argued that courage, regardless of how it expresses itself, is an affirmation of life in spite of the fact that nothingness or "non-being" continuously threatens us.[3] We typically think of courage as a specific response to a localized situation: bravery on the battlefield or in defying unjust authority. But Tillich believed that courage is something else as well. It's a general attitude toward life that colors all our individual decisions and actions, an attitude that says "yes" to our existence against the threats to it that we face daily. This fundamental affirmation, which serves as the taproot for all specific acts of courage, is what Tillich called the "courage to be." It is the resolve to face the fact that our very being is fragile and always at risk, and yet nonetheless to affirm and even celebrate it. The cowardly person tries to repress his disturbing knowledge of just how tenuous his hold on life is. The person of courage embraces his fragility, recognizing it as an unavoidable aspect of who he is. To evade the non-being that threatens us, even if it were possible, would be to lose part of what makes us distinctively human. What right-thinking person would be willing to pay so high a price?

The nothingness that haunts us and is the source of our deepest anxiety reminds us that our existence is never as secure as we would like to believe. The most obvious way in which nothingness threatens us, and certainly the one we most consciously fear, is death. Like Jesus in Gethsemane, we can experience paralyzing waves of hot panic at the thought that one day death will come for us, that we will cease to be, and that there's absolutely nothing we can do to escape this fate. But another way in which nothingness threatens our stability is the uncertainty that comes with making moral decisions. We can almost never be totally confident that the choices we make are the right ones, and so our moral lives are tinged with an abiding sense of uneasiness and even guilt. Yet a third way we're threatened by nothingness is our occasional uneasy suspicion that our life in particular and existence in general is without rhyme or reason, an ultimately meaningless tale told by an idiot. We emerge from the void and we eventually return to it, filling our empty days as best we can. That's all there is to life.

These three experiences of nothingness profoundly threaten us because we want to think of ourselves as stable, enduring, and secure creatures. The experiences of nothingness force us to acknowledge that we're riddled with the possibility of physical, moral, or spiritual collapse. For many and perhaps most people, this is just too much to bear. So we contrive strategies that shield us from our fragility. We refuse to think about our own mortality by adopting a "What, me worry?" attitude, we embrace formulaic ethical rules that promise easy solutions to life's moral dilemmas, we frenetically focus on the minutiae of everyday life to avoid thinking about whether there's an overall pattern behind them, or we try to bluster our way through all our anxieties with a two-fisted defiance. Some of us become loners, isolating ourselves from the physical dangers of the world and the responsibilities that come from being moral agents. Others of us immerse ourselves in collective movements or ideologies, hoping to find strength in numbers. But ultimately these sorts of strategies fail, because to be human simply *is* to be threatened by nothingness. Each of us knows we *will* die. Each of us *will* sometimes wonder if the moral choices we make are the right ones. Each of us *will* have the occasional dark night of the soul when life seems absurd and burdensome.

Tillich accepted the inevitability of human fraility while warning that we can never really escape the anxiety it provokes. So the courage he has in mind isn't fearlessness so much as a steadfast loyalty to life that endures in spite of death-fear, moral uncertainty, and moments of despair. For people of faith, courage is buttressed by belief in a God in whom there is no possibility of non-being and who consequently grounds and ultimately sustains our own nothingness-haunted existence.[4] But religious faith can't and shouldn't erase the primal uncertainties and anxieties with which humans must cope. As one commentator puts it, "no religion can make anyone secure, though it, like the drugs on which our society is so dependent, can give the illusion of security." Instead, "true religion enables one to grasp life with its radical insecurity and to live it with courage. It does not aid us in the pretense that our insecurities have been taken away."[5]

Bonhoeffer wrestled with all three of the anxiety-provoking experiences of nothingness examined by Tillich. His opposition to the Nazis put him in actual physical danger as early as 1936. But the thought of his own mortality had begun to haunt him years earlier when he was still a child. Moreover, he certainly had despairing moments in which he called into question the meaningfulness of his life and the authenticity of his identity. Some of the most poignant letters he wrote from prison in the final months of his life record them. But, as we'll see, it's Tillich's second form of nothingness, the uncertainty of moral decision-making, that especially challenged Bonhoeffer.

Nothingness, Freedom, and Courage

From Tillich's perspective, experiences of nothingness are all negatively anxiety-provoking. But there's a less bleak way of thinking about them that ought not to be neglected. The experience of nothingness also points to a human quality that most of us consider a positive attribute: free will. When experienced as death-fear, moral confusion, or the despair of meaninglessness, nothingness arouses in us an anxiety that, in the absence of the virtue of courage, can crush the spirit. But the nothingness we experience whenever we exercise our free will, although also anxiety-provoking, can also make us feel exuberantly alive and fulfilled. We feel the vertigo of nothingness alongside the thrill of self-direction. The nothingness of freedom, paradoxically, is the source of both deep anxiety and deep affirmation of our humanity.

How is nothingness connected to free will? It's simple. Whenever faced with the need to make a choice—to exercise free will—we stand in the present moment, gaze into the not-as-yet future, and try to predict the consequences of our choice. What will happen if I do this instead of that? If I take this path rather than the other one? If I walk away from this opportunity instead of embracing it? Quite often, there's little riding on our choices: should I see this movie or that one? Eat dinner now or in an hour? But sometimes the choices that present themselves to us carry colossal weight, and we know beyond doubt that whatever we decide will affect the course of our lives. This in itself is enough to provoke anxiety, but what really shakes us is our realization that making the decision is a leap out of the secure present into the unknowable and hence frightening future. Every time we make a free choice that has some weight, we step out of the familiar into the not-as-yet future—nothingness—knowing that the stakes are high and knowing equally well that we don't know where the chips will fall. Who wouldn't feel apprehensive under these circumstances? But at the same time, we experience the sheer thrill of being the sort of creature— a free one—who is capable of making the decision to venture into the unknown. Free will has a price as well as a reward, and both are traceable to the experience of nothingness.

What this means is that the relationship between fear and courage is more complex and less ominous than Tillich imagined. The nothingness which is an essential part of who we are unpleasantly reminds us that we're mortal creatures, but also, more positively, that we're free ones. Our anxiety in the face of death or moral dilemmas or a sense of meaninglessness is simultaneously an acknowledgment of our ability to choose, our status as free subjects rather than futureless things. So courage isn't merely the affirmation of being in spite of the non-being that threatens it. It's also, as Bonhoeffer discovered, the affirmation of freedom in spite of the anxiety it inevitably provokes.

Death and the Outsider

Dietrich Bonhoeffer was born in the winter of 1906, ten minutes before his twin sister Sabine, a fact that he good-naturedly never let her forget. He was the sixth child of parents who embodied the stolid values of Wilhelmine Germany's upper classes. Karl, Bonhoeffer's father, was a noted psychiatrist and neurologist. His mother Paula was an aristocrat whose own mother had studied music with no less a teacher than Franz Liszt. The Bonhoeffers were well-off, with the usual assortment of domestic servants expected in a family of their social class. When Karl was awarded a prestigious professorship at the University of Berlin, the family moved from Breslau, Dietrich's birthplace, to a huge house in the Tiergarten, an exclusive Berlin suburb.

As a boy, Dietrich had little contact with the world outside his family circle. Like all his siblings, he was educated in his early years at home by tutors. The gardens surrounding the mansion were large enough for Dietrich to roam to his heart's content, and his playmates were limited to his siblings, his cousins, and a handful of children from families with the same social standing as his. He felt little curiosity about what lay beyond his small, protected world.

Then, in August 1914, World War I erupted. Suddenly the outside world intruded on the Bonhoeffer household. Eight-year-old Dietrich was swept up in the war fever that gripped the nation, and he played endlessly in the garden at marching, drilling, and soldiering. But soon shortages of food and fuel began to dampen his enthusiasm. Then came reports that fathers of some of his playmates had been killed. Three of his own older cousins also fell in battle, and a fourth was blinded. War was no longer a game.

It was around this time that Dietrich became both fascinated and terrified by the prospect of death. His sister Sabine recalled how the two of them lay awake in the night trying "to imagine what eternal life and being dead were like. We endeavored every evening to get a little nearer to eternity by concentrating on the world and eternity and excluding any other thought."[6] Dietrich, saturated with wartime propaganda that extolled heroic battlefield sacrifices, often dreamt of a glorious warrior's death for himself. But sometimes he was also terrified at the very thought of it. Occasionally, overwrought by the news of the day, he would climb into bed convinced that he was going to die before morning. Then, he wrote (referring to himself in the third person), "in his innocence he cried out to God, asking to be granted a deferment. These experiences dismayed him to some extent. For obviously he did not want to die, he was a coward."[7] In such conflicted moments, Bonhoeffer recalled, he felt great self-contempt. To his shame, he realized that he "could tolerate the thought of the inevitability of death for only a few moments."[8]

Bonhoeffer's death-fear was climaxed by the fate of his brother Walter. Walter and Karl Friedrich, the two eldest Bonhoeffer brothers, were called up for military service when Dietrich was eleven. Just a couple of weeks later, in April 1918, Walter was mortally wounded. He left his Bible to Dietrich, who soon afterwards decided to study theology when he went to university and seek ordination in the German Evangelical Church.

Dietrich waited a couple of years before announcing the decision to his family. There were probably two reasons for the delay. The first was the emotional tailspin into which Walter's death sent his parents. Paula was especially overcome and actually left the household for a few weeks to grieve in private. It was more than a year before she was able to resume even a somewhat normal life. The second reason was that Dietrich felt reluctant to announce a plan that he knew would bewilder his family. Although there were formal prayers at table and bedtime, the Bonhoeffers weren't particularly religious. Karl, in fact, was something of a freethinker who prided himself on his fidelity to science and expressed skepticism about any claim not based on hard empirical evidence.

He thought his son too clever by half for theology. Nevertheless, the family rallied behind Dietrich's decision.

Young Bonhoeffer began his theological studies in 1923 at the University of Tubingen and finished up four years later at the University of Berlin. He was a brilliant student. His professors admired him and he got along well enough with his fellow students. But just as he'd been isolated from the world during his Tiergarten childhood, he was also something of an outsider in the German church community. The other students preparing for ordination came from pious families and had been raised in the church. Bonhoeffer's liberally skeptical family's church attendance was generally limited to Easter and Christmas. All his life, Bonhoeffer would be uncomfortable with churchy piety, worrying that the church, at least in Germany, was often little more than a social club for self-satisfied burghers.

After receiving his degree, Bonhoeffer spent the better part of 1928 serving a German-speaking Lutheran church in Barcelona. Although he enjoyed Spain, he wasn't particularly enthusiastic about parish work. At this point in his life, Bonhoeffer thought of himself more as a scholar than a pastor. He was intrigued by theology, but felt out of his depth when it came to hands-on ministry. It was no surprise to those who knew him when he plunged into academic research and teaching on his return to Berlin. But although he worked tremendously hard, Bonhoeffer later came to see this period of his life as lonely, overly ambitious, and inauthentic. "I plunged into work in a very un-Christian way," he wrote. "An ambition that some noticed in me made my life difficult and robbed me of the love and trust of my fellow human beings. At that time I was terribly alone and left to myself... I know that at that time I turned the doctrine of Jesus Christ into something of personal advantage to myself, for my crazy vanity."[9]

By the time he was twenty-four, Bonhoeffer had succeeded in making his mark as a rising theologian. But his detachment from other people, his discomfort with parish work, and his cerebral approach to religion suggests that the choice he made in 1918 to study theology was motivated more by a need for a safe haven than a heartfelt desire to serve God. Like many intelligent youths who find the realities of the world threatening, Bonhoeffer sought escape in books, ideas, and the safety of academia. He had yet to grapple with either his own mortality or the burden and thrill of freedom. He was still an outsider, a spectator rather than a participant in both religion and life. But all that began to change when he sailed to New York for a year of study at Union Theological Seminary.

Two Journeys to America

His accomplishments notwithstanding, Bonhoeffer was too young in 1930 to be ordained in the German Evangelical Church. The minimum age was twenty-five, and he was still a year short of that. So when the opportunity arose in 1930 for a Sloan Fellowship at Union Theological Seminary, Bonhoeffer jumped at it. It would give him a whole year to continue his studies before returning to Berlin and taking a pulpit.

Bonhoeffer was excited about going to America, but less enthusiastic, on arrival, about the caliber of theology he found there. Under the influence of luminaries such as Reinhold Niebuhr, who had joined the faculty only two years earlier, Union was heavy on the social gospel and light on systematic theology. For a German-trained theologian who had cut his teeth on systematics, this was a bewildering state of affairs. Shortly after arriving in New York, Bonhoeffer disdainfully concluded that "there is no theology here."[10]

It wasn't long, however, before Bonhoeffer began to see things differently. He struck up a friendship with a black student named Frank Fisher who introduced him to the African American spiritual tradition. Bonhoeffer was soon worshiping every Sunday at Harlem's Abyssinian Baptist Church, bowled over by the spontaneity in worship, emotional freedom, and lively music he discovered there. All three were unheard of in the sober, buttoned-down Lutheran services he was used to, and for the first time in his life Bonhoeffer caught a glimpse of what it was like to worship God with one's whole being. The experience began to put some iron into his own thin-blooded faith.

Bonhoeffer also learned to appreciate the importance of the social gospel during his year at Union. In wandering through Depression-era Harlem or the South Bronx, he came closer to poverty than he ever had back in Germany, and what he saw shook him. As far back as his undergraduate days, Bonhoeffer had argued that the church should advocate for the poor. But like most of the convictions of his youth, this one had been abstract and out of touch with the real world. Now he gained concrete, firsthand experience of the squalor and misery of poverty, and this prompted him to read the Bible with fresh eyes that focused especially on the Hebrew prophets and the Sermon on the Mount.

It was during his stay in America that the Sermon on the Mount—the "canon within the canon," as it's often been called—became the single most important scriptural text for Bonhoeffer. Its influence upon him can't be exaggerated. Before his exposure to the social gospel and African American spirituality, Bonhoeffer had conventionally interpreted the Sermon not as a set of principles for transforming the world but as a vision of the future Kingdom of God. Jesus' words about loving one's enemy or turning the other cheek may be inspiring, but they were hardly possible, and surely not obligatory, for fallen human beings. But under the guidance of pacifist students at Union, most notably a young French pastor named Jean Lasserre, Bonhoeffer began to read the Sermon as both social document and personal spiritual standard.[11] He came to believe that the challenge of Christianity—the challenge to *himself*—was to take the Sermon on the Mount as a guideline for everyday living. Reminiscing a few years later about this time in his life, Bonhoeffer wrote,

> For the first time I discovered the Bible . . . I had preached, I had seen a good deal of the Church, and talked and preached about it—but I had not yet become a Christian, but was my own master in a quite wild and unrestrained way. . . For all my loneliness, I was quite pleased with myself. Then the Bible, and above all the Sermon on the Mount, freed me from that.[12]

When he returned to Germany in the early summer of 1931, Bonhoeffer was a different person. "There are things which it is worth supporting without compromise," he now realized. "And it seems to me that these include peace and social justice, or in fact Christ."[13] It was a new way of thinking and a new embrace of the responsibility of freedom for a young man who had entered the ministry at least in part to shelter himself from the hard facts of life.

Those facts were becoming harder to ignore. The Germany to which Bonhoeffer returned was in turmoil. Years of grinding poverty, inflation, unemployment, social unrest, and political chaos, all exacerbated by resentment at the humiliating peace treaty Germany was compelled to sign at the end of World War I, had created a climate that bred political extremism. Hitler's National Socialist party was on the move, having won 107 seats in the Reichstag while Bonhoeffer was away in America. In July 1932, a year after he returned to Germany and seven months after he was ordained, the Nazis won nearly 40 percent of the vote in national elections, increasing their Reichstag presence to 230 seats. Six months later, Hitler became chancellor and the thousand-year Reich was launched.

The Nazis's political ascendancy was bad enough. But it was paralleled by an equally alarming trend in the German Evangelical Church: the emergence, in 1932, of the German Christian movement. German Christians were fanatical supporters of Hitler who believed that National Socialism was the fulfillment of both Christianity and German destiny. Proclaiming the advent of a new "heroic piety," they sought to purge the Old Testament, "with its Jewish morality of reward" and its "stories of cattle breeders and concubines," from churches and Christian memory.[14]

After Hitler's appointment as chancellor, the German Christian movement, which quickly grabbed all the leadership positions in the German Evangelical Church, became a spiritual rubber stamp for the regime. When the Nazis set fire to the Reichstag in February 1933, blamed the arson on communists, and cynically issued an emergency decree restricting personal freedoms, German Christian Bishop Otto Dibelius defended the new law. "When the life or death of the nation is at stake," he declared, "state power must be used thoroughly and powerfully... The church may not get in the way of legitimate state force if it is doing that to which it is called. Not even if it acts harshly and ruthlessly."[15] Shortly afterwards, Reich Bishop Ludwig Mueller ordered all church youth organizations to be folded into the Hitler Youth. Just a year later, school children across Germany were reading passages in their textbooks that compared Hitler to Jesus. "As Jesus set men free from sin and hell, so Hitler rescued the German people from destruction . . . Jesus built for heaven; Hitler, for the German soil."[16]

Astoundingly, about a third of Germany's ordained pastors supported the German Christian movement. Another third stood by, too intimidated by the champions of "heroic piety" to speak out. Even the remaining third who publicly opposed the movement's identification of church and state worried about going too far. When World War I hero and Lutheran pastor Martin Niemoeller formed the Pastors' Emergency League to protest a new Reich law that excluded "non-Aryans" from ordained ministry, he hedged his bet by sending a telegram to Hitler obsequiously assuring him of his loyalty. In 1934, the Emergency League morphed into a new entity that called itself the Confessing Church. Although intended to be a public repudiation of the German Christian movement, many Confessing Church members shared Niemoeller's timidity. They objected to the German Christian control of the church, but stopped short of publicly criticizing Hitler.

Bonhoeffer, who joined the Confessing Church early on, felt no such inhibition. The Nazis sickened him, and he attacked the ideal of heroic piety as blasphemous. Shortly before the Nazis gained power in 1933, Bonhoeffer challenged their militaristic nationalism in a speech before a student organization. "Every form of war service," he said, "unless it be Good Samaritan service, and every preparation for war, is forbidden to the Christian."[17] Two months after the Reichstag fire and Bishop Dibelius's "Christian" defense of a strongarm state, Bonhoeffer gave a thunderously dissenting lecture to a group of Berlin pastors. The church, he said, can choose one or more of three possibilities in dealing with the state. It can challenge the legitimacy of the state's actions and demand moral responsibility from political leaders, or it can come to the assistance of victims of state injustice because "the church has an unconditional obligation to the victims of any ordering of society." These first two options, given the times, were incendiary enough. But the third one positively crackled: "not just to bandage the victims under the wheel, but to put a spoke in the wheel itself."[18] If Bonhoeffer expected a courageous response to his courageous words, he was disappointed. The atmosphere in Germany had already grown so chilly that most of his audience walked out in real or feigned indignation.

Bonhoeffer braved the increasingly wintry climate for another six months. But by October 1933 he was so disheartened by the capitulation of the German Evangelical Church and the wishy-washiness of the Confessing Church that all he could think about was getting out of the country. He felt a growing sense of isolation from both popular opinion and even from some of his closest friends. So, thinking "that it was probably time to go into the wilderness for a while," he accepted a call to pastor two German-speaking congregations in London.[19]

Although Bonhoeffer left Germany, he didn't desert the Confessing Church. Its leadership was too timid for his taste—by now he considered himself a resister to Nazi rule, not merely a critic—but he also recognized that it was the only ecclesiastical option available to him. So, shortly after settling in London, he attended the Confessing Church's first synod. While there, he implored foreign churches to recognize the Confessing Church's legitimacy, spoke out against German Christian nationalism, and was appointed director of the Confessing Church's seminary, scheduled to open the following year.

Bonhoeffer returned to Germany in April 1935 to begin his duties as seminary director. Twenty-three students had been recruited, and the first order of business was to make their learning and living quarters at the seminary site (located initially at Zingst and later at Finkenwald) habitable. They aired rooms, painted walls, cleaned windows, repaired furniture, and took turns preparing meals. Bonhoeffer donated his considerable personal theological library to the seminary.

Over the two years during which the seminary operated, Bonhoeffer worked hard to make it an experiment in communal Christian living and spiritual growth, not just a place of book learning. He urged students to meditate on biblical passages and to spend much of their week in prayer. He also introduced them to his passion for African American gospel music, frequently playing them the records he'd brought back from America. The theologian who earlier in life had immersed himself in safe abstractions wanted to make sure that the students in his care didn't make the same mistake. He wanted to create an environment that would help them mature emotionally and spiritually as well as intellectually.

The Finkenwald years were good for Bonhoeffer. His life at the seminary gave him the peace and quiet he needed to think through the relationship between his commitment to Christ and his resistance to the Nazi state. It was during this time that he wrote what many consider to be his single greatest book, *The Cost of Discipleship*. In it, Bonhoeffer reflected on the nature of courage and the difficulty of practicing it. Too many faint-hearted Christians, he concluded, try to avoid the need for courage by simply refusing to think about their mortality or by abdicating moral responsibility. Instead, they fall into a self-deceptive and unfree type of existence that Bonhoeffer famously called "cheap grace."

According to Bonhoeffer, living in the world as a Christian requires a willingness to accept the anxiety that freedom brings. Followers of Christ can't retreat into a safe, danger-free spiritual realm of private piety where they're never called on to examine their own motives, make hard decisions, or take risks. Nor can they submerge their identity in a group-think corruption of the gospel, such as the German Christian movement, that promises salvation through power or success. All of this, said Bonhoeffer, is cheap grace, "the deadly enemy of our church." Cheap grace is "grace without price; grace without cost."[20] Painless, free, and popular: these are the characteristic values of a life of cheap grace.

Genuine discipleship requires something more strenuous. It demands loyalty to the Sermon on the Mount, which in turn means exercising our terrifying but exhilarating freedom to make moral choices. Living as Jesus commands calls for physical as well as moral courage because taking his words seriously not only requires resisting popular culture but may even demand prophetic denunciations of unjust social practices and policies. The unstated but transparent message in Bonhoeffer's analysis was that the official German church establishment had settled for cheap grace, and that members of the resistant Confessing Church needed to find the courage to repudiate, once and for all, everything that the Nazis and the German Christians stood for.

The Cost of Discipleship was published in 1937. But even before it appeared, Bonhoeffer was tagged as an enemy of the German state. In 1936 the authorities stripped him of his right to teach theology. In August of the following year, the Finkenwald seminary was shut down by the Gestapo, and in just a few months nearly thirty of its former students were either in prison or had been conscripted into the army. Bonhoeffer's friends and family members worried that he would soon follow them.

On the night of November 9, 1938, Nazi thugs rampaged through the cities of Germany in a coordinated attack against Jews. Almost every synagogue in Germany was damaged or destroyed, as were thousands of Jewish-owned shops.

Nearly a hundred Jews were beaten to death and thousands more dragged off to concentration camps. The night of terror came to be called *Krystallnacht* because of the shattered glass from the vandalized synagogues and storefronts.

The Confessing Church was utterly silent in the face of this atrocity, and Bonhoeffer was nearly as outraged and disgusted by its failure of courage as he was by the state-sponsored hooliganism. Two years later, in drafting the book that was posthumously published as *Ethics*, Bonhoeffer passionately condemned the church's refusal to denounce *Krystallnacht*. "The church was silent where she should have cried out," he wrote. "She has witnessed the lawless application of brutal force, the physical and spiritual suffering of countless innocent people, oppression, hatred and murder, and she has not raised her voice on behalf of the victims and has not found a way to hasten to their aid. She is guilty of the deaths of the weakest and most defenseless brothers of Jesus Christ."[21]

By early summer of 1939, Bonhoeffer once again felt suffocated in Nazi Germany. His sense of entrapment was aggravated by the fact that he was at risk of military conscription. In fact, given his reputation as a dissenter, it was more than likely that he would be called up. So, when an offer to return to Union Theological Seminary to teach a series of courses arrived, he decided to sail to New York.

Almost immediately after arriving, however, he began to have second thoughts. He worried that he was betraying the Finkenwald students whom he had encouraged to resist the very political situation he was fleeing. Even worse, Bonhoeffer felt that he was betraying Christ. "We ought to be found only where He is ... Have I, after all, avoided the place where He is? The place where He is for me?"[22] Bonhoeffer feared that any failure of nerve now would deprive him of whatever spiritual influence he might have in rebuilding a post-Nazi Germany. Yet at the same time he knew full well that returning meant forced enlistment, possible imprisonment, or worse.

Bonhoeffer agonized for just over a month about what to do. The beginning of July saw him on a ship back to Germany. The turning point for him came while he was meditating on the New Testament passage where St. Paul implores his absent friend Timothy to "Come before winter!" (2 Tim 4:21). Bonhoeffer felt as if Paul was speaking directly to him.

> That [verse] follows me around all day. It is as if we were soldiers home on leave, and going back into action regardless of what . . . to expect. We cannot be released from it. Not as if we were essential, as if we were needed (by God?!), but simply because that is where our life is and because we abandon, destroy, our life if we are not back in the fight. It is not a matter of piety, but of more vitality.[23]

As he sailed back to Germany and the Nazis, Bonhoeffer must have felt somewhat dazed by the vertigo of freedom. He'd freely chosen to return in hopes of wresting some meaning out of the chaos into which Germany had fallen. He'd made a decision to leap into the unknowable future that called for the greatest display of moral and physical courage he had ever mustered. But it was only a prelude to what would soon be asked of him.

Ultimate Necessities

When Bonhoeffer arrived in Germany, one of his brothers-in-law, Hans von Dohnanyi, eased his worries about conscription by getting him a military-exempt job in the *Abwehr*, the German government's office of intelligence. It may seem strange that someone so opposed to the Nazis accepted a civil service job in Hitler's government. But in fact the *Abwehr* was a secret center of resistance to the regime. Its chief, Admiral Wilhelm Canaris, had disliked Hitler from the start. *Krystallnacht* and later reports from Poland of the mass murder of Jews ratcheted up his opposition to active resistance. He was convinced that Hitler had to be stopped before he destroyed Germany. As the man in charge of the Reich's intelligence service, Canaris was in an excellent position to find and recruit like-minded men and women. Hans von Dohnanyi, a lawyer who had been compiling a secret file on Nazi crimes since 1933, was one of them. Bonhoeffer became another.

As a member of the *Abwehr*, Bonhoeffer was one of the few German civilians permitted to travel regularly outside of Germany. Under the guise of intelligence work, he made several trips to Switzerland to arrange the escape of German Jews and to provide the Allies with news about the German resistance. Although he wasn't directly involved in the July 1944 plot to kill Hitler, Bonhoeffer had come to the conclusion that Germany's only chance lay in Hitler's death. He even expressed the willingness to kill the Fuhrer himself if the opportunity arose.

It wasn't at all the type of life he'd planned for himself. Bonhoeffer's secret resistance to the regime required a suspension of conventional ways of thinking about morality. Extraordinary situations, he decided, called for hard choices that inevitably left the actors with dirty hands. To insist on an ethical purism in the face of the unspeakable situation Germany and the rest of Europe endured was, he believed, a rationalization born of a failure of courage. Insisting that it wasn't proper for a Christian to become entangled in the messy affairs of a world in crisis was symptomatic of the cheap grace Bonhoeffer had condemned in *The Cost of Disci-pleship.* He wanted no part of it.

At the same time, Bonhoeffer fully recognized that the choice to resist Hitler through deception and even violence ran against both the letter and the spirit of Jesus' teachings, and that whoever took this route was guilty—and justly so— in the eyes of God. Yet when confronted with an evil of the magnitude of Nazi aggression and genocide, refusing to act in order to avoid guilt was unacceptable. Whoever sought to escape "guilt in responsibility," wrote Bonhoeffer, incurred the far greater guilt of passivity in the face of evil. "He sets his own personal innocence above his responsibility for men, and he is blind to the more irredeemable guilt which he in-curs precisely in this."[24] When confronted by unimaginable evil, a person of conscience is called to a "deed of free re-sponsibility" that "leaves behind it the domain of principle and convention, the domain of the normal and regular, and is confronted by the extraordinary situation of ultimate ne-cessities, a situation which no law can control."[25]

The dreadful weight of Bonhoeffer's words—and the courage of his decision to live by them—are missed if his po-sition is confused with conventional civil disobedience. The person who performs civil disobedience is willing to go to jail for her violation of the law, but she doesn't see her action as unjust or immoral. On the contrary, she breaks the law because she believes that obeying it is immoral. In violating the bad law, she follows a "higher" one. Her hands are clean, as is her conscience. She remains righteous, despite scorn and persecution from the establishment she opposes.

But for Bonhoeffer this wouldn't do. He took seriously the "free" in "deed of free responsibility." So far as he was concerned, dirtying his hands to destroy Hitler was an irre-ducibly free choice for which he had to assume sole responsi-bility. There was no honest way to justify it or dilute personal responsibility by appealing to higher laws or special insight into God's will. This was the ultimate paradox he faced: working for the murder of Hitler and the liberation of Germany was right but also wrong. So in doing what he believed a "situation of ultimate necessity" demanded, Bonhoeffer freely chose to risk estrangement from God, painfully aware that he would have to face the spiritual and worldly consequences of his decision: possible damnation in the first case, possible torture and execution in the second. Genuine courage consisted in accepting these two horrible dangers, one of spiritual and the other of physical nothingness. Confining one's actions to "the limits of duty" might maintain personal purity, not to mention safety, but would never "score a direct hit on evil and defeat it. The man of duty will in the end have to do his duty by the devil too."[26]

The courage exercised by Bonhoeffer in making his choice is underscored by the fact that it was impossible to eliminate all doubts or uncertainties as to whether his choice was the best one. He was convinced that an other-worldly disregard of the current crisis was a cowardly rationalization. But how could he be sure that his willingness to step over a moral line in defense of Germany wasn't a rationalization? Who was he to set himself against both scripture and tradition, to betray the very Sermon on the Mount to which he had pledged himself during his first visit to America? Which was more likely to be correct: his personal conviction that Hitler needed killing, or Jesus' command not to resist evil with evil? A wicked culture, Bonhoeffer knew, is like a "great masquerade of evil . . . disguised as light."[27] In such a through-the-looking-glass environment, how could he be sure that he wasn't deceiving himself?

The answer, of course, is that he couldn't. Bonhoeffer accepted both the uncertainty of his own position and the dreadful weight of performing an act of free responsibility in obedience to "a God who demands responsible action in a bold venture of faith." In his eyes, this made him a sinner. So all he could do, he concluded, was to throw himself on God's mercy, hoping but not expecting with any confidence that "forgiveness and consolation" would be given him and that he wouldn't be cast into the outer darkness.[28]

Bonhoeffer also had other, more worldly reasons to be anxious. Despite the protection afforded him by his position in the *Abwehr*, he was under suspicion by the Gestapo. Anyone who had publicly denounced the Nazis as frequently as he had was watched closely. Bonhoeffer was frequently tailed by Gestapo agents who also tapped his telephone and read his mail. In September 1940, he was forbidden to speak in public. In March 1941, he was forbidden to publish. By the Christmas of 1942, he felt that his freedom of action had been constricted almost to the vanishing point. But instead of fleeing Germany, he resolved to stay and resist as best he could.

> There remains for us only the very narrow way, often extremely difficult to find, of living every day as if it were our last, and yet living in faith and responsibility as though there were to be a great future... It may be that the day of judgment will dawn tomorrow; In that case, we shall gladly stop working for a better future. But not before.[29]

In mid-1942, a major change in Bonhoeffer's life brought him great joy in the midst of the darkness: his engagement to Maria von Wedemeyer. The daughter of an aristocratic, landed family, she was half Bonhoeffer's age and quite different from him in temperament and interests. She once confessed to him that she found theology incomprehensible, prompting Bonhoeffer to lecture her at times on the finer points of his discipline. Maria endured his tutorials with good grace. She in turn schooled him in domestic matters, china patterns, and the superiority of cupboards over sideboards, teaching which he endured with somewhat less patience. But they were good for each other. Maria opened Bonhoeffer up emotionally and her steady loyalty would help him endure the hard days ahead. Under Bonhoeffer's guidance, she blossomed intellectually.

Then the moment Bonhoeffer feared finally arrived. In April 1943, he and his brother-in-law Hans von Dohnanyi were arrested by the Gestapo. Incriminating documents had been discovered which implicated the two of them in a plot to get Jews out of Germany. Bonhoeffer was sent to Berlin's Tegel prison, a military rather than a Gestapo facility, to await trial. He felt utterly helpless and was tortured by loneliness at a point in his life when he had finally fallen head over heels in love. "Separation from people, from work, from the past, from the future, from marriage, from God, impatience, longing, boredom, sick," he scribbled in despair. "Profoundly alone, suicide, not because of consciousness of guilt but because basically I am already dead."[30]

Bonhoeffer spent the next year and a half at Tegel. Because the prison was run by the *Wehrmacht* instead of the Gestapo, he was treated relatively well, and there is no evidence that his regular interrogations included physical torture. He was allowed books and writing material, and he resumed work on his unfinished *Ethics*. Unusual for Bonhoeffer, he also wrote some fiction—a play and part of a novel—and several poems. But perhaps the most important work to come out of Tegel were the letters in which he explored the possibility that conventional religion, with its comfortable sedatives against death-fear, moral fear, and physical fear, no longer worked in a world of evil and suffering. Christians, he concluded, needed to forgo any trappings of religion that substituted for genuine discipleship. The point wasn't to be a good churchman or churchwoman, but rather to be a human in good relationship to God, and this required the courage to step outside the comfort zones provided by popular piety. "The Christian," he wrote, "is not a *homo religiosus,* but simply a man, as Jesus was man."[31] Mechanical observance of religious customs and creeds doesn't make a Christian; "participation in the sufferings of God in the secular life" does.[32] Bonhoeffer, who'd never really been comfortable with conventional religion anyway—"I am not religious by nature," he once wrote[33]—now rejected it outright as another one of those masquerades worn by an evil culture.

> Our church, which over these years has fought only for its self-preservation as though that were an end in itself, is incapable of being the vehicle of the reconciling and redeeming word for human beings and the world. The former words must become powerless and fall silent, and our being Christians today must consist of two things: in praying and doing what is right among men.[34]

For a while it seemed as if the imprisoned Bonhoeffer had been forgotten by the Gestapo and that he just might survive a war which he and most other Germans realized was lost. But in October 1944 the wheels of Nazi "justice" began to turn. The security police at last found what they were looking for. In Zossen, a town to the south of Berlin, agents ran across a cache of papers, dating as far back as 1939, that documented *Abwehr* plans to overthrow Hitler. Von Dohnanyi was especially implicated, and so, by association, was his brother-in-law. Bonhoeffer was immediately transferred from Tegel to the Gestapo prison in Prinz Albrecht Strasse, a place notorious for its abuse of prisoners.

He was interrogated often, even though the Gestapo really had all the information it needed or wanted from the Zossen papers. But much worse than the interrogations was the fact that the small comforts Bonhoeffer had gotten used to at Tegel, including regular communication with the outside world, were forbidden. During the four months he spent in Prinz Albrecht Strasse prison, he was allowed only three letters to his loved ones.

In February, Bonhoeffer was, ominously, transferred to Buchenwald. At the beginning of April, he and five other members of the *Abwehr* resistance were transported to Flossenburg concentration camp. They arrived there on April 8 and were hanged the next morning. A few days later, von Dohnanyi, as well as another brother-in-law and Bonhoeffer's elder brother Klaus, were also executed. The family had paid a terrible price for resisting the Nazi evil.

Bonhoeffer's final words when summoned to the gallows were "This is the end, for me the beginning of life."[35] After the execution, his body was burned. His friends and family received no notice from the Nazi authorities about his execution. So far as they knew, he had just vanished in the fog of war. It was only toward the end of July, after Hitler was dead and the Third Reich fallen, that they learned of his fate, and then only through a BBC broadcast of a memorial service held for him in London.

Courage and "God's guiding hand"

Life is a gift that offers us wondrous moments of joy, companionship, and insight. But it is also frightening. The very freedom that makes us human and allows us to experience the wonder of life is also a permanent source of anxiety. Whenever we exercise that freedom, we find ourselves confronting the nothingness of a not-as-yet future. There are no guarantees that our choices will work out the way we hope they will. So the exhilaration of freedom is always shadowed by the sobering realization that we, unlike inert objects whose destiny is irrevocable, have life trajectories that are open. Our faces are always pointed toward the future, and the unknowability of that future is especially troublesome when the choices before us are heavy with moral weight. We recognize that whatever comes of them, the responsibility is ours. There's no passing the buck.

At the far end of our future, we also know, lies death. A sense of our mortality haunts even our most joyful moments, and sometimes it so rattles us that all of life seems a meaningless, pointless farce. The nothingness of moral freedom, of death, and of meaninglessness: these are the specters that both vivify and haunt us.

Confronting death at life's end is, for most of us, an inevitably frightening affair. But our ability to face it with courage—to affirm the value of life even as life departs—is proportionate to how courageously we face our experiences of nothingness during our lifetimes without clutching at false hope. Many of us may be tempted to insulate ourselves from nothingness behind a barricade of comfortable, no-risk piety. Others, like the young Bonhoeffer, may seek safety in the realm of neat, nonthreatening intellectual abstractions. Most of us will use the busyness of everyday life as a bulwark against our anxiety. But none of these strategies do anything to prepare us for our appointment with death. This ultimate rendezvous with nothingness can be fruitful only if we have practiced courage throughout our lives by accepting the uncertainty that our freedom brings.

Bonhoeffer went to his own death fully affirming his life even though circumstances had taken him in directions he never could have imagined. In resisting the Nazis, he defied the death-fear that had troubled him as a youth and young man. In making the moral choice to resist Hitler, he hazarded the vertigo of freedom and accepted responsibility for his decision, even if, as he feared, it meant exile from the Kingdom of God. In a Germany gone mad, he courageously insisted that life was still meaningful, even if the old religious standards that had once served as points of orientation needed to be rethought.

Buttressing Bonhoeffer's courage was his conviction that underneath the threat of nothingness lay an unassailable foundation of divine Being. Shortly before he was transferred from Tegel to Prinz Albrecht Strasse prison, he wrote that he was "so sure of God's guiding hand that I hope I shall always be kept in that certainty."[36] Bonhoeffer's faith in an enduring God didn't make his way easier or his anxiety any less real. He, like the rest of us, dreaded the prospect of death, particularly after his engagement to Maria von Wedemeyer. But in the darker moments—and in that darkest moment when he climbed the gallows steps—his confidence in God's guiding hand sustained him. A lifetime of habituating himself to the courageous affirmation of life helped him meet death with some degree of equanimity. It's an example worth remembering.

CHAPTER SEVEN

PATIENCE

John Paul II

"Endurance brings with it patience;
patience helps you to find the way ahead,
and gives you courage for your journey."

Death of a Pope

"No pope is sick until he's dead." For years this was conventional wisdom among Vatican watchers. The secrecy that traditionally cloaked a pontiff's state of health was unsurpassed.

All that ended with the dying of Pope John Paul II. He refused to shield his final weeks from continuous media scrutiny. His suffering during this time, just like his steady physical deterioration over the previous few years, was totally in the open. The world watched as he aged from a sturdy outdoorsman at the beginning of his pontificate—the "pope athlete," as the press enthusiastically called him—to an old man with slurred speech, uncontrollable tremors, frozen expression, and crooked body. None of his infirmity was hidden, none of his suffering concealed.

The climax of John Paul's public dying occurred on Easter Sunday, March 27, 2005. A few days earlier, the pope, suffering from horrible episodes of suffocation, had been given an emergency tracheotomy. Afterwards, his voice was too impaired for him to read the traditional Easter address to the faithful assembled in St. Peter's Square. So he contented himself with standing hunched and trembling at a window that overlooked the square for the thirteen minutes it took Cardinal Angelo Sodano, Vatican Secretary of State, to read it for him. Then came the moment for the traditional papal *Urbi et orbi* blessing.

Thousands of people in St. Peter's Square and millions of television viewers across the world watched as John Paul struggled to pronounce the simple blessing. Finally he gave up. Whispering "my voice is gone," he silently raised his arm to make the sign of the cross and then allowed himself to be helped back to his bed. Stanislaw Dziwisz, John Paul's personal secretary, fellow Pole, and friend of forty years, later said that at that moment the pope "felt the whole weight of [his] powerlessness and suffering." "Maybe," John Paul whispered to Dziwisz, "it would be better for me to die if I can't fulfill the mission that has been entrusted to me." But then he characteristically added "Thy will be done . . . *Totus tuus*"—"totally yours," an affirmation of complete dedication to God that was John Paul's personal and papal motto.[1]

The pope's public dying lodged in the memory of everyone who followed it. The most powerful man in a church of more than a billion members, a man who was the most influential spiritual leader in the Western world, lay dying, and neither his vast authority nor the prayers of millions of Catholics could do a thing to save him. Like every other mortal, John Paul II had to endure suffering and death.

But throughout his dying, the pope displayed a fidelity to St. Paul's injunction "Be patient in suffering" (Rom 12:12) that astounded and moved the world. A lifetime of suffering had schooled him in the virtue of patience. John Paul, born Karol Wojtyla, was orphaned by the time he was twenty; endured the Nazi occupation of his native Poland, followed by years of Communist repression; survived a nearly successful assassination attempt in the third year of his papacy; and, although once robust, experienced a steady and eventually shocking decline in health during the final two decades of his life. John Paul, in short, was no stranger to the suffering that comes to all humans, and the drama of his dying was but the culminating act in the long passion play of his life.

What made that drama so extraordinary was the intensely spiritual character of his patience. He was convinced that there is a deep redemptive meaning to suffering, and that the person who suffers participates in Christ's atonement. By drawing back the Vatican's curtain of secrecy to reveal his own suffering, John Paul sought to share that message of redemption with a hurting world. As one of his associates said, he transformed his final illness into a living homily about the virtue of patience in the face of suffering.

The Virtue of Patience

Misconceptions

There's probably no virtue more misunderstood or undervalued than patience. Despite the fact that we customarily pay lip service to patience, especially when paternalistically lecturing young people, it's not a habit of the heart that too many adults really want to spend a lot of time cultivating. As Lucy says in an old Peanuts cartoon, "I was praying for patience but I stopped. I was afraid I might get it."

Our lack of enthusiasm for patience stems partly from our cultural mania for busyness. We associate success, public reputation, and self-esteem with being on the go, getting things done, moving onwards and upwards, never being satisfied. In this buzzing kind of atmosphere, recommending or practicing patience comes across as an excuse for "settling."

Our culture also puts a high premium on painlessness. We avoid any kind of physical, mental, or emotional suffering, especially when it appears pointless, and we automatically presume that anyone *not* doing so is neurotic. Patience in the face of suffering comes across as either a pathetic kind of denial born of cowardice or a masochism that masquerades as piety or stoic indifference.

Patience is also popularly associated with powerlessness or vulnerability, both of which stick in the craw of a culture that values strength, health, and celebrity. A person should be patient, we think, only as a last resort. The appropriate time for patience is when all our efforts to fix things have failed and our backs are against the wall. Patience isn't an option for people who are still able to take the initiative and shape their destiny. Instead, it's for those who have lost agency and opportunity and have no choice but to put up with what's left them.

In short, our fast-paced, success-oriented, pain-avoiding, and assertive culture is impatient with patience. We so misunderstand its true nature that what we reject is a caricature of it. Genuine patience is neither passive nor lazy. On the contrary, it's a deliberate act of the will that requires colossal self-discipline. The patient person isn't withdrawing from the world so much as resolutely participating in it in a special way.

Similarly, patience in the face of suffering is neither cowardly denial nor a masochistic reveling in pain. It's an effort to recollect oneself so that the ability to relate to the broader world beyond one's own pain doesn't get buried in self-absorption or self-pity. As one commentator puts it, patience is actually "attentive" suffering.[2] Everyone suffers. It's inescapable. But while the impatient person tries to shield himself in one way or another from suffering, the patient one makes herself present to it, listens to it, tries to discern what it might have to tell her, and responds to it. In disciplining herself to patience, she transforms her relationship to the experience of suffering. In attending to suffering, she turns it into something other than an external force or event that knocks the wind out of her. She makes it part of who she is. It's still an unwelcome presence, but it's no longer completely alien.

Theologian Dorothee Soelle echoes this understanding of patience in the face of suffering. "The Christian idea of the acceptance of suffering," she writes, "means something more than and different from what is expressed in the words 'put up with, tolerate, bear.' With these words, the object, the suffering itself, remains unchanged." But when I accept or attend to my suffering, it "belongs to me in a different sense from something I only bear...I take on an assignment; I say yes, I consent, I assent, I agree with."[3]

Finally, while it's true that situations typically calling for patience are ones in which we're at our most vulnerable, it's not at all the case that vulnerability is necessarily a bad thing. Although it may be difficult for a culture fixated on pain-avoidance to appreciate, vulnerability is a necessary condition for both self-knowledge and the ability to relate meaningfully to other people and God. Individuals who experience vulnerability lose the inflated ego so characteristic of worldly go-getters. They have a good sense of their fragility as well as their dependence on others, and this in turn helps them empathize with other fragile people. A patient person, precisely because he's vulnerable, is strong in ways that really count.

Patience and Meaning

But a question immediately arises: *why* should we attend to, much less accept, suffering? Why be patient with it? What's the point?

In the Christian context, patient assent to suffering is based on the conviction that suffering is neither absurd nor pointless, but deeply saturated with meaning. All of us crave meaning and purpose in our lives. The mistake we often make is to presume that meaning always rides on pleasant experiences and meaninglessness on painful ones. But of course many pleasant experiences—absent-mindedly humming a catchy advertising jingle, doodling, daydreaming—can be quite pointless, while unpleasant experiences—the death of a loved one, the collapse of a cherished hope, the trauma of betrayal—can be heavy with meaning.

We've already noted one way in which suffering is laden with meaning: when it opens the way to self-insight and empathy for others. Attentive patience doesn't necessarily lessen our suffering, but it can help us touch deeper levels of meaning than we may hitherto have reached.

Suffering is also meaningful when it serves as a salutary example to others. It's a rare person who isn't afraid of suffering, especially the kind that precedes death. We don't like to think about the prospect of our own suffering, and we don't like to be around persons who are suffering. So we usually scramble to avoid both the thought and the reality of suffering.

But the living example of someone who displays patience in the face of great pain or misfortune is a remarkable tutorial. It shows us that suffering need not rob us of freedom or dignity, and so strengthens us to cope with our own suffering when it comes. It also inspires us to want to be salutary examples in our own turn for others. The manner in which we patiently embrace our suffering, especially at the end of life, may well be one of the finest gifts we can pass on to those we love.

For John Paul II and countless other Christians, the deepest meaning embedded in suffering is a theological one.

When we suffer, we participate in the atoning Passion of Jesus Christ. Because we are one both in (Gal 3:28) and with (Eph 5:30) Jesus, our suffering is his and his is ours. Consequently, the suffering that comes to us is never private, although it is personal. It implicates all of creation, because we are inextricably connected through Christ to everything that is, and it continues the redeeming work of Christ.

We'll explore John Paul's understanding of the deeply redemptive meaning of suffering later. For now, it's enough to point out that this way of thinking about suffering provides a foundation for enduring it patiently and even with a certain degree of sober gratitude. Once we think of suffering as participation in Christ's Passion, there's no way, except in occasional moments of despair (which themselves are participations in the Passion), that we can ever again dismiss it as meaningless. It will still be unpleasant and perhaps even excruciating, but will now be viewed as an opportunity for insight and growth. This conviction guided John Paul from his boyhood right up to the moment of his death in the Vatican.

But a word of caution is in order. It's important not to romanticize or glamorize suffering in the way that certain Christians have in the past. Suffering in itself is an evil. It can debilitate body and mind and sap life of enjoyment. Anyone who has experienced genuine suffering knows how easily it can imprison its victims in misery that shuts them off from the rest of the world and, sometimes, even from God.

So to be patient in the face of suffering because one believes that it is a participation in Christ's Passion doesn't mean that one should go looking for suffering, or that suffering which can be alleviated should be allowed to go untreated. Life is God's great gift to us, and it's only fully appreciated when we enjoy the well-being God wishes for us. We ought never to scorn the gift by actively seeking to suffer. Even Jesus asked for the cup to be taken away. Eagerly grasping it would have been the act of a neurotic. Suffering is inevitable for all humans. Sooner or later, it comes to *us*, so there's no good reason to go in search of *it*.

A Long Training in Patience

The infant who grew up to become the first Slavic pope was christened Karol Wojtyla and affectionately nicknamed "Lolek" by family and friends. He was born in 1920 in Wadowice, Poland, a town of about ten thousand souls located just seventeen miles south of Oswiecim, a place better known by its German name of Auschwitz. Less than a year after his election to the papacy, John Paul visited the site of the death camp to pray for its victims. He'd been there many times before. But it was impossible, he said, "for me not to come here as pope."[4]

Part of the reason it was so important for Karol to return again and again to Auschwitz is that his own experiences of suffering nurtured in him a deep compassion for the suffering of others. In three different periods of his pre-Vatican life, the future pope endured great tragedy and hardship: the loss of his entire family by the time he was twenty, the Nazi occupation of Poland during World War II, and the post-war communist repression in Poland. Each of these periods schooled him in the virtue of patience.

Deaths in the Family

The first period of suffering began in 1929 when Lolek's mother, Emilia, died of heart and kidney disease. In the weeks preceding her death, she fell into a deep depression that threw up a barrier between her and her bewildered, frightened nine-year-old son. Lolek was devastated when she died, withdrawing from schoolmates and family friends into a private world of grief. A poem written about his mother twenty years later expresses the emptiness he continued to feel long after her death:

> Over this your white grave
> the flowers of life in white—
> so many years without you—
> how many have passed out of sight?[5]

At the time of her death, however, Lolek's only recorded comment was a terse "It was God's will."[6] If the account is true (it smacks a bit of hagiography), the nine-year-old boy may have been trying to repress his grief with a pious platitude. But it's also possible that the comment reflected a childish awareness, as yet undeveloped, of the spiritual significance of patience.

Three years later, tragedy struck again. Lolek's only brother Edmund, a young physician just two years out of medical school, caught scarlet fever from a patient and died. Once more Lolek was shattered by loss, dismally realizing that he and his father had no one in the world now except each other. But again he is reported to have said with "grave face" and "resoluteness," "It was God's will."[7]

The shared grief of Lolek and his father, also named Karol, strengthened their already close relationship. Karol Sr. was the most important person in his son's life. That's why his father's death eight years later, when Lolek was twenty, was the heaviest blow of all. Karol Sr. died alone while his son was away at work. Lolek discovered the body when he returned to the apartment they shared. He was now utterly on his own. As he later said, "At twenty, I had already lost all the people that I loved . . . I never felt so alone."[8]

Nazi Terror

It was around the time of his brother Edmund's death that Lolek's faith noticeably deepened. Like most Poles in the early twentieth century, he was already deeply devout. But the loss of half their family in the space of three years drew the grieving son and father to frequent prayer, daily attendance at Mass, and regular religious retreats. Karol Sr.'s fervor inspired his young son; many times Lolek awakened in the morning to discover that his father had been on his knees all night long. It was also during this period, again inspired by the example of his father, but also prompted in part by his yearning for a mother, that Lolek's lifelong devotion to the Blessed Virgin began.

When he was eighteen, Lolek matriculated at Krakow's Jagiellonian University, the same place his brother Edmund had studied medicine. Shaken by the thought of separation from his son, Karol Sr. also moved to Krakow, and the two lived in a bleak basement apartment that a visitor dubbed "the catacomb." Lolek studied Polish language and literature and began writing poetry. He was also passionate about the theater. He continued writing verse (all of it religious, and some of it, if truth be told, dense to the point of incomprehensibility) until he became pope, and he published a play, "The Jeweler's Shop," in 1960, when he was auxiliary bishop of Krakow.

Lolek's formal studies at Jagiellonian didn't last long. On August 31, 1939, Hitler invaded Poland. Just a few days later, Krakow was occupied by the German army and the second great period of the future pope's suffering began. The Nazis, who looked on Lolek and his fellow Poles as subhumans good only for physical labor, launched a systematic campaign to eradicate every vestige of Polish culture. Secondary schools and universities, including Jagiellonian, were shut down, churches were closed, priests were murdered or sent to the camps, Polish books were banned, and feast days of Polish saints were ripped from the calendar. Lolek and his fellow students studied secretly with their professors for a time after the university was closed. But somehow the Nazis caught wind of what was going on and shipped the entire faculty of Jagiellonian to a concentration camp. Only a handful returned at war's end.

Basic necessities of life also became scarce as the Nazis looted Poland to aid the German war effort. The occupation put an end to Karol Sr.'s only source of income, a retiree's pension from the Polish army, leaving the Wojtylas even harder up than they had been before. As Lolek wrote a friend during the war's first winter, "Now life is waiting in line for bread, scavenging for sugar, and dreaming of coal and books."[9]

There was the real threat of personal danger too. Young Poles of Lolek's age faced deportation to work camps in Germany unless they already held jobs approved by the occupation authorities. Through family friends, Lolek managed to land a common laborer's position at the Eastern German Chemical Works, just outside of Krakow. The factory made caustic soda, a necessary ingredient in explosives. Lolek was assigned to the quarry, first laying railroad tracks, then working as a brakeman. The labor was backbreaking and the hours were long. Lolek soon lost weight and felt hungry and worn-out all the time. But the job protected him from deportation, brought in a meager and much needed income, and allowed him to continue living with his father.

Lolek was eventually given a less exhausting task at the quarry which allowed him more free time to study and pray. His new job was helping the foreman to place quarry explosives. Although physically easier, the new position was dangerous in two ways: it involved handling dynamite, and Lolek and his boss faced severe punishment if any of the explosives in their care went missing.

It was during this anxious period that Lolek realized he had a calling to the priesthood. Archbishop of Krakow Adam Sapieha immediately accepted the promising youth as a postulant. This added yet another element of danger to Lolek's life. The Nazis had closed down all the seminaries in Poland, and priestly training had to be done in secret while students held down worldly jobs for the sake of appearance. Despite precautions, the Gestapo occasionally discovered the identities of secret seminarians and either shot them out of hand or sent them off to perish in the camps.

In 1944, a little over a year after he began his seminary training, young Karol Wotyla narrowly missed death on two separate occasions. The first occurred on a frigid night in February. Walking home after his workday at the quarry, he was hit by a German army truck. If a passerby hadn't discovered him some time later he would've frozen to death. Karol was hospitalized for three weeks with a bad concussion, dislocated shoulder, and multiple lacerations and bruises. During his convalescence, he embraced his suffering as "a spiritual retreat sent from God."[10]

In August of that same year, Karol nearly fell victim to the Nazis on what came to be known as "Black Sunday." A month earlier, Polish partisans had launched a coordinated attack against the Nazi occupiers of Warsaw. After a few days of desperate fighting, the partisans were slaughtered and the uprising quelled. But the revolt surprised and frightened the Nazis. Determined to forestall the possibility of a similar uprising in Krakow, German soldiers rounded up hundreds of Polish men, including those with work permits, and either executed or imprisoned them. When Karol caught wind of what was going on, he fled to the basement apartment he'd once shared with his father and spent the entire day facedown, arms outstretched in cruciform fashion, praying fervently. Had he been captured, he would

have confessed to being a seminarian and almost certainly
would have been shot.

Krakow was liberated by the Russian army in January
1945. By March, Karol had returned to Jagiellonian University. He was ordained nearly two years later. His religious devotion, sense of dedication, and personal austerity made him
a favorite of Archbishop Sapieha. It was clear to those who
knew Karol that he was destined for greatness.

Communist Oppression

Karol's early years of schooling in patient suffering served
him well during his later career as priest, bishop, archbishop,
and cardinal in communist Poland. There's the sharply
poignant suffering of the sort that he experienced in early
life—the death of loved ones, severe injuries, the perils of
warfare—and there's the less traumatic but wearing suffering
of daily irritations, harassment, and oppression that he and
all of Poland's Roman Catholics endured under post-war Soviet domination. Coping with both kinds of suffering requires strength for the long haul which can be sustained only
by attentive patience.

From the end of the war until the collapse of the Soviet
empire in 1990, the Polish church and Poland's communist
government were locked in a continuous and exhausting struggle. Sometimes the tussle erupted in bursts of anti-religious
propaganda and the arrest and imprisonment of priests. More
typically, the government's strategy was a less dramatic one of
passive aggression. Permits to build churches got tangled in
bureaucratic red tape, permit applications for outdoor religious
processions or Masses went missing, seminarians were hassled
by police, the telephones of priests were tapped and their passports confiscated, and seminaries and university theology departments were either closed down or had their budgets

slashed to the bone. The game of governmental stalling, periodically punctuated by repressive crackdowns, was maddening.

Shortly after his ordination, Karol was sent to Rome for doctoral studies. When he returned to Poland, he spent three years in parish work before earning a second doctorate and moving on to teach philosophy at the University of Lublin. He was appointed auxiliary bishop of Krakow in 1958, then archbishop of Krakow in 1963 and cardinal in 1967. His participation in Vatican II brought him to the attention of Pope Paul VI, who admired Wojtyla for his intelligence as much as for his devotion. Most of Paul's famous encyclical about birth control, *Humanae Vitae,* was probably drafted by Cardinal Wojtyla.

Ironically, the Polish government, which insisted on vetting all nominees for episcopal office in the country, welcomed the rise of Wojtyla as a prince of the church. The presumption was that he was too much of an egghead to cause any great trouble. But to the authorities' surprise, Wojtyla proved to be a persistent and painful thorn in their side.

As cardinal, Wojtyla's style was to avoid public confrontation with the regime. Instead, he doggedly worked behind the scenes to defend the church against governmental restrictions and bureaucratic stonewalling, refusing to take no for an answer to his persistent requests for greater freedom of religion for Catholic Poles. He didn't go out of his way to provoke the authorities, but was tireless in his insistence that they respect the human rights of all Polish citizens, Catholic or not. It was an exhausting cat-and-mouse game in which Wojtyla frequently felt he took one step back for every two forward. By the time he was elected pope in October 1978, his twenty-year struggle with the Polish authorities had honed his patience to a fine edge. Very few occupiers of the throne of Peter have been as well trained in endurance and forbearance.

The Bullet That Missed

Although he'd suffered much in his life and learned from an early age to use the suffering as an opportunity to cultivate patience, John Paul's afflictions during his first sixty years were never really health-related. His only experience of serious bodily harm was when he had been hit by the German lorry in 1944. As priest, bishop, cardinal, and pope he displayed great pity and spiritual concern for sick people, regularly ministering to them and meditating on the deep and mysterious connection between their suffering and Christ's. But he had nearly no firsthand knowledge of what they endured.

That all changed in May 1981. Pope for a little over two-and-a-half years, John Paul had already made a much-publicized visit to his homeland, blessed the rise of the trade union Solidarity, and encouraged resistance to Poland's communist government—as well as, by implication, the Kremlin. He'd also published his first encyclical, *Redemptor Hominis,* which affirmed the dignity of human beings while condemning human rights abuses, militarism, and environmental devastation. Although he criticized capitalism in the encyclical for its addiction to consumerism, it was pretty clear that the papal finger pointed mainly at Eastern Bloc totalitarianism. The new pope, in short, almost immediately riled the Soviet Union by showing more willingness to go on the offensive than he'd displayed as a cardinal in Poland. In hindsight, it's not surprising that the KGB, acting through the Bulgarian government, arranged for his assassination.[11]

The man hired to shoot the pope was a twenty-three-year-old Turk named Mehmet Ali Agca, a freelance assassin who worked at different times for both right- and left-wing groups. On the day of the hit, May 13, 1981, Agca joined a crowd of pilgrims cheering John Paul as he made his way through St. Peter's Square while standing in a slowly moving jeep. As was his custom, the pope reached out to touch hundreds of outstretched hands and embrace children held up to him. He'd just kissed and returned a little girl to her parents when shots rang out. The pope crumpled into the arms of the man sitting next to him in the jeep, his secretary and long-time friend Stanislaw Dziwisz. The time was 5:13 in the afternoon.

Agca was no more than ten feet from the pope when he fired. One bullet smacked into John Paul's stomach. The other grazed his right elbow and broke his left index finger before going on to wound a couple of nearby American tourists. As quick-thinking bystanders grabbed Agca, the pope was rushed to an ambulance kept on standby by the Vatican health services. His personal physician, Dr. Renato Buzzonetti, gave the order to head straight to Gemelli Hospital. En route, the ambulance's siren gave out, and the driver had to lay on the horn in a desperate effort to clear a path through Rome's congested rush hour traffic.

By the time he arrived at the Gemelli's emergency room, John Paul had lost consciousness, his blood pressure was dropping, and his pulse was faint. Right before the pope was wheeled into the operating theater, a tearful Dziwisz gave him last rites.

The damage caused by Agca's first shot became horribly apparent as soon as the surgeons opened John Paul up. The pope was hemorrhaging badly into his abdominal cavity—he had lost more than six pints of blood—and the first urgent priority was to locate and staunch the source of the bleeding. When this was done and John Paul was no longer in immediate danger of slipping into shock, surgeons turned their attention to the multiple wounds caused by the bullet. The pope's peritoneum and colon had been perforated and his small intestine had no fewer than five wounds. Over the next few hours, surgeons removed almost two feet of intestine and performed a temporary colostomy. The surgery lasted until nearly midnight.

John Paul was in intensive care for five days before he was finally moved to a regular hospital room on May 18, his sixty-first birthday. He was weak and in great pain most of that time, and was able to take a little solid food again only on May 20. It was a period of great darkness for him. As Dziwisz later described it, "For many days he experienced what he had been talking about, with sensitivity and tenderness, in his many speeches to the sick:... powerlessness, weakness, pain, sadness, isolation, and dependence upon others."[12] But throughout the ordeal, the pope struggled to hang on patiently and hopefully to the deeper meaning of human suffering, a meaning he had slowly discerned during his years in Poland. Just four days after the shooting, John Paul recorded a message to the faithful, declaring in a faint voice: "United with Christ, priest and victim, I offer my sufferings for the Church and the world."[13] His suffering—all human suffering—was connected to Christ's for the good of the world: this was the message the pope wanted people to hear, the great spiritual truth he clung to during his ordeal.

John Paul left the Gemelli and returned to the Vatican on June 3. But shortly afterwards his condition nose-dived. He developed a dangerously high fever and was bent double at times with severe abdominal pain and breathlessness. He lost so much weight that Vatican staff, alarmed at his haggard appearance, implored him to return to the Gemelli.

Doctors were baffled about the cause of the pope's distress and Vatican insiders began to panic. But finally the culprit was diagnosed: a cytomegalovirus picked up from one of the blood transfusions received during surgery. Since antibiotics are useless against viruses, the only therapy was to treat

John Paul's symptoms and wait for the bug to wear itself out. This meant several more weeks of suffering—a "second agony," as one Vatican priest said.[14] Slowly but surely, however, the pope recovered. His colostomy was reversed on August 5 and he finally left Gemelli Hospital nine days later to spend the rest of the summer convalescing at Castel Gandolfo, the papal summer quarters.

The attempt on John Paul's life fell on the anniversary of Mary's first appearance at Fatima in 1917, and the pope became convinced during his convalescence that her intervention had saved his life. "In everything that happened to me that day," he later said, "I felt her extraordinary protection and concern, which showed itself to be more powerful than the assassin's bullet."[15] "One hand fired," he concluded, "but another guided the bullet."[16] The pope later installed the bullet that did so much damage to him in the crown of the statue of Our Lady of Fatima at her shrine in Portugal.

The attack in St. Peter's Square brought John Paul greater physical and psychological suffering than he had known up to that point in his life. It was an agonizing and frightening ordeal. But it was also, he decided, a gift: "God permitted me to experience suffering; he permitted me to experience the danger of losing my life."[17] The trial gave him firsthand experience of what it was like to endure the intense suffering of agonizing pain and panicky death-fear as well as the physical and emotional suffering of a drawn-out illness. If John Paul had ever romanticized suffering in even the slightest way before the assassination attempt, any further temptation to do that was seared away by his encounter with Mehmet Ali Agca. It was during the pope's long convalescence that he began thinking about the apostolic letter on the meaning of suffering that he was to publish three years later.

Salvifici Doloris

John Paul released his apostolic letter *Salvifici Doloris*—"Redemptive Suffering"—on February 11, 1984. The date, the feast of Our Lady of Lourdes, was chosen to honor Mary, whose hand John Paul believed had "guided the bullet," and to encourage all those who, like the thousands of yearly pilgrims to Lourdes, suffer in body and mind.

In his letter, John Paul leads off with a bleakly honest acknowledgment of the centrality of suffering in the human condition. Suffering is the "universal theme that accompanies man at every point on earth . . . It co-exists with him in the world."[18] This isn't to deny that life deserves to be celebrated, but only to say what everyone knows: beautiful as life can be, suffering is an inevitable part of it. John Paul is forthright about a second point as well: suffering is an evil. In no sense can it be seen as a good. To suffer is to undergo a diminution of well-being, at least so long as the suffering lasts.[19]

Suffering isn't only physical or psychological distress caused by painful stimuli such as injury, illness, bankruptcy, or divorce. It also torments its victims with the profound spiritual fear that suffering is senseless, a calamity that befalls us for no reason whatsoever, which points to nothing beyond itself, and which proclaims the utter meaninglessness of life. "With each form of suffering . . . there inevitably arises the question: Why? It is a question about the cause, the reason, and equally, about the purpose of suffering."[20] Bewilderment in the face of suffering, especially when illness or crisis stretches our resources to the breaking point, can easily plunge us into despair, overwhelming us with a sense of abandonment and betrayal that often stokes nihilistic fury. As John Paul wrote elsewhere, seemingly purposeless suffering "can make us cruel, it can embitter not only the one who is directly affected but also those who are close to him, and who, powerless to bring aid, suffer on account of that powerlessness."[21]

Can we find some meaning in suffering that keeps us from sinking into anger, cruelty, and bitterness? John Paul thinks that the suffering or Passion of Jesus provides the answer. Jesus endured public humiliation, torture, and a horrific death in order to overcome evil. The suffering he experienced didn't defeat him. Instead, it served as a vehicle for showing once and for all that evil—even the evil of death—doesn't have the final word. The Resurrection is a sign of "the victorious power of suffering."[22]

Even more, Jesus' conquest of suffering is redemptive. In suffering and dying to conquer evil, Jesus liberates us from our bondage to suffering and death. But none of this would have been possible except through his own suffering. God tamed suffering and death for us not by waving a magic wand from on high, but by becoming human, patiently enduring the evil of suffering, and defeating it. "Precisely by means of his suffering," John Paul wrote, Jesus "must bring it about that man should not perish, but have eternal life. Precisely by means of his Cross he must strike at the roots of evil...Precisely by means of his Cross he must accomplish the work of salvation."[23]

So suffering, in the first place, has what might be thought of as a negative meaning: although an undesirable and inevitable evil, it is *not* the final word, *not* the ultimate destroyer of well-being, *not* the implacable harbinger of decay and dissolution. Jesus submitted himself to suffering to give it purpose, and his mastery of it promises victory to any human who also suffers.

But, additionally, there's also a positive meaning to suffering, heralded in the very first paragraph of *Salvifici Doloris* when John Paul quotes the apostle Paul (Col 1:24): "In my flesh I complete what is lacking in Christ's afflictions for the sake of his body, that is, the Church."[24] Paul's assumption is that Christ is now indissolubly grafted into all Christians. We are the members and Christ is the head of the Mystical Body called the Church. Because we now live in Christ, and because Christ's suffering is redemptive, our suffering must be too. By patiently accepting our suffering, then, we participate in Jesus' "work of saving the world."[25] Because of our union with Christ, we have "the certainty that in the spiritual dimension of the work of Redemption [we are] serving, like Christ, the salvation of [our] brothers and sisters."[26] Or as Paul wrote in Romans (8:17), "we share in his sufferings in order that we may also share in his glory."

There's nothing radically new in *Salvifici Doloris*. The claim that the redemption of the world is rooted in Christ's suffering is as old as the Resurrection itself, and the intuition that human suffering can participate in that redemption dates, as we've seen, at least as far back as Paul. But in writing his apostolic letter, John Paul offered the world a fresh and inspiring reminder of the truth that suffering, when endured patiently, can be unimaginably fruitful. In the months following the assassination attempt, John Paul must've thought often of the darkest moments in his own life and concluded that they'd all been occasions for redemptive suffering. In offering a final word of counsel to the faithful at the end of his letter, he wrote out of personal experience: "We ask precisely you who are weak *to become a source of strength* for the Church and humanity. In the terrible battle between the forces of good and evil, revealed to our eyes by our modern world, may your suffering in union with the cross of Christ be victorious!"[27]

"I offer my sufferings"

John Paul was one of the most physically robust popes ever enthroned on Peter's chair. But the bullet that nearly killed him two and a half years into his papacy, together with the crushing schedule he set for himself over the next decade, seriously undermined his health.

During his pontificate, John Paul wrote fourteen encyclicals, traveled to 129 countries and nearly 150 locales in Italy, and was a significant player in world affairs, especially the 1990 collapse of the Soviet empire. The pope's day typically began at 5:30 AM and ended late at night. Prayer and devotions, paperwork, public audiences, meetings with officials of the curia, pastoral duties, hosting visiting dignitaries, study and writing—all on top of his constant world travel—filled his schedule to overflowing. The regimen would've exhausted anyone. Even the relatively strong John Paul began to feel its cumulative effects as he approached his seventies.

The first obvious warning that the pontiff's health was breaking came in 1991. A tremor in his left hand prompted his physician, Dr. Renato Buzzonetti, to order diagnostic neurological tests which eventually revealed that John Paul had early-stage Parkinson's disease. Pharmaceutical treatment and physical therapy were begun, but they had little effect on the disease's progress.

In the summer of 1992, John Paul was admitted to the Gemelli Hospital—which, after the weeks he'd spent there following the assassination attempt, he jokingly called "Vatican III"—for the removal of a benign colon tumor. He'd been experiencing symptoms for several months but had ignored them in order to maintain his busy schedule. The recovery period lasted until early autumn.

In November of the next year, at the conclusion of a public audience, John Paul tripped on the hem of his vestment and tumbled to the floor in the Vatican's Hall of Blessings. He dislocated his right shoulder: a minor injury, but a portent of things to come. Dr. Buzzonetti knew that the fall in all likelihood was related to the pope's increasingly troublesome tremors. A more serious Parkinson's-related mishap occurred six months later when John Paul fell in his private apartments and broke his right hip. Back in the Gemelli for surgery, he endured a lengthy recovery period followed by exhausting physical therapy. Afterwards, John Paul began using a cane, which was eventually replaced by a wheelchair.

On Christmas morning 1995, while reading his Christmas message to the faithful gathered in St. Peter's Square, John Paul suddenly grimaced and gasped, "Excuse me, I need to stop." He was diagnosed with acute appendicitis, but refused surgical treatment. Treated with antibiotics, the pope recovered, with only occasional flare-ups, until August 1996, when he suffered a severe relapse. Buzzonetti insisted on removal of the appendix. But John Paul refused to interrupt his schedule, so surgery was postponed until early October. It was the pope's sixth time in the Gemelli's operating theater.

The tumbles, surgeries, and Parkinson's—not to mention his advanced age—wore the pope down as the twenty-first century approached. To add to his troubles, he developed severe osteoarthritis in his right knee, which not only caused him great pain but made him even more immobile. Understandably, given the cumulative amount of time he'd been confined to the Gemelli Hospital over the previous few years, the pope adamantly refused to consider knee replacement.

Looking back over his years of tending to John Paul, Dr. Buzzonetti concluded that "in a physical sense, the pope grew old before his time, worn down by the difficult years of his youth; by uncommon burdens, discomforts, and privations; and by the challenging ministry he carried out first in Poland and then as pope."[28] Vatican observers marveled at John Paul's staying power, and attributed it to his strong determination to see the church into the third millennium. Nearly everyone agreed that he kept going through sheer will power.

Vatican insiders noticed something else as well: the pope's patience with his steadily increasing infirmity. According to Buzzonetti, "he always displayed an attitude of profound interior serenity."[29] Growing old and sickly is a burden for anyone, but especially for a person who in earlier years enjoyed a physically active life. Yet all who knew John Paul during his last decade and a half testify to the fact that he tolerated his condition with remarkable forbearance. Even allowing for the hagiographical gloss that inevitably polishes the memory of a pope, especially one as beloved as John Paul, it's clear that he endured his decline with striking gentleness of spirit. He knew that the suffering brought by advancing debility is also part of Christ's Passion.

This isn't to say that the pope was indifferent to his suffering. He would've been less than human had that been the case. John Paul neither desired nor enjoyed infirmity, and his reluctance to undergo yet another surgery when his right knee went bad testifies to his weariness with hospital stays. It's not hard to imagine that in the privacy of his apartments he experienced moments of bewilderment, regret, anger, and perhaps even despair as he contemplated his progressively impaired body. Powerless to control the trembling in his limbs or to walk unaided, stunned when he gazed in a mirror at his Parkinson's-frozen expression and the spittle that perpetually threatened to drop from the right corner of his mouth, often in pain from the scars of his bullet wound, his replaced hip, and his disintegrating kneecap: how could John

Paul not have rebelled occasionally at the all-too-evident signs of his physical degeneration? At times he must've felt trapped inside his own body.

But patience in the face of suffering isn't fearlessness or unrealistic optimism. The person of patience resolutely faces up to her frailty. In the case of a Christian, this patience rests on the conviction that suffering has a meaning which, while not mitigating its unpleasantness, certainly allows the sufferer to accept and even gratefully assent to her decline. As we've seen, the meaning is found partly in the self-insight and empathy for others that suffering can bring. But the deepest source of meaning in suffering is the opportunity it affords the sufferer to participate in the ongoing redemptive suffering of Christ.

In his final years, as his own health declined and his suffering increased, John Paul returned to this conviction again and again, frequently referring to his own afflictions in homilies and writings. His purpose wasn't to solicit pity, but rather to offer his physical decline as an example to the faithful of how to cope patiently with suffering. As one of his aides noted, the pope transformed "the stigma of suffering" into "an instrument of the apostolate."[30]

On his last trip abroad, for example, John Paul visited the shrine at Lourdes and assured the thousands of sick and dying pilgrims gathered there that "with you I share a time of life marked by physical suffering, yet not for that reason any less fruitful in God's wondrous plan."[31] Just a few months later, during one of his final stays at Gemelli Hospital, he proclaimed to the world that "I continue to serve the Church and the whole of humanity, even here in the hospital among other sick persons."[32] And shortly before his death, John Paul issued this Lenten message: "If growing old, with its inevitable conditions, is accepted serenely in the light of faith, it can become an invaluable opportunity for better understanding the mystery of the Cross, which gives full meaning to human existence."[33]

His message was always the same: illness, even the illness that is a prelude to death, can be fruitful rather than barren because at its deepest level it connects the sufferer with both the atoning Christ and a world hungry for salvation. John Paul's words assured fellow sufferers that they had a vital spiritual role to play even when their physical strength waned. By enduring their suffering and debility with patience, they aided Christ in saving souls. Their groans of pain, seen from this perspective, were also the groans of birthing. "If you join your suffering to the suffering of Christ, you will be privileged cooperators in the salvation of souls . . . your suffering is never wasted! Indeed, it is valuable, for it is a mysterious but real sharing in the saving mission of the Son of God."[34]

John Paul believed that assent to this task was not simply a privilege; it was also an obligation. "The adoration of the Cross directs us to a commitment that we cannot shirk," he wrote in one of his Lenten messages for 2005. "It is the mission that St. Paul expressed in these words: 'In my flesh I complete what is lacking in Christ's afflictions for the sake of his body, that is, the Church.'" Then, characteristically, John Paul added this personal note: "I also offer my sufferings so that God's plan may be completed and his Word spread among the peoples."[35] The pope wanted to make clear to the faithful that he was practicing what he preached. A priest, he believed, was "sent in a special way, *in persona Christi*, to serve the community of the saved."[36] How much more, then, was demanded of the pope, the servant of the servants, when it came to patiently assenting to personal suffering?

During his final five years, John Paul's health became so precarious that medical personnel and equipment were installed next to his living quarters in the Vatican and a series of medical specialists from around the world routinely consulted. His medical team, which Dr. Buzzoneti remembers as "discreetly follow[ing] the pope each time he left his private apartment," was in a "constant state of tension and alarm."[37] But with very little interruption, the pope maintained his heavy schedule, especially the hours he devoted each day to prayer.

The beginning of the end came in early 2005. Observers noticed that John Paul's recitation of the Angelus on January 30 was raspy and halting. The very next day, the Vatican press office announced that the pope had come down with flu and that his audiences for the day were cancelled.

Flu is a worrisome illness for any octogenarian, but it posed a special threat to the fragile John Paul. The simple sore throat that annoyed him in January soon developed into an acute inflammation of the larynx whose swelling partially blocked his windpipe. This was a serious turn of events because the pope's Parkinson's had already compromised his ability to swallow. By February 1, John Paul was in such respiratory distress that he had to be rushed to the Gemelli. He stayed there for the next week and a half, returning to the Vatican on the second day of Lent. Before he left the hospital, he signed copies of his just-released (and final) book, *Memory and Identity.* In the book's concluding chapter, which dealt with the 1981 assassination attempt, John Paul reflected once more on the theme of suffering that had occupied him most of his life. "The passion of Christ on the Cross gave a radically new meaning to suffering, transforming it from within . . . It is this suffering which burns and consumes evil with the flame of love."[38] In the weeks to follow, the pope would offer his own suffering as a flame of love.

Less than a fortnight later, John Paul was back at the Gemelli with breathing problems, this time nearly to the point of asphyxiation, because of laryngeal spasms. His condition was so serious that he received last rites shortly before going to the hospital. On his arrival, doctors performed a tracheotomy they hoped would stabilize his breathing. Awakening from the anesthesia to discover that he could no longer speak because of the procedure, the pope scribbled a note in Polish to his old friend Stanislaw Dziwisz: "See what they have done to me!" But this plaintive cry of distress, so unusual for John Paul, was immediately followed up with "But... *totus tuus!*"[39] This latest bout of suffering, like all the others, would be endured patiently for the sake of Christ's Passion.

The pope stayed in the hospital a full two weeks before returning to his papal apartment. He did his best while in hospital and back in the Vatican to keep up with the daily paperwork that required his attention. But what little strength he still had was trickling away. He found it too difficult to swallow, and his inability to take food so weakened him that his physicians made the decision to commence tube-feeding. By the time he stood at his open window on Easter Sunday and found himself unable to pronounce the *Urbi et orbi* blessing, it was clear to everyone who saw him that he had little time left.

On March 31, Thursday of Easter Week, John Paul began shivering uncontrollably while in his private chapel. His temperature spiked to 103 degrees and he rapidly fell into septic shock and cardiovascular collapse. Tests later revealed that the source of the crisis was a urinary tract infection. Aware that this was his final trial, the pope insisted on remaining in his apartment rather than returning to the Gemelli. He wanted to die in the Vatican.

Over the next two days, he said his farewells to members of the papal household, concelebrated Mass, listened to the Divine Office, and prayed. On Saturday, April 2, his temperature shot up again and he began to flicker in and out of consciousness. Shortly before slipping into a coma, he muttered in Polish, "Let me go to the Lord."[40]

Six hours later, at 9:37 PM, the suffering that John Paul had endured so patiently finally ended.

A Divine Promise

In the speech quoted at the beginning of this chapter, John Paul said that patience in the face of suffering gives us courage to continue our journey. Sustained by the virtue of patience, by the realization that suffering is neither gratuitous nor absurd, we are enabled to endure without falling into hopelessness or anger. By patiently assenting to suffering, we make the choice to affirm and collaborate in its meaning. And, for John Paul, the most profound level of suffering's meaning is participation in the redemptive Passion of Christ.

We *will* suffer throughout our lives. Most of our suffering will probably be the low order irritations, anxieties, and worries that routinely bedevil people. In the grand scheme of things, the hassle of morning rush-hour traffic or the sleepless night spent worrying about how to pay for a child's college education may not seem so awful. But embracing these things as opportunities to practice the virtue of patience not only is an acknowledgment that all *suffering,* when assented to, is made fruitful by virtue of its participation in Christ's atoning work. It is also preparation for coping with much greater suffering when it comes to us, especially the suffering unto death. As the sixteenth-century Cambridge theologian William Perkins put it,

> He that would be able to bear all the crosses, namely death itself, must first of all learn to bear small crosses, [such] as sicknesses in body and troubles in mind,

with losses of goods and of friends, of good name, which I may fitly term little deaths . . . we must first of all acquaint ourselves with these little deaths before we can be able to bear the great death of all.[41]

A lifetime of experience in patiently assenting to inevitable suffering ensures that when our time to die comes, we won't be caught short. We won't waste our final days and squander our remaining resources ranting against the coming darkness or desperately trying to deny what's happening to us. Instead, knowing that our suffering has a purpose that extends far beyond our own personal interests—knowing, as John Paul said, that "every form of human pain contains within itself a divine promise of salvation and glory"[42]—our dying can be fruitful, just as our living was.

CHAPTER EIGHT

CHRISTING

Caryll Houselander

"We are other Christs.
Our destiny is to live the Christ-life:
to bring Christ's life into the world;
to increase Christ's love in the world;
to give Christ's peace to the world."

"Christ in them all"

Picture a young woman in her early twenties riding on a London underground train filled, as she later described it, with "sitting and strap-hanging workers of every description going home at the end of the day." Her appearance is striking, even bizarre. She is wearing oversized, thick eyeglasses and has flaming red hair. Her face is painted white with, in the words of an acquaintance, "some abominable chalky-white substance" and her upper lip is stained "dandelion-yellow" from the cigarettes she endlessly smokes.[1]

The young woman has a troubled inner life. A miserable and lonely childhood has left her somewhat reclusive, susceptible to panic attacks, and probably afflicted with eating disorders. She has a sharp tongue and is sometimes too fond of gossip. An intense seeker of God, she is deeply alienated from the Roman Catholic Church in which she was confirmed. She still reels from a recent unhappy love affair whose aftermath left her even more lonely than she normally is. She's at a low point in her life.

And then out of the blue, jostling along on the tube and gazing wearily at her fellow passengers, something happens to her that transfigures her jaded way of seeing the world.

> Quite suddenly I saw with my mind, but as vividly as a wonderful picture, Christ in them all. But I saw more than that; not only was Christ in every one of them, living in them, dying in them, rejoicing in them, sorrowing in them—but because He was in them, and because they were here, the whole world was here too, here in this underground train; not only the world as it was at that moment, not only all the people in all the countries of the world, but all those people who had lived in the past, and all those yet to come.[2]

Nor does the vision end as soon as the young woman arrives at her station. When she walks out onto the street and gazes at all the pedestrians scurrying to wherever they're going, she sees the same thing. "On every side, in every passer-by, everywhere—Christ."[3]

The young woman who experienced this vision was Caryll Houselander. Although sadly neglected today, she was an influential British spiritual author in the 1940s and early 1950s. By training a woodcarver and religious artist, Houselander began writing in earnest only in 1941. But at her death thirteen years later, she left behind fifteen books and over seven hundred articles, short stories, and poems. All of them reflected to one extent or another what she had learned from her London underground vision, the revelation that became the grand theme of her life: seeing Christ in all things.

After her experience on the tube, Caryll was convinced that the universe is Christ-saturated, and that a life well-lived gives us the spiritual clarity to discern Christ's presence in others and in ourselves. It also enables us to face our own mortality with a certain degree of composure, knowing that because Christ lives and dies with us, we are resurrected with him. We cannot understand precisely what that means. But we can know that if Christ indwells us, our "mortality" is not what it seems. If our destinies are tied to Christ's, death has no lasting power over us.

This general way of looking at the world, one which Caryll sometimes called "christing" (pronounced with a long "i"), is a habit of the heart that incorporates and brings to fruition all the virtues for living and dying well that we've explored. Christing, like the other virtues, is built on a bedrock of *trustfully* letting go of our need to control and letting reality be, which in turn helps us become more *lovingly available* to God, fellow humans, and ourselves. This willingness to make ourselves available encourages the attentiveness necessary for *gratitude,* and gratitude in turn inclines us to want to *obey* God's word by aligning our wills with the divine will. Finally, obedience girds us with the *courage* to embrace our freedom and the *patience* to endure suffering. Each of these virtues awakens our souls and strengthens our characters, preparing us to discern the steady presence of Christ in the world and to comport ourselves in a Christ-like manner. A lifelong habituation to the virtues that culminate in christing puts us in a state of being very much like that described in the well-known prayer attributed to St. Patrick:

Christ with me, Christ before me, Christ behind me;
Christ within me, Christ beneath me, Christ above me;
Christ to right of me, Christ to left of me;

Christ in my lying, Christ in my sitting, Christ in my
    rising;
Christ in the heart of all who think of me,
Christ on the tongue of all who speak to me,
Christ in the eye of all who see me,
Christ in the ear of all who hear me.[4]

In practicing christing, we live and we die surrounded by
Christ.

Christing as a Virtue

Christing involves a conversion or "transubstantiation,"[5] as
Caryll put it, of our way of seeing the world, understanding
our place in it, and relating to other people. When we cultivate the virtue of christing, we discern God's presence in creation, our true identities as "other Christs,"[6] and our duty—
our *privilege*—to help others likewise see and embrace the
holiness that birthed them, surrounds them, flows through
them, and nurtures them.

Christ before Me, Christ behind Me

One of the most remarkable consequences of christing is
that it enables us to see creation for the God-saturated thing
it is. Nothing seems commonplace or uninteresting any
longer. Every object and person encountered is a revelation
of the plenitudinous presence of Christ.

Caryll sometimes appealed to the Jesuit poet Gerard
Manley Hopkins (1844–1889) to get across her sense of the
christic nature of reality. Like her, Hopkins had a sensitive eye
for signs of God's presence in creation. He was convinced

that God is discernible in created things because the uniqueness of each of them reflects the uniqueness of their Creator.
The "thisness" of each thing—its uniquely singular identity—
is God's thumbprint.

Hopkins called the divine thumbprint "inscape." Inscape
trumpets its presence—or, as Hopkins sometimes said, "selves"
forth—to human awareness. That's why the apprehension of
it often feels forcefully revelatory. Discernment of inscape
should never be confused with the mere perception of an
object. Instead, it's an intuitive grasp of the object's underlying pattern, a pattern linked but not limited to the object's
perceptible qualities.[7]

For Hopkins, "all the world is full of inscape,"[8] and in
his journal entries and poetry he beautifully describes his
many experiences of it. He writes, for example, of the inscape of "greenwhite tufts of long bleached grass like heads
of hair or the crowns of heads of hair, each a whorl of slen-
der curves, one tuft taking up another."[9] Stars, speckled
trout, piebald cows, clouds, dew-dappled grass, moonlight,
golden bees, undulating waves, spider webs: for Hopkins,

> Each mortal thing does one thing and the same:
> . . . Selves—goes itself: *myself* it speaks and spells,
> Crying *What I do is me: for that I came.*[10]

And what all this selving-forth shows, says Hopkins, is the
deep-down christic nature of things:

> . . . for Christ plays in ten thousand places,
> Lovely in limbs, and lovely in eyes not his.[11]

When Caryll read Hopkins, she knew exactly what he
was talking about. Like him, she saw Christ—God's unique
stamp—selving forth everywhere. "The inward meaning of

life," she wrote, "is Christ." God created the world, in fact, "to be the womb and cradle of Christ"—and that divine intention is discoverable in even the most everyday object.[12]

> The pattern of the universe [is] within a little thing, like a flower, the ring on a bird's feather, a fish's scale and so on. The pattern within it, not reflected on it, but integral to it, and whole and complete in it, so that in a sense it is true to say of such a little created thing that its very being *is* the pattern of its Creator's mind.[13]

But if, as St. Patrick's prayer says, Christ is before, behind, beneath, and above us, why do so many of us *not* sense Christ's presence in the world? Gerard Manley Hopkins and Caryll Houselander offer two explanations. The first is that we allow ourselves to be distracted from the close attentiveness necessary for noticing Christ. Preoccupation with the affairs of the world or our own particular troubles can make us spiritually myopic.

But we can also miss the deep-down Christ-pattern of reality because of its sheer elusiveness. God's presence in the singularity of created objects—the infinite housed in the finite, the shoreless ocean absorbed in a sponge—can be glimpsed but never held for long. It flashes before us like lightning, illuminating everything for a brief second before vanishing again. As creatures with finite rational powers, we find it impossible to hold in our minds the spiraling depths of inscape in a bird feather or fish scale. "Our vision fails, our thought fails, we cannot follow it home, we cannot reach its littleness or its vastness, for the end of both is God."[14] We must be content with the realization that "God's way with us [is] to hide and reveal Himself at the same time"—not because God is coy, but because we can only take in so much.[15]

Like an Expanding Rose

It's not just the natural world that's charged with God's grandeur. We are too. Alone of all created things, we humans are made in the divine likeness, an imprint that, although tarnished by the Fall, is subsequently polished and restored by Christ. In becoming human, Christ, the New Adam, shares and salvages our humanness. Grafted into him as we now are—"I am the vine, you are the branches" (John 15:5)—we share Christ's life. And because the branches of the vine are all vitalized by the same spirit, we share one another's life as well. Individual Christians are never isolated or solitary. As branches of the vine we are always in relationship to both God and other humans.

As we've seen, one aspect of the virtue of christing is awareness of Christ's deep-down presence in the things of the world. A second is recognizing Christ in ourselves. Habituation to christing helps me realize Christ as my center and so, as St. Patrick put it, "within me." Once I come to that realization, I can't but see Christ in everyone else as well, "to right and left of me." All of us, wrote Caryll, are "syllables of the Word."[16]

This way of thinking about our spiritual identity is tied to the doctrine of the Mystical Body of Christ, introduced two millennia ago by St. Paul: "In Christ we who are many form one body, and each member belongs to all the others" (Rom 12:5). Just as an organic body has many parts, each with a specific function that works in coordination with all the others, so individual Christians are the organs and limbs of the Body of Christ, each with his or her own identity but also part of a greater whole. Each of us, says Paul, is called to a unique task within the Body proportionate to our talents and dispositions (1 Cor 12:12–31) and each of us is integral to the functioning of the whole. Christ is the head of the

Mystical Body (Eph 5:23; Col 1:18), and we are energized by the vitality that flows from him.[17]

Caryll unreservedly accepted the doctrine of the Mystical Body. In one of her poems, she noted that "Christ is among us, His heart like a rose expanding within us."[18] As Christ's heart expands—as we, the members of his Body, mature in Christ-like compassion and love—we grow into our true inscaped identities as "other Christs." The growth is both individual and collective. My progress (or regress, for that matter) necessarily affects the state of the Body because, as Caryll knew, "we are really part of a vast rhythm."[19] Cultivation of the virtue of christing brings the awareness that "Christ on earth, what we call the Mystical Body, means one great *living* in all spiritual life...we, who all have the same life, are made into *one* person in Him."[20]

So everything we do as inscaped Christs has consequences whose scope is breathtaking. "We are all good with others' goodness," Caryll realized, "and guilty with others' guilt, praying with others' prayers and so on."[21] My very identity as a branch of Christ's vine makes me inescapably responsible for all the other branches, even to the point (as John Paul II taught) of shouldering as best I can the suffering of humanity. In serving these "other Christs" to the right and left of me, I minister to Christ himself.

Caryll had a special love for wounded people—those suffering from mental or physical illness, those who felt unloved or betrayed, those whose appearance or mannerisms made them social pariahs, and those who were poor and hopeless. She often said that the unhappiness she endured in her early years made her especially sensitive to the unhappiness of others. But it's also true that Caryll took Christ at his word when he said that he was in the poor, the homeless, the sick, and the imprisoned (Matt 25:34–40). It's dangerous, she believed, to cling to conventionally pious (and safe) ideas of what Christ looks like. If we do, we risk missing his presence in others. Christ doesn't indwell only the saints. He's found and should be "reverenced" even in "very unlikely people," including the very worst or the most broken of us.[22] "We should never come to a sinner without the reverence we would take to the Holy Sepulchre."[23] This, too, is what it means to practice christing.

Setting Christ Free

Caryll's suggestion that we should approach the sinner as we would the Holy Sepulchre is striking. It points to her recognition that although Christ indwells everyone, our sinful behavior often blinds us to his presence. But even then, the Christ entombed in our hearts patiently waits for us to roll back the stone.

The third aspect of the virtue of christing is a commitment to helping others roll back the stone of their own tomb-hearts so that they can sense the presence of Christ within themselves and in the world. Christing calls us to speak and behave in ways that reveal to others the christic nature of reality.

This is no small task. The great malady of our time, Caryll believed, is repression of the indwelling Christ. Even those who consider themselves Christians find it difficult to embrace their Christ-selves, because doing so requires a daunting level of trust. To discover our Christ nature, advised Caryll, "we've just got to shut our eyes and dive into this sea of Christ, dive with the trust of people who can't swim and yet go straight into the dark water."[24] But few of us can bear this, and least of all those in most need of diving into the sea of Christ. It's no accident that Jesus ministered to those broken in spirit and sunk in sin.

Jesus advised them to become childlike in order to over-come their anxiety. Childlikeness, wrote Caryll, ought not to be confused with childishness. The latter is the attitude of the "perpetual adolescent" who "does not grow up because he— or she—is afraid to do so. Afraid of life: of grown-up respon-sibilities, of working for a living, of independence, of making decisions, of taking risks; afraid of falling in love, of making a home, of having children; afraid of sickness, of growing old and of dying."[25] But *childlikeness*, ironically, is spiritual matu-rity, a resolve "to grow up, to give ourselves to life, to accept life as it is . . . to accept ourselves as we are."[26] In becoming childlike, we liberate the repressed Christ within our hearts.

Practicing the virtue of christing encourages childlikeness in others too. First and foremost, this is done by modeling the Christ-life for them, helping them cultivate the spiritual clarity to discern the inscaped Christ for themselves, and above all treating them with the reverence that is their due, even if they don't yet know their own worth. Caryll believed that as humans we are not only "one of God's creatures . . . , but we are also His Christ, His only Son, the sole object of His whole love."[27] When we practice the virtue of christing, we see others and in turn help them to transfiguratively see themselves as the "sole objects" of divine love they are. But we must be gentle and patient with them, as God is with us, lest in our zeal we overreach and "unwittingly tear out the tender little shoot of Christ-life that [is] pushing up against the dark heavy clay" in which they have entombed Christ.[28]

"I had to be healed of myself"

When Caryll was born in October 1901, she was such a "small and odd" infant that neither her mother nor her maternal uncle, a gynecologist who assisted at the delivery, expected her to live for more than a few hours.[29] A Protestant clergyman was urgently summoned to baptize her, but mother and uncle so offended him with their nervous giggles that he stomped out of the house in the middle of the ceremony. So Caryll's uncle completed the baptism, using a salad bowl as a font and naming his niece after a favorite sailing yacht.

Whenever Caryll told this story, her aim was to get a chuckle out of her audience. But there's as much sadness as humor in the tale, presaging as it does a childhood of parental neglect, loneliness, and fragile health. That Caryll wasn't poisoned by her early years is a testament to her spiritual resilience.

Caryll's mother and father, Gertrude and Wilmot, were singularly unsuited for parenthood. Fond of sports and society life, both were much more comfortable on horseback or a tennis court than in a nursery. Wilmot was pretty much an absentee father, while Gertrude ran emotionally hot and cold, sometimes smothering Caryll and her older sister Ruth with attention, sometimes exiling them to the exclusive care of nurses and nannies.

During one of Gertrude's smothering periods, she got it into her head that it would be good for her two daughters to become Catholics. Caryll was six years old at the time, and the sudden switch from living in a religiously indifferent household to living in one that revolved around Gertrude's newly-found and rather manic faith was hard on her. She especially resented having to spend all her pocket money on "deplorable statues, flower vases, flowers, lamps and candles and candlesticks, as well as lace and linen cloths" for the homemade altars Gertrude insisted the girls make. The long hours of kneeling before them demanded by Gertrude rankled as well.[30] When as an adult Caryll warned against heavy-handed zealotry, she knew what she was talking about.

Incredibly, none of this forced piety was supplemented in the slightest way by religious instruction. Gertrude either saw no need to teach her daughters anything about the faith or, just as likely given her hot-and-cold temperament, she lost her fervor just as suddenly as she had found it. In either case, whatever Caryll learned of Christianity in those early years was picked up from a family friend named George Spencer Bower, whom she affectionately called "Smoky." Bower was an agnostic who admired the intellectual rigor of the Catholic tradition even though he couldn't accept its beliefs, and he shared his love of Catholic theology and English literature with Caryll. The two of them often read Shakespeare together. Caryll remembered once reciting Lady Macbeth's sleepwalking scene, "but hindered from giving it the full dramatic force that I should have liked to do by Smoky's little dog, Spot, who, used to nothing but gentleness and welcome from Smoky and me, would look bewildered and startled at the words, 'Out, damned Spot!'"[31] Caryll discovered in Smoky not only an able teacher but also a surrogate parent. He gave her the loving attention her own parents didn't.

Despite Bower's tutelage in theology, Caryll, put off by Gertrude's zeal, was conflicted about her faith. She made her first Confession and Communion when she was eight, but only after weeks of inner turmoil almost unthinkable in so young a child. Emotionally exhausted by the ordeal, she fell mysteriously ill the very next day. When she finally left her bed three weeks later, right before she was to receive her second Communion, she collapsed in a paralysis, punctuated by frightening bouts of breathlessness and fever, which lasted for several weeks. During this time, Caryll suffered agonies of conscience about dozens of imagined transgressions and

obsessively insisted on confessing over and over again to an
increasingly bewildered priest. Clearly both her bouts of illness were hysterical in nature, stirred up by her loneliness,
her unfulfilled hunger for love, and her guilt-stricken religious ambivalence.

Caryll's second mysterious illness reached a turning
point when the reason for her morbid sense of guilt dawned
on her. She realized "in a dim, intuitive way that it was not
something I had done that required forgiveness, but everything that I was that required to be miraculously transformed. It was of myself that I required to be healed."[32]
This harsh self-appraisal reflects Caryll's unhappy awareness
of the damage done her by her dysfunctional parents. As she
later recognized, her illnesses certainly sprang from "anxiety
neurosis."[33] But there was nothing neurotic about the sense
of relief that came to her when she recognized her deep
woundedness for what it was: injury caused by others, not
sinfulness on her part. Her physical symptoms ceased immediately and her religious ambivalence was replaced with a
grateful sense of dependency on God's grace. "I was instantly at peace," she recalled, "as if I had simply woken
from a long nightmare to the security and blessedness of a
sunlit morning."[34]

Caryll sorely needed her new faith in God over the next
few years. Shortly after her breakthrough, her parents di-
vorced. The split was no surprise to family acquaintances,
but it dealt a devastating and totally unanticipated blow to
Caryll. Writing about the divorce years later, she still felt a
desolate sense of abandonment:

> Come, let us walk for a time
> among ghosts and memories.
> Let us forget
> that not only home was lost,

not only Father and Mother
(Home,
and Father
and Mother
were God.)[35]

After their parents went their separate ways, Caryll and Ruth were sent to a boarding school which Caryll described as a "refuge for the children of broken marriages and unhappy homes."[36] Once planted there, the girls, virtually forgotten by their parents, were left in the care of the sisters even during school holidays. Thanks to the Reverend Mother's maternal instincts, Caryll wasn't miserable. But her parents' desertion of her continued to hurt.

Caryll was still at the school when World War I erupted in the summer of 1914. It was during the early days of the war that Caryll had the first of three christing visions that culminated in the one described at the beginning of this chapter. Her first one lasted less than a minute, but influenced the rest of her life.

One of the lay sisters in the Convent of the Holy Child was a young Bavarian woman who spoke hardly any English. The language barrier already isolated her from the other nuns and students, but anti-German sentiment ostracized her even more. "What her loneliness must have been when the war broke out," wrote Caryll, "I cannot imagine."[37]

One day Caryll happened to come upon the sister sitting alone in a small room cleaning shoes and silently weeping. "Speechless with embarrassment," Caryll stood in front of her, not knowing what to do. "I saw her large, toilworn hands come down onto her lap and fold on the little shoes, and even those hands, red and chapped, with blunted nails, were folded in a way that expressed inconsolable grief." When Caryll looked up from the sister's hands to her face, she saw to her astonishment that she was "crowned with the crown of thorns... That bowed head was weighed under the crown of thorns."[38] In that vision, which Caryll believed lasted no more than thirty seconds, she realized that Christ's Passion is played out again and again in every instance of human misery. It was her first experience of inscape, her first hint of the christic nature of reality.

Not long afterwards Caryll's mother, now trying to make ends meet as a single woman by operating a boarding house in Brighton, pulled her out of the school. For the next couple of years she was in and out of a number of cheaper boarding schools, lived for a time with a friend of the family, and eventually moved back to Gertrude's boarding house to help out with the chores. She was generally unhappy and unfulfilled, both creatively—she was beginning to feel the artistic stirrings that eventually led her to drawing and woodcarving—and spiritually. She hadn't lost the deep sense of connection with Christ that came to her after her childhood illness and was reinforced by the vision of the crown of thorns. But she was disenchanted with what she took to be the shallowness of the Catholics she knew (especially her mother), and when an usher treated her rudely at Mass one day she stalked out of the chapel and, for nearly a decade, out of the Church. She was sixteen years old and ready to be on her own in the world.

Over the next couple of years, Caryll began to find herself. She won a scholarship to London's Saint John's Art School and gratefully discovered a kinship with its bohemian students. Her hunger for a new religious home sent her exploring Judaism, and Buddhism as well as a number of non-Catholic Christian denominations including Anglicanism, Methodism, Russian Orthodoxy, and the Salvation Army.

Caryll's reading of Orthodox spirituality especially stirred her and certainly colored the second of her three christic experiences. This one occurred when she was seventeen years old. She was hurrying to market late one day to buy some potatoes when suddenly "in front of me, above me, literally wiping out not only the grey street and sky but the whole world, was something which I can only call a gigantic and living Russian icon. I had never seen a Russian icon at the time . . . It was an icon of Christ the King crucified."[39] The next day she read in the *London Times* about the execution of the Russian Tsar Nicholas and his family. When she saw his photograph in the paper, she was stunned to see that it was identical to the face of Christ the King in her vision.

In her first christic vision, Caryll saw the presence of Christ in the poor and lowly. In this one, she recognized Christ in the high-born. "It was not for nothing that my first glimpse of Christ in man was in the humblest of lay sisters, bowed by a great crown of thorns, and my second a king in splendor, bowed under a great crown of gold. I realized that every crown is Christ's crown, and the crown of gold is a crown of thorns."[40] Christ made no distinction between persons, and in realizing this Caryll edged closer to an awareness of the Mystical Body where "in Christ everyone exists." Christ "has the qualities of [both] heroes and helpless children."[41]

By the time she was in her early twenties, Caryll was supporting herself by a number of odd jobs, some of them artistic —painting lampshades and drawing commercial prints—and others not—working as a charwoman and a "professional" letter writer. She fell head over heels in love with a man twenty-six years her senior, the Russian-born spy Sidney Reilly, who eventually broke her heart when he left her for another woman. It was in the aftermath of this brutally painful betrayal, a period in which she forlornly saw herself a displaced person without Church, family, or friends, that she experienced the third, culminating vision of Christ in *all*

persons, high or low born. Suddenly, in a flash, her desolate
sense of loneliness was replaced by one of connectedness to
everyone.

After her third vision, Caryll knew with absolute certainty that "Christ is everywhere; in Him every kind of life
has a meaning and has an influence on every other kind of
life."[42] She also recognized that because Christ *is* everywhere, he's also in sinners, and that the spiritual shallowness
of her mother or of the rude church usher oughtn't to blind
her to the christic identity of even them. "Realization of our
oneness in Christ is the only cure for human loneliness," she
concluded, and "oneness in Christ" didn't discriminate between sinners and saints.[43] Fortified now by an abiding awareness of the ocean of Christ in which she swam, Caryll returned
to the Church.

Stretching Christ

In 1925 Caryll met a woman who would become her close
companion for the rest of her life. Iris Wyndham, a wealthy
young Londoner, hired Caryll to decorate a nursery for her
only child Joan. The two became friends, and when Iris di-
vorced a short while later she invited Caryll to come live
with her. Some of Iris's friends disapproved, believing that
the eccentric young artist was an opportunistic moocher.
Caryll's own mother also disapproved, although it's not clear
why, causing in their already tense relationship a rift that
lasted for some time. But the friendship between Iris and
Caryll was genuine and deep. As Caryll described it,
"though in temperament we are so unlike, the friendship
and love between us is like a rock: it is a thing we both do
not cease to thank God for."[44]

The decade leading up to World War II was busy and
fulfilling for Caryll. After years of free-lancing as an illustra-

tor and wood-carver, she landed steady employment with a firm that specialized in church decoration and restoration. She also began contributing stories to a couple of Catholic periodicals. Most of them were written for children and often reflected her deepening awareness of Christ's presence in the world as well as her attraction to Orthodox spirituality. When the elderly editor of the two periodicals grew too infirm to handle the day-to-day business of running them, Caryll took over much of the responsibility for their publication. Later, during the war years, she sometimes wrote and illustrated entire issues.

In the late 1930s, with England reeling like the rest of the world from the Great Depression, Caryll organized several of her friends into a society called "The Loaves and Fishes." Caryll loved to tell the story of how it came about. She and the friends were wondering one day how they could ever find the money to help all those in need. Their conversation eventually turned to the biblical story of Jesus miraculously feeding the multitude, and Caryll suddenly suggested that each person lay down a penny on the table around which they were seated. "If God wants us to do something," she said, "He will multiply it." No sooner had she spoken the words when the father of one of her friends entered the room, gazed down at the coins for a few seconds, and said, "Whatever those are for, I will multiply them." Then he put five shillings on the table.[45]

The society's purpose was to aid the "unofficial poor," as Caryll called them: members of the middle class who had fallen on hard times, the aged and the ill, and the steadily swelling stream of refugees from Hitler's European expansion. The society members, playfully dubbed "Sprats," worked hard at soliciting contributions in money or supplies from wealthy patrons which they then distributed anonymously and secretly to those in need. By the end of its first year, The Loaves and Fishes had recruited nearly one hundred Sprats, including Caryll's mother Gertrude, with whom she had reconciled, and her sister Ruth.

For Caryll, her work with The Loaves and Fishes had a deeply christic significance. She believed that when the Sprats offered aid, they served both the immediate recipients as well as the Christ who indwelt the hungry, the homeless, the lonely, and the ill. Moreover, she was firmly convinced that it was Christ himself who inspired and worked in and through the Sprats. In behaving in a Christ-like manner to those who carried Christ within their hearts, Caryll believed the Sprats were operating as conduits of Christ's ubiquitous presence in the world. As she put it in one of her poems,

> ... For me the miracle was this:
> that a clear stream of the Lord's love—
> not mine—
> flowed out of my soul,
> a shining wave over my fellow men.[46]

The clear stream of God's love was difficult for many to discern as the 1930s drew to a close. Economic hard times showed few signs of going away, and Hitler's saber-rattling on the Continent was getting louder by the day. Prime Minister Neville Chamberlain embodied the naïve hopes of many that Hitler could be appeased. But Caryll and Iris were among those who saw that war was inevitable and in September 1939 they began taking classes in first aid and civil defense. "I hate war," Caryll wrote to an acquaintance, "[but] I would never be a pacifist because in taking part in a war one takes one's share of the common burden."[47]

When the Nazi bombing of London began, Caryll worked for a few months in a First Aid Post, a position she found physically and emotionally exhausting. "I have had some very, very bad moments, with a sheer physical desire to weep."[48] As if the work wasn't taxing enough, the reclusive Caryll found the dormitory sleeping arrangements for first aid workers horrid. Every hour spent in them felt like an assault. After a few months, friends worried about her health convinced her to take a less stressful day job in the Censorship Office. At night, she served as a fire spotter.

Her wartime activities left Caryll in a more or less permanent state of exhaustion. In addition, she suffered personally from the Blitz's violence. One night while she and Iris were at their First Aid Post, the flat they shared in another part of London was leveled. Another time, after they moved into a new apartment, Caryll was blown clear across the room by the concussion from a nearby bomb explosion.

Despite all this, Caryll's faith in the christic nature of reality not only endured but flourished during the war years. She saw the war as a "great chance of proving our Christhood."[49] For herself, she desired nothing more than to be "a kind of simple breath in the sighing of Christ in the Lost Jerusalem."[50] For her countrymen as a whole, she prayed that they would resist embittered hatred of the enemy and the bloodlust-driven desire for vengeance, both of which would blunt "the sharp edge of the uncompromising simplicity of the love of Christ."[51] Her hope was that they would "stretch" the Christ in themselves large enough "to fit the size of this war"[52] and come to see that the suffering they and the enemy endured was also Christ's. "All men's sorrows are Christ's sorrows ... The healing and service given to each other is given to Christ ... What we refuse to each other, we refuse to Christ."[53] The key to stretching Christ was to embody his love.

> We are in the world now as Christs; in the midst of this storm. We are here to keep Christianity alive, to keep Christianity pure, intact, to ensure by our own lives in

Christ that the gates of hell shall not prevail against
Christendom. This cannot be done if there is the least
compromise of love ... If we do not imitate Christ literally, we shall succumb to hate or to despair.[54]

In 1941, Caryll published her first book, *This War Is the
Passion,* in which she introduced her notion of christing. By
war's end she had published two more books—*The Reed of
God* (1944), a meditation on the Blessed Virgin, and *The
Flowering Tree* (1945), a collection of poetry—and started a
third, *The Dry Wood* (1947), her only novel. She also worked
steadily as an illustrator and woodcarver. For all its horrors,
the war freed Caryll's creativity.

Loving into Life

At the beginning of the war, Caryll wrote that "nothing now
is more needed than a continual Christ bearing into this
world."[55] Her phrase "Christ bearing" is richly evocative,
suggesting *birthing* Christ, *carrying* Christ, and *comporting*
oneself in a Christ-like manner. At war's end, bearing Christ
in all three senses remained just as important. The killing
may have ceased, but the long and bloody struggle that had
consumed Europe had inflicted long-term spiritual and psychological damage on millions. Caryll knew that only Christ-
like love would ease their suffering.

After the publication of *This War is the Passion,* Caryll
was flooded with hundreds of requests for spiritual advice.
Letters arrived daily, unannounced visitors showed up on her
doorstep, and Caryll found herself spending hours offering
counseling. Her reputation as a sensitive spiritual director
grew, and in 1942 the eminent British psychiatrist Dr. Eric

Strauss invited her to work with war-traumatized patients. Much of the aid Caryll offered them was in the form of art therapy. By encouraging patients to express themselves in paint, modeling clay, or wood, Caryll helped them break through their pain and repression to make healing contact with the Christ within. "Every human being is an artist, simply because he is made in God's image and indwelt by His spirit ... The artist has been submerged in most men, but because it is his true nature, it can always be restored."[56] Strauss, who called Caryll a "divine eccentric," was impressed with both her methods and her cure rate. According to him, she loved her patients back to life.

Caryll continued her therapeutic work after the war ended. For nearly two years, until her health broke under the strain, she made weekly train trips from London to a Surrey village to teach art in a special school for war-traumatized adolescents. Her students, each of whom had suffered terribly in the war, hailed from all over Europe. (One of them, a Polish boy, stunned Caryll by emotionlessly telling her that the Nazis had shot his father in front of his eyes.) Caryll saw these wounded youths as "Christ-children," and gently encouraged them to touch and transfigure their pain by expressing it artistically.

In an interview a couple of years before her death, Caryll recalled one of them in particular. He was a youth "full of turmoil and bitterness," utterly crushed, in her opinion, by "the weight of the Cross." The boy chose to work with wood, and spent days huddled in a corner, his back to the rest of the class, carving his block. When he finally showed Caryll what he'd done, she saw "it was a crucifix, carved crudely, yet with amazing skill. And the *face of terrible suffering was smiling*. It was the face of the young carver himself, his own features unmistakable, but transformed by that amazing smile on the face of the Crucified Christ." In touching his own wounds, the youth saw that he wasn't abandoned in his suffering and that his pain wasn't the last word. The breakthrough, said Caryll, changed him. "The sudden realization of himself, *indwelt by Christ*, flooded the bitterness out of him, and he became a Christ to the others."[57]

A couple of years after the end of the war, Caryll's awareness of Christ around her reached a new depth, although it's one she initially resisted. Iris's daughter Joan became pregnant. Both she and her husband, still university students, seemed even more helpless when it came to raising children than Caryll's own parents had been. Understandably, Iris felt obliged to step in when her granddaughter Clare was born. With her daughter's relieved consent, she brought the infant back to the flat she shared with Caryll.

Equally understandably, Caryll wasn't crazy about the idea. Although in the postwar years she occasionally dreamed of several big projects—opening a Catholic bookstore was one of her favorites—what she really wanted to do was devote herself to writing. But the steady stream of people seeking her spiritual counsel whittled away at her time, and she found herself forced to grab moments of undisturbed privacy in which to write whenever she could. She feared that the addition of an infant to the household would interfere with her writing even more. To make matters worse, she knew nothing about caring for babies.

But Caryll soon discovered that Clare immeasurably enriched her life. The middle-aged spinster with next to no experience of infants was awed and delighted by the child's presence, and before long loved her with all her heart. A photograph of the two of them taken in 1948 tells the whole story. Caryll, seated on a bench, holds Clare in her lap. Clare stares boldly at the photographer, while Caryll's gaze is characteristically shy, focused downward and inward. But there's an expression of such deep maternal love on her face that the photograph looks like an icon of the adoring Madonna holding the Christ child.

Caryll discerned in Clare's delight in the world the childlikeness that, as we've seen, became an integral aspect of her understanding of christing. Through her relationship with the infant, she came to appreciate as never before the wisdom of Jesus' observation that "unless you become like little children again, you shall not enter the kingdom of heaven" (Matt 18:3). A child, Caryll discovered firsthand, is innocently receptive. His way of looking at the world isn't cluttered with theories, abstractions, presuppositions, and judgments. Instead, he gratefully accepts the world for the enchanted thing it is. "In little things of no value he receives the Sacrament of the Universe; his jewels are chips of salted and frosted glass that he finds on the sea-shore; he listens for the sound of the sea in a hollow shell, and he hears the song of God."[58]

The wonder with which the child looks at his or her world is the same wonder with which Christ beholds creation. As we mature, we typically lose touch with this innocent and wonder-filled way of experiencing reality, and the doors of our heart slam shut. But the presence of children reminds us of who we truly are: bearers of the Christ child and sharers in the Christ child's delight in life. "Christ rests [in us] as He rested in Mary. From the moment when the Christ-life is conceived in us, our life is intended for one thing, the expression of His love."[59] Our task is simple: "to treasure the Infant Christ in us; to be not the castle but the cradle of Christ," so that we may recapture "the amazement of seeing for the first time and with the spontaneous giving of the whole heart that is the unique joy of first love."[60]

These Things Must Come

Caryll was never robust. When she was a child, one of her physicians predicted, accurately as it turned out, that her health would always be indifferent. Her weak constitution was further undermined by her adult lifestyle. She kept irregular hours, never got enough sleep, and her eating habits were abysmal. Sometimes she starved herself, at other times she gorged. When she worked on a new book or piece of art, she threw herself into her task with such exhausting intensity that she often collapsed at its completion. And then there was the chain-smoking, an addiction that caused chronic bronchial difficulties.

In what must've been a colossal struggle, Caryll finally managed to wean herself from tobacco in the last few years of her life. But by then her health was so shattered that she suffered from an ever-widening range of afflictions including gastritis, earache, toothache, hernia, and periodic pneumonia. A few months after the end of the war she underwent surgery that sapped her energy for months. She suffered another collapse in 1949 which forced her to give up her work in Surrey with the disturbed boys. She was ill for most of 1950 with "inflammation of the lungs," and confessed she'd been brought so low that "for more than a year my senses have been dead to beauty, and anything like music or even looking at a beautiful scene has only seemed to add to the effort of being alive almost unbearably."[61] To top things off, no sooner did Caryll begin to feel better than her mother fell terminally ill with breast cancer. When Gertrude was taken to the hospital, Caryll arranged with the staff to stay with her mother day and night, leaving for only a few hours each morning to bathe and catch a little sleep. Her mother suffered terribly—"more," observed Caryll, "than I have ever seen anyone suffer before."[62] After Gertrude finally died, Caryll was stricken with remorse that she hadn't been a better daughter.

Just a few months later, a cancer was found on Caryll's left breast, exactly where her mother's tumor had been located. Caryll half-jokingly and half-superstitiously called the diagnosis "Gert's revenge." Surgery was performed, followed by a difficult recovery. The wound became infected, throwing Caryll into what she described as "a week of real agony" and eventually requiring a second round of surgery to clean and drain the infection. Caryll tried to be a good patient, despite loathing everything about the hospital, especially the lack of privacy. But she also recognized that her illness was an opportunity to grow in childlikeness because it made her utterly dependent on caregivers and, especially, on God. "God now gives me the chance of being quite helpless, literally knocked out, and committed helpless into His hands."[63]

Six weeks after her operation, Caryll was discharged from the hospital with instructions to return daily for radiation treatments. She sensed that she was on the downward slope of life, and resolved to exult in simple everyday pleasures while she could. She regretted having been too preoccupied earlier in life to really enjoy "the sheer loveliness of the world, the people in it, and even the material things in it, food, drink, the sun, spending money, etc."—the world's glorious range of singularities. Now she vowed to "enjoy everything in life that I can, for as long as I can, and as wholly as I can."[64] Caryll wanted to spend whatever time she had left celebrating the inscapes discernible in even the most commonplace objects and acts.

During her last three years, despite steadily failing health, Caryll remained creatively active. She completed a delightful memoir posthumously published as *A Rocking-Horse Catholic,* remained productive as an artist, and spent as much time as she could with Clare, who was now walking and talking. But her energy continued to decline, and despite her resolve to accept her helplessness as an opportunity to connect with God, she felt anxious in the long intervals between medical check-ups. Still, Caryll sensed that what was happening to her was yet another manifestation of the christic nature of reality, that even ill health was somehow an inscape of Christ. As she wrote in one of the last manuscripts she completed,

> Sickness, old age, death, these must come; and when they come it seems that our service is ended. There is an exhaustion which makes it first an effort, then an impossibility, to lift the hand up to make the sign of the cross; no more liturgical acts in daily life, gestures and symbols that worship God and give Christ's love. Everything falls away from us, even memories—even the weariness of self. This is the breaking of the bread, the supreme moment in the prayer of the body, the end of the liturgy of our mortal lives, when we are broken for and in the communion of Christ's love to the whole world.[65]

The liturgy of Caryll's life came to an end in October 1954, shortly before her fifty-third birthday. During the spring of that year she began to fail noticeably, losing the little energy and appetite she had left and occasionally falling into periods of mental confusion. Shortly before she died, she told Iris: "I've been doing a big think and I'm not afraid of death any more." Iris rarely left her bedside. At the end, Caryll whispered to her: "You must be very tired."[66] Then she was gone.

We Fall and We Rise

When we cultivate the virtue of christing, we attune ourselves to the presence of Christ. We gaze through Christ's eyes, as it were, seeing the world as Christ does. But we also see Christ everywhere in the world. "You can think of anyone you like," said Caryll. "In that person Christ is, and is there to be known and loved and served in this world."[67] Additionally, we know ourselves as members of the Mystical Body and feel our deep-down kinship through Christ with all of God's creation. Nothing looks ordinary anymore. Everything reflects the glory of God simply by being what it is.

In saying that everything reflects God's glory, the emphasis should be on every *thing*. Like Gerard Manley Hopkins, Caryll Houselander believed that the uniqueness which each and every object and creature and event displays is Christ's own seal on creation. "The more intensely and completely that an individual is himself," she wrote, "the more completely is he the part of the whole—the whole of Christ." Moreover, given the spiritual interconnectedness that defines the Mystical Body of Christ, the uniqueness of each of the Body's members constitutes the strength of the Body as a whole. "Each one *owes* it to all the others to be himself, in the extreme."[68] Caryll's point is especially appreciated if one stops to consider how impoverished the Body would be without her own eccentric genius.

Practicing christing is life-enhancing because it corrects our spiritual myopia and allows us to see the world as the Christ-saturated thing it is. But christing also helps us to accept our dying with courage, trust, and love. If, as Caryll believed, we indeed are other Christs, participants in Christ's life, then we must also participate in his suffering and his death. But no one who is a member of the Mystical Body ever dies once and for all. As for Christ, so for us: resurrection follows death. As Caryll wrote, "All of us know that when a Christian dies it is Christ Who is dying, and his love has overcome death."[69]

If during life we have learned to discern Christ in everything, why would we not likewise sense his presence at the moment of our death? This most likely won't take away death's sting. After all, even Christ feared death. But it can bring us the deep and abiding confidence that our death is no more our end than Christ's death on the Cross was his. Even when standing in the shadow of the rood, those who cultivate christing can still proclaim:

> Break, spring;
> break
> from the ageless tree![70]

Death is bitter, but it's not the final word.

CONCLUSION

The Great Test

Before each person are life and death,
and whichever one chooses will be given.
—*Sirach 15:17*

Dying isn't just the inevitable terminus of life. It's also a test. As with all real tests, especially ones where the stakes are high, there's always some anxiety about how we'll do. Will we pass with honors, barely squeak by, or utterly fail?

What exactly does death test? Ultimately, our grip on reality, how well we managed over a lifetime to forthrightly face the truth about the way the world is, who we are, and what we must do to live the good life and be good persons. As we saw in chapter 1, such honesty doesn't come easily for many of us.

An observation by C. S. Lewis is helpful here. In his memoir *A Grief Observed* (which, by the way, is about death and dying), he reminds us of our all-too-human tendency to construct comfortable illusions which we then mistake for reality. Our expectations, desires, and fears—especially the latter—color the world with the hues we want it to have. This may work for us for a while, but sooner or later there's a price to be paid. We wind up loving the beloved as we've remade her, not as she really is; worshiping our idea of god rather than God; practicing a make-believe religion that shields us from life's unpleasantness; and refusing to think about painful subjects like death.

But reality, says Lewis, is iconoclastic. Reality is the hard edge which our fictions inevitably run up against. When we build houses of cards, reality always ends up scattering them, sometimes with revelatory gusts of intense joy but more often with bursts of unexpected suffering. When we are confronted by public disgrace, the traumatic end of a relationship, or the death of a loved one, the imaginary constructs that we've mistaken for reality can collapse in an instant. Those with especially good defense mechanisms may be able to weather a good many of these crises. But eventually even they run up against the greatest challenge to fictions and denial that anyone ever faces: dying. Dying is The Great Test.

If we're ill-prepared for it—if part of our retreat from reality has been a refusal to think much about our own mortality, or if we've managed to convince ourselves that dying is as easy as falling asleep—we'll fail The Great Test miserably. We'll be like the lazy student who cuts classes, refuses to crack open a book, and then, at the end of term, gets blown out of the water by the final exam. Reality will rush in and deliver us a stunning blow: this is what it *really* means to die, you fool! But unlike failing a school exam, there's no possibility of a retake here. We can sit for The Great Test only once.

Habituating ourselves to the virtues that make for a good life is the preparation needed to pass the final exam of dying. Virtues keep us resolutely in contact with reality, making it difficult to sequester ourselves in make-believe houses. When we cultivate courage, for example, we face rather than flee the things in the world that frighten us. When we learn obedience, we attend to where God wants us to go, even if we're not particularly crazy about the idea at the start. When we practice christing, we train our spiritual vision to see God in all aspects of life, the bleak as well as the bright. When we cultivate love, we learn to care for the well-being of everyone, not just those people who are easy to love. The practice of virtue builds spiritual muscles that prepare us to cope with the challenges of life and the ultimate challenge of death. Granted, there's no *absolute* guarantee that the person of virtue will rise to the occasion and pass The Great Test with flying colors. Anything can happen, anyone can stumble. But the odds are stacked incredibly in such a person's favor.

No *ars moriendi*—or *ars vivendi,* for that matter—can supply quick and convenient crib notes for The Great Test. What it can do is help us build the strength of character essential for a good life and a good death. It would be naïve to presume that our dying can be made any less uncanny through our efforts. Dying is a hard business. Given its strangeness, its unfamiliarity—remember my friend who didn't quite know how to go about dying because she had no experience at it?—it will always defy attempts, religious or otherwise, to domesticate it.

Yet the resolute honesty that comes from thoughtful and virtuous living can help us face up to the untamable reality of death so that when it finally comes for us—when it ceases to be a future possibility we pretend will never arrive and becomes a present actuality—we can meet it with some degree of equanimity. The fundamental rule, as we've seen in this book, is that we die as we live. This principle is so reliable that the sort of life a person lived can actually be inferred from the way he or she dies. Lives can be read backwards from deathbeds. The resolve with which we lived or the denial under which we crept carry through to the very end.

Two stories from my own pastoral experience come to mind.

The first is about a man in his late fifties who was dying of lung cancer. He didn't belong to my parish, or any other for that matter. But his wife, whom I knew, asked me to attend to him in his final weeks. He was under hospice care in the apartment they shared. It didn't take a lot to see that he was dying badly. He was surly with hospice nurses, testy with his wife, and tolerated my presence only under the condition that the word "death" was never uttered. Talk about God was okay, just so long as the conversation never strayed into the no-fly zone. Whenever he felt that our conversation had veered too close to the forbidden topic he generally flew into a tantrum, ordered me out of the apartment, and afterwards (I learned) vented his spleen on his poor wife. Even in the best of times his moods shifted unpredictably from anger to despair to maudlin sentimentality to apathy. In his relatively pain-free moments, he talked excitedly about all the things he planned to do once he was "up and about again," even though some part of him must've known perfectly well that his up-and-about days were over. He was clearly in the grip of a powerful death-fear and trying to protect himself with all sorts of denial and diversionary tactics.

More than once his wife called me late at night with frantic pleas for help. Sometimes his midnight crises were physical in nature, precipitated by especially bad pain or near suffocation. But most of the time they were spiritual, sparked by a nighttime encounter with Death every bit as horrifying as Tolstoy's experience in Arzamas. In those moments I'd find him flailing in panic on the hospital cot that had been set up for him in the living room screaming "No! No!" and "Help! Help!" A bit of quiet prayer and a dose of morphine usually calmed him down. Afterwards, when I encouraged him to talk about his death-fear, he'd clam up or become so agitated that he'd have another bout of breathlessness.

The morning of the day he died he was so furious with his wife for some imagined offense that he sullenly kept her at arm's length right up to his death struggle. There were no goodbyes, no embraces, no sharing of memories, no holding of hands. In his final moments, even though there were three people in the room with him—his wife, shattered by his rejection of her, the hospice nurse, and me—he still died utterly alone, frightened and angry. His last word was a tremulous "Don't!"

Witnessing this man die was one of the most chilling experiences I've ever had. God help him, he failed The Great Test just about as badly as anyone can. If we believe that there's some connection between living and dying, the sad conclusion must be that he died so badly because he'd failed to cultivate the strength of character needed to live well and die well. Virtues such as courage, patience, love, and trust could have helped him cope with his dying because they would have given him the tools needed to keep a firm hold on reality and face what it had to throw at him. But if his dying is any evidence—and it is—he instead developed an irresolute character that was short on all of them and long on ill-temper, fearfulness, suspicion, and especially denial. He died as he lived. We oughtn't to judge him so much as pity him and, in a way, be thankful to him. His manner of dying is a cautionary tale for all of us.

Here's the other story.

I was the on-duty chaplain at the hospital one Sunday morning when I was paged to visit a patient in the Intensive Care Unit. He was a man in his mid-sixties suffering from advanced cirrhosis. He'd been bleeding internally all week. Blood transfusions were keeping him alive, but his liver and veins were so brittle that he kept bleeding out. Just that morning his doctor had told him that the hemorrhaging couldn't be stopped. The patient opted for no more transfusions, and was told that he'd likely die by the end of the day.

As I walked toward the ICU, I prepared myself for ministering to a distraught man. But I was in for a surprise. I found the patient sitting up in bed, reading glasses perched on the end of his nose, calmly turning the pages of the Sunday newspaper. Except for a jaundiced complexion, he looked healthy enough. His wife sat in a chair next to the bed, knitting. I noticed a Bible in her lap. She looked less calm, as if she was struggling to keep it together.

My first thought was that this was a guy in deep denial. What normal person would sit calmly reading a paper after hearing that this was his final day of life? But as I talked with him and his wife, it dawned on me that his equanimity in the face of death was the real deal. He admitted that he was sad to leave his wife and worried about how she would cope with his dying, and he got misty-eyed (the only time during our entire conversation) when he reached out to take hold of her hand. But otherwise he was, as he put it, "ready to pack it in." "I've had a good life," he told me. "I wish I could've had a few more years, but it's okay. I can..." His voice trailed off and he smiled a little sadly. "I started to say, 'I can live with it,'" he continued. Then: "It's hard to get out of the habit of living."

I stayed with the patient and his wife a bit longer, prayed with them, and left. My shift ended two or three hours later. He died later that day.

I know nothing more about the man than what I've recorded here. But the way he dealt with his imminent death—the love he clearly felt for his wife, his compassion for her grief, the gratitude with which he looked back on his life, his courage in leaving the world, his trust that things would be "okay"—surely suggests that his life had been equally loving, courageous, and trusting. Simply being with him for a single hour on the day he died was enough to convince me that here was a man who had lived a good life in both the descriptive sense of personal fulfillment and the prescriptive one of treating others with decency and kindness. How else could he have died so well? How else could he have passed The Great Test with such flying colors? Whereas the first patient's dying exhausted and rattled me, this one filled me with awe and admiration. It made me want to be a better person.

The difference between these two deaths can be put simply: the first patient chose death even in the midst of life, while the second affirmed life even in the midst of dying. Judging from the way he died, the first patient's manner of living cut him off from the virtues whose cultivation builds a spiritual center of gravity, gives us strength to face reality, and encourages a joyful vitality. Instead, somewhere along the way he shut down, alienating himself from other people, from God, and from the chance of a genuinely fulfilled life. His miserable dying was the predictable culmination of a tragically stunted life.

Judging from the way the second patient died, he, like the seven people whose living and dying we've explored in this book, re-affirmed even at death's door a longstanding allegiance to the goodness of life. He lived with resolve, trust, and gratitude, not denying the bad moments that undoubtedly punctuated his life as much as anyone else's, but instead facing them, putting them in perspective, and continuing to celebrate life. His dying was a bittersweet capstone to a life well lived. He regretted leaving life. It's hard, as he said, to give up the habit of living. Yet he was able to die with grace, dignity, and peace.

These two stories underscore the fact that preparation for The Great Test begins long before death actually comes for us. Every choice we make that influences our characters for good or ill, and every opportunity for the practice of virtue that we embrace or let pass by, is part of the preparation.

Whether or not we know it, life and death are always present before us as we make our journey, and they demand that we choose: reality or denial, trust or distrust, love or selfishness, obedience or deafness, courage or cowardice, patience or restlessness, christing or blindness. No decision we make is insignificant because, as the Book of Sirach tells us, we become what we choose. Our choices not only determine the quality of our living. They also dictate how we finally comport ourselves when we head westward to that land from which no one returns.

NOTES

Introduction. An *Ars moriendi* for Today

The epigraph is from Arthur E. Imhof, "An *Ars Moriendi* for Our Time: To Live a Fulfilled Life; to Die a Peaceful Death," in *Facing Death: Where Culture, Religion, and Medicine Meet*, ed. Howard M. Spiro, Mary G. McCrea Curnen, Lee Palmer Wandel (New Haven, CT: Yale University Press, 1996), 119.

1. Living toward a Good Death

The chapter epigraph is an inscription from a New England tombstone, quoted in *A Sourcebook about Christian Death*, ed. Virginia Sloyan (Chicago, IL: Liturgy Training Publications, 1989), 13.

1. Quoted in *Tolstoy*, ed. Henri Troyat, trans. Nancy Amphoux (New York: Dell, 1969), 391.

2. Ibid., 392.

3. "Pious 'fight death the hardest,'" BBC News (17 March 2009). Available at <http://news.bbc.co.uk/2/hi/health/7949111. stm>. Accessed September 28, 2009.

4. Henri Nouwen, *Our Greatest Gift: A Meditation on Dying and Caring* (San Francisco: SanFranciscoHarper, 1994), 108.

5. Libby Purves, "Something in the Way He Died," *The Tablet* (December 8, 2001), 1734.

6. Epicurus, "Letter to Menoeceus," in *The Stoic and Epicurean Philosophers*, ed. Whitney J. Oates (New York: Random House, 1940), 31.

7. Martin Heidegger discusses being-towards-death in *Being and Time*, trans. John Macquarrie and Edward Robinson (New York: Harper & Row, 1962), 279–311.

8. Sir Thomas Browne, *Christian Morals* (1670), quoted in *Death: A Book of Preparation and Consolation*, ed. Barry Ulanov (New York: Sheed and Ward, 1959), 55.

9. Quoted in "Death as Friend and Enemy," by Martin E. Marty, *Christian Century* (September 25, 1996). Available at <http://findarticles.com/p/articles/mi_m1058/is_n27_v113/ai_18760995/>. Accessed December 8, 2009.

10. The classic account of the virtues is found in Aristotle's *The Nichomachean Ethics*, trans. David Ross (New York: Oxford University Press, 1986).

11. Christopher Vogt, *Patience, Compassion, Hope, and the Christian Art of Dying Well* (Lanham, MD: Sheed & Ward, 2004), 9.

12. Nouwen, *Our Greatest Gift*, 38.

13. Ibid., 47.

2. Trust: Joseph Bernardin

The chapter epigraph is from a 1995 Christmas sermon preached by Cardinal Bernardin at the Cook County Correctional Facility. Quoted in *This Man Bernardin*, by John H. White and Eugene Kennedy (Chicago, IL: Loyola Press, 1996), 167.

1. Joseph Bernardin, "The Cancer Has Returned," in *The Final Journey of Cardinal Joseph Bernardin*, by John H. White, Raymond E. Goedert, Kenneth Velo, Mary Brian Costello, Mary Lucia Skalka, and Ellen Gaynor (Chicago, IL: Loyola Press, 1997), 19.

2. Ibid.

3. Ibid, 21.

4. Faith has become such an overworked word in our day, meaning so many things to so many people, that it's sometimes difficult to know what sense to make of it. To avoid this baggage, I've preferred to use instead the word "trust."

5. Henry Nouwen, *Our Greatest Gift: A Meditation on Dying and Caring* (San Francisco: HarperSanFrancisco, 1994), 14.

6. See Karl Rahner, "The Christian Understanding of Death," in *The Content of Faith: The Best of Karl Raher's Theological Writings,* ed. Karl Lehmann and Albert Raffelt, trans. Harvey D. Egan (New York: Crossroad, 1999), 629.

7. John Macquarrie, *Principles of Christian Theology* (New York: Charles Scribner's Sons, 1977), 113.

8. Rowan Williams, *Tokens of Trust: An Introduction to Christian Belief* (Louisville, KY: Westminster John Knox Press, 2007), 16.

9. Joseph Bernardin, *The Gift of Peace* (Chicago, IL: Loyola Press, 1997), 86.

10. Tim Unsworth, *I Am Your Brother Joseph: Cardinal Bernardin of Chicago* (New York: Crossroad, 1997), 58.

11. Bernardin, *The Gift of Peace,* 4-5.

12. Ibid., 6.

13. Kenneth L. Woodward and John McCormick, "The Art of Dying Well," *Newsweek* 128, no. 22 (November 25, 1996): 62.

14. Quoted in *My Brother Joseph: The Spirit of a Cardinal and the Story of a Friendship,* by Eugene Kennedy (New York: St. Martin's Press, 1997), 164. These retreat notes later became the opening pages of Bernardin's *The Gift of Peace.*

15. Ibid., 164, 165.

16. Bernardin, *The Gift of Peace,* 9.

17. Quoted in Kennedy, *My Brother Joseph,* 166.

18. Joseph Bernardin, "Christ Calls Us Who Are Many to Be but One," Grant Park, Illinois (August 29, 1982) in *Selected Works of Joseph Cardinal Bernardin,* vol. 1, *Homilies and Teaching Documents,* ed. Alphonse P. Spilly (Collegeville, MN: The Liturgical Press, 2000), 297.

19. Joseph Bernardin, "It is a Spiritual Event," installation homily (August 25, 1982), in Spilly, *Selected Works of Joseph Cardinal Bernardin,* 295.

20. Joseph Bernardin, "I Am Joseph, Your Brother," evening prayer with presbyterate (August 24, 1982), in Spilly, *Selected Works of Joseph Cardinal Bernardin,* 288.

21. Bernardin, *The Gift of Peace,* 26.

22. Ibid., 31.

23. Quoted in White and Kennedy, *This Man Bernardin,* 133.

24. Joseph Bernardin, Homily (18 November 1993), in Spilly, *Selected Works of Joseph Cardinal Bernardin,* 581.

25. Bernardin, *The Gift of Peace,* 30.

26. Kennedy, *My Brother Joseph,* 102.

27. Joseph Bernardin, "A Sign of Hope: Pastoral Letter on Health Care" (October 18, 1995), in Spilly, *Selected Works of Joseph Cardinal Bernardin,* 82.

28. Joseph Bernardin, Homily, communal anointing of the sick (August 24, 1996), in Spilly, *Selected Works of Joseph Cardinal Bernardin,* 593.

29. Bernardin, *The Gift of Peace,* 59.

30. Joseph Bernardin, Homily, "Theology on Tap" Mass (August 11, 1996), in Spilly, *Selected Works of Joseph Cardinal Bernardin,* 590.

31. Bernardin, *The Gift of Peace,* 59.

32. Quoted in Unsworth, *I Am Your Brother Joseph,* 24–25.

33. Joseph Bernardin, "A Sign of Hope: Pastoral Letter on Health Care" (18 October 1995), in Spilly, *Selected Works of Joseph Cardinal Bernardin,* 85.

34. Quoted in White and Kennedy, *This Man Bernardin,* 149.

35. Bernardin, *The Gift of Peace,* 71.

36. Ibid., 93.

37. Ibid., 95.

38. Ibid., 89.

39. Ibid., 71.

40. Quoted in White et al., *The Final Journey of Joseph Cardinal Bernardin,* 13.

41. Ibid., 19.

42. Charles Curran, "Death 'as friend'—But...", *America* 176, no. 10 (March 29, 1997): 10–14.

43. Joseph Bernardin, Homily, prayer service with priests (October 7, 1996), in Spilly, *Selected Works of Joseph Cardinal Bernardin,* 607.

44. Bernardin, *The Gift of Peace,* 126.

45. Ibid., 133.

46. Quoted in White and Kennedy, *This Man Bernardin,* 167.

47. Bernardin, *The Gift of Peace,* 3, 6.

48. Ibid., 136.

49. Kennedy, *My Brother Joseph,* 170–71.

50. Quoted in H. White et al., *The Final Journey of Joseph Cardinal Bernardin,* 59.

51. Joseph Bernardin, Homily, prayer service with priests, in Spilly, *Selected Works of Joseph Cardinal Bernardin,* 607.

3. Love: Thea Bowman

The chapter epigraph is from an 1989 speech Thea Bowman gave at Viterbo College (now Viterbo University), quoted in *Thea's Song: The Life of Thea Bowman,* ed. Charlene Smith and John Feister (Maryknoll, NY: Orbis, 2009), 253.

1. Celestine Cepress, ed., Sister Thea Bowman, *Shooting Star: Selected Writings and Speeches* (Winona, MN: Saint Mary's Press/Christian Brothers Publications, 1993), 26. Hereafter *Shooting Star.*

2. Paul Gray, Hannah Bloch, and Sally B. Donnelly, "What Is Love?" *Time* (15 February 1993). Available at <http://www.time.com/time/magazine/article/0,9171,977763,00.html.> Accessed 15 April 2010.

3. C. S. Lewis, *The Four Loves,* originally published in 1960, is still a good introduction to this topic.

4. Fyodor Dostoyevsky, *The Brothers Karamazov,* trans. Constance Garnett (New York: Signet, 1980), 62.

5. Thomas Aquinas, *Summa Theologica,* trans. Fathers of the English Dominican Province (New York: Benziger Brothers, 1948), II–II, 27, 2.

6. For an analysis of availability, see Gabriel Marcel, *The Mystery of Being,* vol. 1, *Reflection and Mystery,* trans. G. S. Fraser (London: The Harvill Press, 1951), 181.

7. Marcel calls this the "*avec.*"

8. Martin Buber, *I and Thou,* trans. Walter Kaufmann (New York: Charles Scribner's Sons, 1970).

9. Smith and Feister, *Thea's Song,* 6.

10. Quoted in Maurice J. Nutt, ed., *Thea Bowman: In My Own Words* (Liguori, MI: Liguori, 2009), 4.

11. Smith and Feister, *Thea's Song,* 18.

12. *Shooting Star,* 76.

13. *Sister Thea: Songs of My People* (Boston: St. Paul Books & Media, 1989), 7.

14. Quoted in Smith and Feister, *Thea's Song,* 26.

15. *Shooting Star,* 18.

16. Ibid.

17. Ibid., 21.

18. Ibid., 93.

19. Smith and Feister, *Thea's Song,* 55.

20. *Shooting Star,* 94.

21. Ibid., 23.

22. Ibid., 65.

23. Ibid., 61.

24. Quoted in Smith and Feister, *Thea's Song,* 197.

25. *Shooting Star,* 45.

26. Quoted in Smith and Feister, *Thea's Song,* 161.

27. Ibid., 205.

28. *The Voice of Negro America,* LP record (Canton, MI: Holy Child Jesus School, 1967).

29. Quoted in Smith and Feister, *Thea's Song,* 90.

30. *Shooting Star,* 32.

31. Smith and Feister, *Thea's Song,* 139.

32. Ibid., 201.

33. Ibid., 157.

34. Quoted in Smith and Feister, *Thea's Song,* 180.

35. Ibid., 96.

36. Ibid., 237. The "bald is beautiful" was Thea's joking reference to the baldness that came from her chemotherapy.

37. Ibid., 188.

38. Smith and Feister, *Thea's Song,* 191.

39. *Shooting Star,* 91.

40. Quoted in Nutt, *Thea Bowman: In My Own Words,* 60.

41. Ibid., 103.

42. *Shooting Star,* 107.

43. Ibid., 113.

44. Quoted in Smith and Feister, *Thea's Song,* 185.

45. Ibid., 195.

46. Ibid., 239.

47. Ibid., 224.

48. Ibid., 267.

49. Ibid., 236.

50. *Shooting Star,* 19.

51. Quoted in Smith and Feister, *Thea's Song,* 249. Two films that are especially good in covering Sister Thea's years of sickness are *Sr. Thea: Her Own Story* (Florissant, MO: Oblate Media and Communication, 1990) and *Almost Home: Living with Suffering and Dying* (Liguori, MI: Liguori, 2008).

52. Smith and Feister, *Thea's Song,* 285.

53. Dorothee Soelle, *Death by Bread Alone: Texts and Reflections on Religious Experience* (Minneapolis: Fortress Press, 1978), 49.

4. Gratitude: Etty Hillesum

The chapter epigraph is from an entry dated May 29, 1942 in Etty Hillesum's diary. In *Etty: The Letters and Diaries of Etty Hillesum, 1941–1943,* ed. Klass A. D. Smelik, trans. Arnold J. Pomerans (Grand Rapids, MI: William B. Eerdmans & Ottawa, ON: Novalis, St. Paul University, 2002), 384. Hereafter referred to as Smelik.

1. Letter to Christine van Nooten, September 7, 1943, in Smelik, 658–59. The scriptural quote is from 2 Samuel 22:2–3.

2. Rowan Williams, Foreword, in Patrick Woodhouse, *Etty Hillesum: A Life Transformed* (New York: Continuum, 2009), ix, x.

3. Diaries, November 23, 1941, in Smelik, 150.

4. Ibid., 640.

5. Quoted in *Sacraments of Life, Life of the Sacraments,* by Leonardo Boff, trans. John Drury (Beltsville, MD: The Pastoral Press, 1987), 30.

6. Martin Heidegger, "What Calls for Thinking?" in *Basic Writings,* ed. David Farrell Kress (San Francisco: Harper, 1993), 371.

7. Henri Nouwen, *The Return of the Prodigal Son: A Story of Homecoming* (New York: Doubleday, 1994), 85.

8. Ibid., 86.

9. Diaries, August 8, 1941, in Smelik, 80.

10. Diaries, 6 December 1941, in Smelik, 168.

11. Diaries, November 30,1941, in Smelik, 160.

12. Diaries, November 21, 1941, in Smelik, 146.

13. Diaries, October 30,1941, in Smelik, 141.

14. Diaries, April 24, 1942, in Smelik, 341.

15. Diaries, November 30, 1941, in Smelik, 160.

16. Diaries, November 22, 1942, in Smelik, 198–99.

17. Diaries, March 9, 1941, in Smelik, 4, 6.

18. Diaries, March 9, 1941, in Smelik, 6.

19. Diaries, September 24, 1942, in Smelik, 530.

20. Diaries, April 5, 1942, in Smelik, 326.

21. Diaries, August 10, 1941, in Smelik, 84.

22. Diaries, December 1, 1941, in Smelik, 162.

23. Ibid.

24. Diaries, September 15, 1942, in Smelik, 516.

25. Diaries, August 10, 1941, in Smelik, 83.

26. Diaries, August 26, 1941, in Smelik, 91.

27. Diaries, December 22, 1941, in Smelik, 198.

28. Ibid.

29. Diaries, December 14, 1941, in Smelik, 181. Denise de Costa offers an insightful analysis of the relationship between sexuality and spirituality for Etty in *Anne Frank and Etty Hillesum: Inscribing Spirituality and Sexuality,* trans. Mischa F. C. Hoyinck and Robert E. Chesal (New Brunswick, NJ: Rutgers University Press, 2008), 141–239.

30. Diaries, December 30, 1941, in Smelik, 209.

31. Diaries, June 8, 1941, in Smelik, 57.

32. Diaries, December 31, 1941, in Smelik, 211.

33. Diaries, September 5, 1941, in Smelik, 94.

34. Diaries, March 16, 1941, in Smelik, 25–26.

35. Diaries, December 12, 1941, in Smelik, 174–75.

36. Diaries, April 3, 1942, in Smelik, 320. April 3 was also Good Friday, which Etty carefully noted in her diary.

37. Diaries, February 27, 1942, in Smelik, 259.

38. Diaries, July 14, 1942, in Smelik, 491.

39. Diaries, July 15, 1942, in Smelik, 495.

40. Diaries, July 3, 1942, in Smelik, 463.

41. For more on Westerbork, see Philip Mechanicus, *Waiting for Death: A Diary,* trans. Irene R. Gibbons (London: Calder and Boyars, 1968) and Jaap Polak and Ina Soep, *Steal a Pencil for Me* (Scarsdale, NY: Lion Books, 2000). Polak and Soep, who subsequently married, survived the war. Mechanicus, one of Holland's most gifted journalists, didn't.

42. Letter to Han Wegerif and others, June 8, 1943, in Smelik, 602.

43. Diaries, September 22, 1942, in Smelik, 527.

44. Diaries, July 22, 1942, in Smelik, 499.

45. Letter to Maria Tuinzing, August 7/8, 1943, in Smelik, 634.

46. Diaries, October 8, 1942, in Smelik, 545.

47. Diaries, October 12, 1942, in Smelik, 549.

48. Diaries, September 17, 1942, in Smelik, 521.

49. Diaries, October 3, 1942, in Smelik, 543.

50. Letter to Han Wegerif and others, August 24, 1943, in Smelik, 647, 646, 647, 644.

51. Letter to Henny Tideman, August 18, 1943, in Smelik, 640.

52. Diaries, July 12, 1942, in Smelik, 488.

5. Obedience: Jonathan Daniels

The chapter epigraph is from one of Jonathan Daniels's letters, dated May 1, 1965, to Mary Elizabeth Macnaughtan, in William J. Schneider, *American Martyr: The Jon Daniels Story* (Harrisburg, PA: Morehouse, 1992), 80. Schneider's book is both a biography and an anthology of Daniels' writings. Hereafter referred to as Schneider. When quoting from the anthology, I reference the specific title of the Daniels piece.

1. Schneider, 45–46.

2. *Here Am I, Send Me: The Story of Jonathan Daniels.* Produced by Larry Benaquist and Bill Sullivan (Atlanta, GA: The Episcopal Media Center, 1999).

3. *The Rule of Benedict,* ed. Timothy Fry, OSB (Collegeville, MN: The Liturgical Press, 1980), 157.

4. Rudolf Bultmann, *Theology of the New Testament,* trans. Kendrick Grobel (New York: Charles Scribner's Sons, 1955), 11–12.

5. Ibid., 13.

6. Ibid.

7. Jonathan Daniels, "Autobiography I, 1957," in Schneider, 58.

8. Ibid.

9. Jonathan Daniels, "Autobiography II, 1963," in Schneider, 60.

10. Jonathan Daniels, "Autobiography I, 1957," in Schneider, 56.

11. Schneider, 16.

12. Ibid., 17.

13. Ibid., 18.

14. Ibid.

15. Jonathan Daniels, "Autobiography II, 1963," in Schneider, 59.

16. Ibid.

17. Charles W. Eagles, *Outside Agitator: Jon Daniels and the Civil Rights Movement in Alabama* (Tuscaloosa, AL: University of Alabama Press, 2000), 19.

18. *Here Am I, Send Me: The Story of Jonathan Daniels.*

19. Ibid.

20. Eagles, *Outside Agitator,* 24.

21. Jonathan Daniels, "Autobiography II, 1963," in Schneider, 61.

22. Schneider, 23.

23. Ibid., 24–25.

24. Jonathan Daniels, "Foreclosure of a Mortgage: Reflections from a Point on the Way of the Cross: A Meditation on Theological Ethics," in Schneider, 105.

25. Schneider, 28.

26. Ibid., 34.

27. Jonathan Daniels to Mary Elizabeth Macnaughtan, April 12, 1965, in Schneider, 72.

28. Jonathan Daniels to James Wilson, April 1964, in Schneider, 64.

29. Jonathan Daniels to Molly D. Thoron, April 15, 1965, in Schneider, 73.

30. Ibid.

31. Jonathan Daniels to the Rev. William J. Schneider, May 1965, in Schneider, 78.

32. Ibid.

33. Schneider, 37.

34. Jonathan Daniels to Mary Elizabeth Macnaughtan, May 1, 1965, in Schneider, 80.

35. Jonathan Daniels to Carl Edwards, June 22, 1965, in Schneider, 82.

36. Jonathan Daniels, "Foreclosure of a Mortgage," in Schneider, 94.

37. *Here Am I, Send Me: The Story of Jonathan Daniels.*

38. For an excellent narrative of the trial and acquittal of Tom Coleman, and its national aftermath, see Eagles, *Outside Agitator,* 185–249.

39. Jonathan Daniels to Mary Elizabeth Macnaughtan, March 29, 1965, in Schneider, 70.

40. Ibid.

6. Courage: Dietrich Bonhoeffer

The chapter epigraph is from a sermon preached by Bonhoeffer on January 15, 1933, two weeks before Hitler became Chancellor of Germany. Quoted in *The Shame and the Sacrifice: The Life and Martyrdom of Dietrich Bonhoeffer,* by Edwin Robertson (New York: Collier, 1988), 85.

1. Robertson, *The Shame and the Sacrifice,* 277.

2. Dietrich Bonhoeffer, Sermon, January 15, 1933. Quoted in Robertson, *The Shame and the Sacrifice,* 85.

3. Paul Tillich, *The Courage to Be* (New York: Collins, 1974), 152.

4. Ibid., 152–53.

5. John Shelby Spong, *A New Christianity for a New World* (San Francisco: HarperCollins, 2002), 68.

6. Eberhard Bethge, *Dietrich Bonhoeffer: Man of Vision, Man of Courage,* trans. Eric Mosbacher, Peter and Betty Ross, Frank Clarke, William Glen-Doepel (New York: Harper & Row, 1970), 23.

7. Ibid., 24.

8. Ibid.

9. Dietrich Bonhoeffer, Letter, January 27, 1936. Quoted in *Dietrich Bonhoeffer: A Spoke in the Wheel,* by Renate Wind, trans. John Bowden (Grand Rapids, MI: William B. Eerdmans, 1992), 46.

10. Eberhard Bethge, Renate Bethge, and Christian Gremmels, eds., *Dietrich Bonhoeffer: A Life in Pictures* (New York: Harper and Row, 1977), 74.

11. Lasserre would go on to write one of the twentieth-century's classics in Christian pacifism: *War and the Gospel* (1962).

12. Dietrich Bonhoeffer, Letter, January 27, 1936. Quoted in Renate Wind, *Dietrich Bonhoeffer: A Spoke in the Wheel,* 52.

13. Ibid., 54.

14. Ibid., 82. For more on the Christian German movement, see Robert P. Ericksen and Susannah Heschel, ed., *Betrayal: German Churches and the Holocaust* (Minneapolis, MI: Fortress Press, 1999); and a documentary film by Martin Doblmeier, *Bonhoeffer: Pastor, Pacifist, Nazi Resister* (South Carolina Educational Television, 2003).

15. Ibid., 68.

16. Edwin Robertson, *Christians Against Hitler* (London: SCM Press, 1962), 18.

17. Dietrich Bonhoeffer, "Christ and Peace" (Fall 1932), in *Dietrich Bonhoeffer: A Testament to Freedom,* ed. Geffrey B. Kelly and F. Burton Nelson (San Francisco: HarperSanFrancisco, 1995), 95.

18. Dietrich Bonhoeffer, "The Church and the Jewish Question" (April 1933), in Kelly and Nelson, *A Testament to Freedom,* 132.

19. Dietrich Bonhoeffer, Letter, October 24, 1933. Quoted in Wind, *Dietrich Bonhoeffer: A Spoke in the Wheel,* 77.

20. Dietrich Bonhoeffer, *The Cost of Discipleship,* trans. R. H. Fuller (New York: Touchstone, 1995), 43.

21. Dietrich Bonhoeffer, *Ethics*, trans. Neville Horton Smith (New York: Macmillan, 1965), 113.

22. Dietrich Bonhoeffer, Letter, June 9, 1939. Quoted in Bethge, *Dietrich Bonhoeffer: Man of Vision, Man of Courage*, 554.

23. Dietrich Bonhoeffer, Letter, June 26, 1939. Quoted in Bethge, *Dietrich Bonhoeffer: Man of Vision, Man of Courage*, 560.

24. Dietrich Bonhoeffer, *Ethics*, 238.

25. Ibid.

26. Dietrich Bonhoeffer, *Letters and Papers from Prison* (New York: Macmillan, 1971), 5.

27. Ibid., 4.

28. Ibid., 6.

29. Ibid., 15.

30. Bethge, Bethge, and Gemmels, *Dietrich Bonhoeffer: A Life in Pictures*, 191.

31. Bonhoeffer, *Letters and Papers from Prison*, 369.

32. Ibid., 361.

33. Dietrich Bonhoeffer, Letter, June 25, 1942. Quoted in Bethge, *Dietrich Bonhoeffer: Man of Vision, Man of Courage*, 626.

34. Quoted in Wind, *Dietrich Bonhoeffer: A Spoke in the Wheel*, 168.

35. Quoted in Bethge, *Dietrich Bonhoeffer: Man of Vision, Man of Courage*, 830.

36. Bonhoeffer, *Letters and Papers from Prison*, 393.

7. Patience: John Paul II

The chapter epigraph is from John Paul II's Speech at Alice Springs, Australia, September 29, 1986. Available at <http://www.acmlismore.org.au/popesSpeech.php>. Accessed February 3, 2010.

1. Cardinal Stanislaw Dziwisz, *A Life with Karol: My Forty-Year Friendship with the Man Who Became Pope*, trans. Adrian J. Walker (New York: Doubleday, 2007), 254.

2. David Baily Harned, *Patience: How We Wait Upon the World* (Cambridge, MA: Cowley, 1997), 37.

3. Dorothee Soelle, *Suffering*, trans. Everett R. Kalin (Philadelphia: Fortress Press, 1975), 103.

4. Quoted in Benedict XIV, Speech at Auschwitz, 28 May 2006. Available at <http://www.vatican.va/holy_father/benedict_xvi/speeches/2006/may/documents/hf_ben-xvi_spe_20060528_auschwitz-birkenau_en.html>. Accessed 15 January 2010.

5. Karol Wojtyla, *Collected Poems*, trans. Jerzy Peterkiewicz (New York: Random House, 1982), p. 2.

6. Jonathan Kwitney, *Man of the Century: The Life and Times of John Paul II* (New York: Henry Holt, 1997), 35.

7. Ibid., 27.

8. Ibid., 70.

9. Ibid, 56.

10. Ibid., 80

11. It's still not entirely clear what Agca's motives were or who hired him. But John Paul and his longtime friend and secretary Stanislaw Dziwisz were both convinced that the attempt was ultimately traceable to the KGB. See Dziwisz, *A Life with Karol*, 137–42 and George Weigel, *Witness to Hope: The Biography of John Paul II* (New York: HarperCollins, 2005), 397–411.

12. Sanislaw Dziwisz, Czeslaw Drazek, Renato Buzzonetti, and Angelo Comastri, *Let Me Go to the Father's House: John Paul II's Strength in Weakness*, trans. Matthew Sherry (Boston: Pauline Books & Media, 2006), 23.

13. Ibid.

14. Weigel, *Witness to Hope*, 416.

15. Dziwisz et al., *Let Me Go to the Father's House*, 25.

16. Weigel, *Witness to Hope*, 413.

17. Dziwisz et al., *Let Me Go to the Father's House*, 25.

18. John Paul II, *Salvifici Doloris: On the Christian Meaning of Human Suffering*. Vatican Translation (Boston: Pauline Books & Media, 1984), 5–6.

19. Ibid., 9–10

20. Ibid., 12.

21. Quoted in Robert G. Schroeder, *John Paul II and the Meaning of Suffering* (Huntingdon, IN: Our Sunday Visitor, 2008), 58.

22. John Paul II, *Salvifici Doloris*, 43.

23. Ibid., 23.
24. Ibid., 5.
25. Ibid., 46
26. Ibid., 47.
27. Ibid., 56.
28. Dziwisz et al., *Let Me Go to the Father's House*, 56.
29. Ibid., 62.
30. Ibid., 5.
31. John Paul II, *Silence Transformed into Life: The Testament of His Final Year* (New York: New City Press, 2006), 111.
32. Ibid., 59.
33. Ibid., 23.
34. Ibid., 120.
35. Ibid., 115.
36. Ibid., 53.
37. Dziwisz et al., *Let Me Go to the Father's House*, 64.
38. John Paul II, *Memory and Identity: Conversations at the Dawn of a Millennium* (New York: Rizzoli, 2005), 167.
39. Stanislaw Dziwisz et al., *Let Me Go to the Father's House*, 68.
40. Ibid., p. 74. This is the account given by John Paul's personal physician, Dr. Renato Buzzonetti. Stanislaw Dziwisz remembers the pope's final words slightly differently as "Let me go to the house of the Father" (p. 37).
41. William Perkins, *A Salve for a Sicke Man*, in *The English* Ars Moriendi, ed. David William Atkinson (New York: Peter Lang, 1992), 141. I've modernized Perkins's spelling in the quoted passage.
42. Dziwisz et al., *Let Me Go to the Father's House*, 33.

8. Christing: Caryll Houselander

The chapter epigraph is from Caryll Houselander's *The Passion of the Infant Christ* (London: Sheed and Ward, 1979), 78.
1. Maisie Ward, *Caryll Houselander: That Divine Eccentric* (London: Sheed and Ward, 1962), 123. Masie Ward was Caryll's friend and publisher. To date, this is the only book-length biography of Houselander. A new one is sorely needed.

2. Caryll Houselander, *A Rocking-Horse Catholic* (London: Sheed and Ward, 1955), 137–38.

3. Ibid., 138.

4. Oliver Davies, ed., *Celtic Spirituality* (New York: Paulist Press, 1999), 120.

5. Caryll Houselander, *The Comforting of Christ* (London: Sheed and Ward, 1947), 8.

6. Caryll Houselander, *This War is the Passion* (Notre Dame, IN: Ave Maria Press, 2008), 1.

7. Gerard Manley Hopkins, Diary (1872), in *A Hopkins Reader*, ed. John Pick (Garden City, NY: Image Books, 1966), 106.

8. Gerard Manley Hopkins, Diary (1873), in *A Hopkins Reader*, 111.

9. Ibid., 110.

10. Gerard Manley Hopkins, "As kingfishers catch fire," in *A Hopkins Reader*, 67.

11. Ibid.

12. Caryll Houselander, *The Passion of the Infant Christ*, 85; Caryll Houselander, *Guilt* (New York: Sheed and Ward, 1951), 72.

13. Houselander, *The Passion of the Infant Christ*, 29.

14. Ibid., 29.

15. Ibid., 30.

16. Caryll Houselander, *The Flowering Tree* (New York: Sheed and Ward, 1945), 91.

17. See Pius XII, *The Mystical Body of Christ (Mystici Corporis Christi)* (New York: Paulist Press, n.d.), 34–35.

18. Houselander, *The Flowering Tree*, 33.

19. Ibid., i.

20. Caryll Houselander, Letter to Archie Campbell-Murdoch (1941), in *The Letters of Caryll Houselander*, ed. Maisie Ward (New York: Sheed and Ward, 1965), 41.

21. Caryll Houselander, Letter to a young friend who married and settled abroad (October 22, 1945), in *The Letters of Caryll Houselander*, 114.

22. Quoted in Ward, *Caryll Houselander: That Divine Eccentric*, 136.

23. Ibid., 200.

24. Caryll Houselander, Letter to Baroness Bosch van Drakestein (August 26, 1939), in *The Letters of Caryll Houselander,* 23.

25. Houselander, *The Passion of the Infant Christ,* 71.

26. Ibid.

27. Ibid., 78.

28. Caryll Houselander, *The Reed of God* (Notre Dame, IN: Ave Maria Press, 2006), 58.

29. Houselander, *A Rocking-Horse Catholic,* 3.

30. Ibid., 31.

31. Ibid., 23.

32. Ibid., 46.

33. Ibid., 49.

34. Ibid., 47.

35. Quoted in Ward, *Caryll Houselander: That Divine Eccentric,* 24.

36. Caryll Houselander, *A Rocking-Horse Catholic,* 63.

37. Ibid., 73.

38. Ibid., 74.

39. Ibid., 111–12.

40. Ibid., 115–16.

41. Caryll Houselander, Letter to Archie Campbell-Murdoch (n.d.), in *The Letters of Caryll Houselander,* 41.

42. Houselander, *A Rocking-Horse Catholic,* 139.

43. Ibid., 140.

44. Quoted in Ward, *Caryll Houselander: That Divine Eccentric,* 153.

45. Ibid., 124–25.

46. Houselander, *The Flowering Tree,* 61, 62.

47. Quoted in *Caryll Houselander: Essential Writings,* ed. Wendy M. Wright (Maryknoll, NY: Orbis Books, 2005), 73–74.

48. Caryll Houselander, Letter to Baroness Bosch van Drakestein (September 17, 1939), in *The Letters of Caryll Houselander,* 31.

49. Caryll Houselander, Letter to Baroness Bosch van Drakestein (September 2, 1939), in *Caryll Houselander: Essential Writings,* 76.

50. Caryll Houselander, Letter to Baroness Bosch van Drakestein (September 21, 1939), in *Caryll Houselander: Essential Writings,* 81.

51. Houselander, *The Passion of the Infant Christ*, 7.

52. Quoted in Ward, *Caryll Houselander: That Divine Eccentric*, 192.

53. Houselander, *This War is the Passion*, 147.

54. Ibid., 25.

55. Caryll Houselander, Letter to Baroness Bosch van Drakestein (September 19, 1939), in *Caryll Houselander: Essential Writings*, 79.

56. Caryll Houselander, "Children and Creativity" (1952), in *Caryll Houselander: Essential Writings*, 156.

57. Ibid., 154, 155.

58. Houselander, *The Passion of the Infant Christ*, 81.

59. Ibid., 22–23.

60. Ibid., 81.

61. Ibid., 287.

62. Ibid., 290.

63. Ibid., 293.

64. Ibid., 297.

65. Caryll Houselander, *The Risen Christ* (London: Sheed and Ward, 1958), 73–74.

66. Quoted in Ward, *Caryll Houselander: That Divine Eccentric*, 319, 323.

67. Houselander, *The Passion of the Infant Christ*, 136.

68. Caryll Houselander, Letter to Maisie Ward (September 3, 1944), in *Caryll Houselander: Essential Writings*, 146.

69. Houselander, *The Passion of the Infant Christ*, 5.

70. Houselander, *The Flowering Tree*, 30.

INDEX